GENDER AND CITIZENSHIP

Politics and Agency in France, Britain and Denmark

BIRTE SIIM
Aalborg University, Denmark

CAMBRIDGE
UNIVERSITY PRESS

PUBLISHED BY THE PRESS SYNDICATE OF THE UNIVERSITY OF CAMBRIDGE
The Pitt Building, Trumpington Street, Cambridge, United Kingdom

CAMBRIDGE UNIVERSITY PRESS
The Edinburgh Building, Cambridge CB2 2RU, UK
40 West 20th Street, New York, NY 10011–4211, USA
10 Stamford Road, Oakleigh, VIC 3166, Australia
Ruiz de Alarcón 13, 28014 Madrid, Spain
Dock House, The Waterfront, Cape Town 8001, South Africa

http://www.cambridge.org

First published 2000

Printed in Singapore by Green Giant Press Pte Ltd

Typeface New Baskerville (Adobe) 10/12 pt.   *System* QuarkXPress® [BC]

A catalogue record for this book is available from the British Library

National Library of Australia Cataloguing in Publication data
Siim, Birte.
Gender and citizenship: politics and agency in France, Britain and Denmark
Bibliography.
Includes index.
ISBN 0 521 59154 6
ISBN 0 521 59843 5 (pbk)
1. Citizenship – France. 2. Citizenship – Denmark. 3. Citizenship – Great
Britain. 4. Women's rights – France. 5. Women's rights – Great Britain.
6. Women's rights – Denmark. 7. Women – France – Social conditions.
8. Women – Great Britain – Social conditions. 9. Women –
Denmark – social conditions. I. Title.
305.42094

ISBN 0 521 59154 6 hardback
ISBN 0 521 59843 5 paperback

10·11·17.

Participation (published in Danish, 1993).

Contents

v

Tables and Figures

Preface

My approach to citizenship reflects inspiration from scholars I have met and collaborated with in different contexts during the last 15 years. I became interested in the concept of democratic citizenship and in the feminist approach to citizenship in the autumn of 1984 while I stayed in Palo Alto as a Visiting Scholar at the Centre for Research on Women (CROW). This was the first time I met Carole Pateman and Wendy Sarvasy – two political scientists and feminist scholars who became important to my thinking in different ways. Carole Pateman gave me her Berkeley Lectures 'Women and Democratic Citizenship' to be delivered in the spring of 1985. Wendy Sarvasy has remained my best friend and critic, and we worked together to develop a new framework to understand the intermeshing of social and political citizenship.

A crucial inspiration for rethinking citizenship in a Danish context was the participation in the research group on Democratic Citizenship in Denmark at Aalborg University (1988–1994). I am grateful to Ann-Dorte Christensen, Johannes Andersen and Lars Torpe, who in different ways have contributed to my understanding of citizenship in Denmark. Together with Anna-Birte Ravn and Anette Borchorst they have made useful comments to the first draft of the chapter on gender and citizenship in Denmark.

The European network for Theory and Research on Women, Welfare State and Citizenship, which was started in 1991, has been another source of inspiration for thinking about social citizenship from a feminist perspective. I am grateful to Mary Daly, Barbara Hobson, Jacqueline Heinen, Trudie Knijn, Arnlaug Leira, Jane Lewis, Ilona Ostner, Bérengère Marquez-Pereira, Liisa Rantalaiho, Chiara Saraceno who have worked with me in the European research project: 'Gender and Citizenship: Social Integration and Social Exclusion in European Welfare

States' (1996–1999). They have encouraged me to think about how different models of citizenship in Europe have influenced the experience of citizens as well as the vocabulary of citizenship.

The serious comparative work on models of citizenship from a gender perspective started in Paris in 1993–95. I participated in the work of the international research group 'L'État et Rapports Sociaux de Sexe' and in the seminars of GEDISST: Groupe d'Études sur la Division Sociale et Sexuelle du Travail. I received invaluable inspiration from seminars and discussions of the group on gender and citizenship from a comparative European perspective. My friends Jacqueline Heinen, Mariette Sineau and Bérengère Marquez-Pereira have enlightened me about the French case and have made useful comments to the first drafts of the chapter about gender and citizenship in France.

I have co-operated closely with British feminist scholars and participated in seminars, conferences, research projects and books with colleagues in Britain since the middle of the 1980s. I have learnt a lot about gender and citizenship in the British context from the work and discussions with Ruth Lister, Anne Showstack Sassoon, and Jane Lewis. The last two have read and made useful comments to the first drafts of the chapter about gender and citizenship in Britain.

The National Danish Research Committee for the Social Sciences gave financial support to my research project 'Gender, Power and Democracy – the interplay between citizenship and political participation' (1993–1995) that enabled me to take leave from the university for one full year. Support from the Department of Development and Planning, Aalborg University enabled me to continue my work on the project in the spring of 1996.

I am grateful to my secretary Line Jacobsen who has helped with the manuscript and tables and the student assistant Tina Kjær Bach who has helped tidy up the bibliography.

My thanks to all the individuals and organisations who in different ways have made this book possible and to the many people, including members of my research networks and colleagues whose ideas have directly or indirectly contributed to the book. Last but not least I want to thank Bengt-Åke for preparing excellent meals for me and my feminist colleagues and for always being prepared to comment on my ideas in spite of his own busy agenda.

Abbreviations

AJE	Allocation Jeune Enfant
APE	Allocation Parentale d'Education
CGT	Conféderation Génerale de Travail
CGTU	Conféderation Génerale de Travail Unitaire
EC	European Community
EU	European Union
MLF	Mouvement Liberation des Femmes
NCW	National Council of Women
NUSEC	National Union of Societies for Equal Citizenship
NUWSS	National Union of Women's Suffrage Societies
NWLM	New Women's Liberation Movement
UFCS	Union Feminine Civile et Sociale
UFSF	Union Française pour le Suffrage en France
WLL	Women's Labour League
WS	Women's Sections

Introduction:
Feminist Rethinking of Citizenship

'Citizenship' has become a key word in academic scholarship and in social and political discourse, and the issues of gender and citizenship have recently been taken up by feminist scholarship (Lister 1997a; Bussemaker and Voet 1998). Citizenship is rooted in philosophical and political traditions. The vocabulary of citizenship is about 'individual rights and obligations' and about 'belonging and participation to political communities'. Citizenship is a contextualised concept and is contested. Vocabularies of citizenship are dependent on the social and political context and historical legacies in which they have been developed (Turner 1992). The European welfare states have different vocabularies of citizenship, but there has been no systematic comparison of the implications of different models of citizenship for gender relations (Bussemaker and Voet 1998).

The political scientist Carole Pateman first raised the question of women's citizenship in modern democracies in a path-breaking article in 1985 that addressed women's exclusion from active citizenship and their specific inclusion as mothers (1985). During the last ten years, gender and citizenship have become key questions in feminist scholarship (Pateman 1988; Phillips 1992; Lister 1997a). One of the central themes in the feminist rethinking of citizenship has been a re-establishing of the link between women's social rights and the democratic citizenship that has been one of the legacies of the history of feminism (Hernes 1987; Pateman 1988; Siim 1988, Sarvasy, 1994; Pateman 1996; Lister 1997a).

The relationship between feminism and citizenship is ambivalent, and feminist scholarship has developed different frameworks and competing visions of women's full and equal citizenship (Phillips 1992, 1993; Lister 1997a). One of the central questions in feminist political theory has been that of analysing women's *exclusion* from citizenship, this

1

emphasis leading to a focus on institutional and structural *barriers* for women's access to democratic citizenship. Carole Pateman's influential approach – I have called it the 'patriarchal hypothesis' – explains women's exclusion from democratic citizenship and their specific inclusion as mothers as a result of the public/private division in modern democracies (1988).

More recently there has been a shift of focus towards an interest in women's agency and women's inclusion in democratic institutions (Phillips 1995; Lister 1997a). Today, the feminist debate about the role of women's agency is often based on a normative vision that aims at increasing women's political participation and representation in politics, for example through the quota system and the legislation of parity (Young 1990a; Gaspard et al. 1992; Phillips 1992). I hope that this work will contribute to shifting the focus of attention in feminist scholarship from a theoretical figure of patriarchy and exclusion to an analysis of the dynamic processes of women's participation in civil society and in public political life.

From a global context, women's exclusion from civil, political and social rights is still important. During the 1990s, globalisation and immigration have created new problems of exclusion and inclusion (Bottomore and Marshall 1992). One of the challenges is to integrate diversity and difference, based on gender, ethnicity and race, within the framework of citizenship (Young 1990a; Phillips 1993; Lister 1997a; Yuval-Davis 1997). Another is to analyse the new problems of exclusion for women that are connected with education, unemployment and marginalisation from the labour market. I suggest that the growth of feminism has at the same time created new possibilities for the inclusion of women in active citizenship in all European welfare states. These are most visible in the Nordic context. Here, women's mobilisation in the new feminist movement has been accompanied by their integration within the political elite, with the result that women today comprise between 30 and 40 per cent of representatives in parliament (Bergquist et al. 1999). This has changed the political meaning of gender and given women a new political presence in politics.

The main concern of this book is with tracing the connection between the social and political aspects of citizenship, especially the bonds between civil society and the public arena from the point of view of women. The notion of women's *agency* plays a crucial role in the framework for several reasons. It is premised on the belief that politics matters. Second, agency provides a link between an active, participatory citizenship and demands for equal civil, political and social rights. Finally the focus on women's agency points to the importance of women's activities as mothers, workers and citizens and of the interconnection of the different arenas of state, market and civil society.

The New Paradigm about Gender in
Modern Democracies

The French Revolution represents a break with the old patriarchal society and traditional gender relations and the beginning of modern post-traditional societies based on a new notion of *equality* among individual citizens (Pateman 1988; Duby and Perrot 1992a). The old patriarchy was overthrown but it gave way to a new gendering of the public sphere, which became a new division between 'public' man and 'private' women. Feminist scholarship has different interpretations of the potential for modern democracy for women, but there is agreement that modern democracies have constructed a new paradigm about gender and that assumptions about gender relations are embedded in them (Landes 1988; Scott 1988; Pateman 1988).[1]

Taking the French Revolution as a point of departure is a methodological choice indicating that modern democracies express a new dynamic between public and private arenas and new visions about citizenship. Key issues are what the assumptions about gender have been in modern democracies and how gender relations have influenced the development of democracy. Feminist scholarship suggests that modern democracies imply new forms of inclusion and exclusion of women citizens in the public, political sphere. The concept of citizenship becomes a central problematic for the analysis of discourses about gender in modern democracies because it expresses a contradiction between the universal principle of the *equality* of men and the *particularity* or *difference* of women and other excluded groups (Pateman 1988; Scott 1988).

Feminist scholarship has begun to examine the contradiction between the universality of man and the particularity of woman, as well as the specific exclusion and inclusion of women in citizenship in different national contexts (Bock and Tane 1991; Bock and James 1992; Koven and Michel 1993). The theoretical and methodological premise of the book is that there is no universal story about gender and citizenship. The story about the constraints on and possibilities for the inclusion of women in full citizenship and of the relation between the social and political aspects of citizenship needs to be told from different national contexts (see Bussemaker and Voet 1998).

In modern democracies, gender and the gender system are dynamic concepts embedded in national histories, institutions and cultures. The guiding hypothesis of this book is inspired by the claim of feminist scholarship that modern democracy represents a break with traditional societies, that it has constructed a new understanding of the public political arena, and that it includes a new discourse about gender. The three cases of France, Britain and Denmark have been selected because they represent three different vocabularies and dynamics of citizenship and gender that illuminate the processes of exclusion and inclusion of women as workers, mothers and citizens (Siim 1999a).

Key Notions: Agency, Power and Discourse

My approach to citizenship is inspired by understandings in sociology, political science and feminism. Citizenship is a status, a practice and an identity, and it has a vertical as well as a horizontal dimension.[2] The framework of citizenship combines two analytically distinct dimensions of citizenship: the social and the political. I focus on the interplay between political, social and civil rights, as well as on the connection between social citizenship, political participation and power (Hernes 1987; Siim 1988).[3]

The notion of agency is contested. According to Anthony Giddens (1984: 14), agency is about action to intervene in the world and about the capacity to 'make a difference' to a pre-existing state of affairs or cause of events. In feminist scholarship women's agency often refers to women's ability to determine their own daily life as well as their collective ability to make a difference on the public arena. In Ruth Lister's recent attempt to synthesise the liberal and civic republican framework of citizenship, human agency[4] is defined as 'a conscious capacity to choose and act at a personal and political level' (1997a: 38). In feminist scholarship women's agency may refer both to women's independent organising and to the capacity of women's collective agency to influence formal politics. In this study the notion of agency is a key to women's active citizenship and refers both to individual actors and to the political influence of women's collective agency. On the analytical level it is a way of connecting the different arenas of state, market and civil society and the different forms of participation, 'from below' and 'from above' (Sarvasy and Siim 1994; Siim 1998a). From this perspective, the notion of agency raises key questions about the relation between women as a social and political group and their political identities and practice, and about cooperation and conflict between women's collective agency and collective actors like the labour movement.

'Politics' is another key term that is contested and has different meanings in different theoretical traditions. Feminist scholarship has criticised the narrow understanding of politics in political science and in civic republicanism, which has politics defined exclusively in relation to political institutions and deliberations about the common good. Feminist scholarship has suggested a broader notion of the political to include the 'politics of everyday life' (Lister 1997a: 29). This does not mean that 'everything is political'. It is crucial to be able to distinguish between political questions and personal questions that we may decide for ourselves without the intervention of the state (see Phillips 1992, 1993; Elshtain 1993). In my understanding, politics is a dynamic concept that is both historical and contextual. The point is that there is a struggle about what politics is, and about where the line should be drawn between what is included and what is excluded as political. In an elaboration of the conventional distinction between politics, policy and polity, Wendy Stokes (1998) gives three dimensions of politics: the actors and the political forms of activities; the content of policies and how politics takes place; and the structure of the polity defined by political institutions, culture, laws and discourses. Politics thus includes citizens' activities in voluntary associations in civil society,[5] which can be defined as the horizontal dimension of citizenship (Andersen et al. 1993). Active citizenship refers both to political activities related to women's everyday life and women's independent organisations outside the political system, as well as to women's integration in political organisations and institutions.

The notion of discourse is inspired by Nancy Fraser's framework and by Chantal Mouffe's (1992a: 11) understanding of the political 'as a discursive constructed ensemble of social relations'. Fraser (1988: 146) distinguishes between the discursive and practical dimensions of social welfare programs and defines the discursive, or ideological, dimension 'as the tacit norms and implicit assumptions that are constitutive of practice'. I find Fraser's understanding useful because it differentiates discourse and practice as two analytical dimensions of the social, and it indicates that the forms used to describe social life are also active forces shaping it. This makes it possible to analyse the interaction between discourse and practice (see also Fraser and Gordon 1994: 5).

In the sociological tradition of Anthony Giddens (1984) and in feminist scholarship, agency thus involves a 'generative' concept of power as enabling, as opposed to 'hierarchical' power, which is 'the ability of individuals or groups to exert their will over others' (Lister 1997a). The present book aims to contribute to a synthesis of the two feminist perspectives or paradigms of power: the concept of empowerment of actors 'from below', which enables them to influence politics and political institutions; and the constraints on actors imposed by macro-sociological structures (Pateman 1988; Scott 1988). In feminist scholarship, empowerment has both an individual and a collective dimension, and is often connected with the autonomy of women to determine their own lives as well as their ability to influence politics. Iris Young (1990a: 251) has defined empowerment as 'the participation of an agent in decision-making through an effective voice and vote'. The argument is that there is space for politics and for women's agency to influence politics.

I find that access to the public, political sphere is therefore a double challenge for both women and modern democracy. Women's presence in politics can be seen as a means of changing sexual power relations in modern democracies. But it can also be seen as a way of gaining a new pluralism and diversity in modern democracy and of creating a new form of solidarity that includes not just women but all marginalised and oppressed social groups (Young 1990a; Phillips 1993; Siim 1994a; Dean 1996; Lister 1997a). Wendy Sarvasy and I used the notion of feminist pluralism to indicate that women as a collective have different political profiles, identities and interests and that citizenship practice must build bridges across the differences among women:

> First, women participate on a number of political arenas – in neighbourhoods, at work places, in formal political institutions, organisations, social movement, and the welfare state. Second, a plurality of different identities and ideologies exists within the category women. Third, each individual woman assumes a number of roles and identities. Fourth, citizens participate in a number of formal levels of political organisation, including global, regional, nation-state, and post-nation state formations. (Sarvasy and Siim 1994: 253)

It also acknowledges that the individual women have a plurality of roles and identities and often construct their own citizenship practice by combining overlapping identities and sometimes contrasting roles.

From this perspective the study of women's equal citizenship includes the dynamic connection between agency, political institutions and political discourse. The different vocabularies of rights and responsibilities, political participation, and power each express different dimensions of citizenship (Siim 1994a).

First, civil, social and political rights raise questions about formal and substantial gender equality, but also about sexual difference. The right to abortion[6] on demand, for instance, has been interpreted as an individual civil right, but it can also be interpreted as a political and social right and a body right based on sexual difference (Shaver 1997). The right to maternity leave can also be interpreted as a social right or as a right based on sexual difference or indeed on human diversity between women and men (see Sen 1992).

Second, active citizenship includes women's multiple activities in civil society as well as their presence in the political arena. This raises questions about strategies that will ensure gender equality in political participation and representation in public life. The quota system and affirmative action – forms of preferential treatment that give women a certain number of seats – have been employed to increase women's political representation. These methods to ensure gender equality are, however, contested and have been interpreted by some feminist scholars as inadvertently reproducing gender differences in politics (Mouffe 1992a,b). Democratic inclusion also raises questions about the right to form political communities and identities, about the right to cultural diversity and difference, and about the ability to create autonomous political communities and identities for ethnic groups. One question is the role of women's organisations and the interplay between the women's movement and the national political culture – that is, the variations in political values and attitudes in national contexts.[7]

Third, democratic citizenship raises issues about unequal power relations between women and men. In feminist theory the notion of power has been reconstructed to include male domination in the governing of society as well as the empowering of women, defined as a dynamic process enabling women to mobilise collectively in order to acquire 'a voice and a vote' (Young 1990a). The challenge is to integrate the two perceptions of power to a comprehensive framework of unequal power relations and to develop a dynamic understanding of power relations.

I suggest that an analysis of citizenship in terms of power contributes to increasing our understanding of both the mechanisms that reproduce sexual power structures and the role of women's agency in determining their own life as well as influencing society. This approach thus combines the question of how and through what processes the sexual hierarchies in society are created and reproduced with the question of how they have changed historically and how they may be abolished in the future.

On the theoretical level, the basic approach is inspired by feminism as well as by post-structuralism. The object of this book is twofold: to confront universal theories of citizenship with a gender perspective that makes the contradictions between the vocabularies of citizenship – freedom, equality and fraternity – visible; and to confront (universal) feminist theories of citizenship with research about the politics and dynamic of gendered citizenship in the national contexts of France, Britain and Denmark. There is a dynamic interaction between theory and research. Feminist theories can help to develop a gender-sensitive framework for comparative studies that will give us new knowledge about women's citizenship and contribute to developing feminist theories of citizenship.

The crucial question is what is the political meaning of gender in different political cultures, in the content of women's social and political rights, in the form of women's political activities, and in the content of women's political identities? This includes an analysis of the interaction between women's social and political citizenship, between women's rights and their political participation, identities and power.

The two crucial elements in my framework for understanding social and political citizenship can thus be summarised as follows:

- Active citizenship and the interaction of institutions and human agency is the key to democratic citizenship. The active/passive dimension is the aspect of citizenship that helps to explain dynamic changes as well as variations in models (Mouffe 1992a; Turner 1992, 1993). The notion of 'active citizenship' includes activities in a number of political arenas, from neighbourhoods, the workplace, informal organisations, social movements, and the welfare state to formal political organisations (Phillips 1992; Sarvasy 1994).
- The discourse about public/private is a second dimension of citizenship that contributes to explaining differences in as well as transformations of citizenship (Turner 1993). The vocabulary of 'public/private' defines the meaning of the public and private arenas and includes notions about gender and the family that are embedded in political institutions and social policies (Pateman 1988; Scott 1988).

The two dimensions of citizenship express who the agents are, the kind of politics and where the politics takes place, that is, the interaction of institutions, culture, discourses, policies and human agency. They can therefore help to explain variations in national models of citizenship as well as in women's citizenship (Siim 1998a).

Methodological Reflections and Outline of the Book

My own point of departure has been my Danish/Scandinavian background, where the political meaning of gender has changed dramatically during the last thirty years when women have been included as active citizens. I am aware that the Danish bias has coloured not only the main questions in this study but also the framework, the key concepts, and interpretations of the three cases. My curiosity for comparative work was stimulated first by the apparent contradictions between the social policy logic of the Danish context and the dominant Anglo-American norm in relation to attitudes towards public childcare that I experienced doing research in Britain and the USA in 1985 (Siim 1988, 1990). It was fuelled again by the puzzling contradiction I became aware of while living in Paris from 1993 to 1995 between the French revolutionary tradition, which excluded women from democratic citizenship, and the Danish democratic tradition, which had apparently managed to include women in the political elite.

My interest in democratic citizenship and women's agency is no doubt influenced by Danish political history as well as by Scandinavian feminist research. I have wondered why it was that women were included in democratic citizenship in Denmark, what the implications of this are for democracy and public policies, and to what extent a similar development can be expected in the French and British cases as well as in other European democracies.

One of the objectives of this study has been to contextualise the framework of citizenship and to challenge the liberal Anglo-American basis for the prevailing theories of citizenship, including the feminist language of citizenship. Feminist theorising during the 1970s and 1980s often had a bias towards liberal Anglo-American theory and practice that focused exclusively on the negative effects of the public/private divide for women (Pateman 1988, 1989).

In comparative feminist research in the 1990s, there has been an increasing interest in understanding the histories and logic of the different European welfare states (Bock and Thane 1991; Koven and Michel 1993). Feminist scholarship has also turned for inspiration to the 'women-friendly' Scandinavian welfare states, and Scandinavian feminists have started to conceptualise women's relations as mothers, workers and citizens (Hernes 1987; Siim 1988). This book aims among other things to deepen the knowledge of the Scandinavian case by presenting new research about citizenship in Denmark.

The new body of comparative feminist research has challenged the Anglo-American dominance in feminist and political theory. The recent interest in France is also part of the growing feminist interest in political and comparative history, which has made visible the gap between the revolutionary democratic tradition and the exclusion of women 'from the city' (Duby and Perrot 1992a; Rosanvallon 1992; Pedersen 1993a,b; Scott 1997a). Feminist scholarship has during the 1980s and 1990s become increasingly sensitive to context, and one of the aims of this has been to develop 'situated' knowledge. Since feminist thinking is embedded in national configurations that influence norms and frames of reference as well as interpretations, it is not surprising that British feminists have raised the issue about the virtues and inadequacies of the liberal discourse of (male) autonomy and (female) dependency and that Scandinavian feminists have criticised the paternalism of the universal welfare states and social democracy (Hernes 1987, 1988; Hirdman 1990, 1991). One of the special contributions of French feminists is the critique of the concepts of universalism and the public good in republican theories, which have made it difficult to integrate women in politics (Gaspard 1994; Varikas 1994). The comparative approach raises important questions about what concepts travel well across national and cultural boundaries and of the different meanings of key concepts like the family, market and the state as well as feminist notions of equality and difference.

The aim of the book is twofold. On the theoretical level it is to gender and degender paradigms of citizenship by confronting mainstream theories with feminist approaches. On the comparative level it is to develop a gender-sensitive framework for citizenship that is dynamic in the sense that politics (in the broad sense, which includes history, institutions, culture, discourse and agency) plays a key role in the determination of gender and citizenship.

Results from comparative studies indicate that there are fundamental differences in the understanding of gender and citizenship in European welfare states, and feminist scholars have started to conceptualise these differences (Koven and Michel 1993; Pedersen 1993b; Lewis and Ostner 1994; Siim 1994). The recent study of shifts in the discourses of gender and citizenship from different national configurations indicates a need for a more systematic analysis of the national histories and dynamics behind the evolution of women's civil, political and social rights (Bussemaker and Voet 1998). Two questions have been the inspiration behind the comparative study. From the perspective of women's social citizenship, to what extent does the male-breadwinner model in Britain represent the exception rather than the rule? To what extent does the inclusion of women in democratic citizenship in Scandinavia represent the exception or the future democratic developments? (Siim 1999b).

The methodological approach aims to develop a gender-sensitive framework for comparative studies of citizenship by examining the interaction of institutions, discourses and agency in France, Britain and Denmark. The focus is on the development of citizenship as a central institution in modern European welfare states. France, Britain and Denmark are selected because these three cases have different discourses, vocabularies and politics of citizenship, with contrasting assumptions about gender and different roles for women's agency (Siim 1999b).

In this study, the French case is taken as the point of departure because it illuminates the contradiction between the active revolutionary model of political equality premised on the exclusion of women from political citizenship (Landes 1988; Duby and Perrot 1992a). In the French vocabulary, citizenship is associated with the struggle for political rights (Rosanvallon 1992). Questions about social rights have not usually been discussed from the framework of citizenship, although feminist scholars have recently tried to re-establish the link between the social and political aspects of citizenship (Jenson and Sineau 1995; Del Re and Heinen 1996). The case thus illustrates the potential and constraints of the republican discourse and solidaristic policies to secure full and equal citizenship for women. From the point of view of political rights, France is the laggard, and the thesis is that the republican heritage helps to explain why up till the general election in 1997 women comprised only 6 per cent of the French parliament (see Chapter 4).

One of the assumptions of the book is that from the context of social policies in the European welfare states Britain represents the exception rather than the rule (Pedersen 1993b). The British case was premised on a strict division between the public and private spheres, between wage work and motherhood, and the male-breadwinner model has until recently been the basis for social policy (Lewis and Ostner 1994). Britain has had a social rights tradition going back to the heritage of social liberalism and to the influential British sociologist T. H. Marshall (1992; Lewis 1994). This tradition was challenged by almost twenty years of conservative governments (1979–97). The debate about civil and political rights has only recently been revitalised by the Left (Lister 1998a). The case thus illustrates the limits and possibilities of social-liberal discourse and politics to secure full and equal citizenship for women. From the point of view of social policies, Britain is the laggard, and my thesis is that the social-liberal discourse helps to explain why British women still lack crucial social rights in relation to maternity and childcare (see Chapter 5).

Denmark has no separate citizenship tradition, and the language of citizenship has only recently been used in political discourse and academic debate. The Danish case combines an active participatory model with a tradition for universal social rights (Siim 1998a, 1999b). Feminist scholarship has suggested that this model has opened up a space for women's agency to influence politics and, more recently, for the inclusion of women in politics (Hernes 1987; Siim 1988). In spite of this, there is no gender equality in terms of political power and there is still a high degree of sexual segregation in the labour market. The Danish case thus illustrates the limits and possibilities of the egalitarian social-democratic discourse and universal social policies for women's full and equal citizenship. It represents a participatory model of citizenship that has constructed citizenship 'from below', and my thesis is that the Danish model of citizenship helps to explain women's specific inclusion in the public arena (see Chapter 6).

On the comparative level, the object of the book is first to analyse the interplay between women's social and political citizenship in crucial periods of formation of the welfare state and democracy. Second, it is to study the way in which demands from women's agency could establish a link between the different political arenas. The emphasis is thus on continuity in discourse and the vocabulary of gender and citizenship in the three cases, as well as on turning-points in political development. The research interest is to discuss the shifts in the discourse and policies of citizenship and gender during the last thirty years. The period of study ends in 1997 with the rise to power of a new Red–Green coalition in France and the victory of New Labour in Britain. It does not address in any detail the recent shifts in the discourse of gender and citizenship in France, Britain and Denmark (see *Critical Social Policy* 18, 1998).

The book aims to trace the logic of women's civil, political and social citizenship in different contexts on the basis of comparative studies of national histories, institutions, cultures and discourses. The first chapter discusses a gender-sensitive framework of citizenship on the basis of critical readings of the classical works of T. H. Marshall and the typology developed by the English sociologist Brian Turner. It is also inspired by the debate about the male-breadwinner model, a notion that was first introduced by Jane Lewis and Ilona Ostner.

The second chapter traces the classical traditions of citizenship, liberalism, socialism and republicanism and the feminist criticism. In the third chapter I have selected three feminist approaches that each represent a dominant paradigm. They tell different stories about citizenship and gender: the patriarchal hypothesis, the maternal-communitarian model, and the pluralist-participatory model. They are each confronted by challenges from the postmodern paradigm.

The next three chapters are case studies of the discourse about gender and citizenship in France, Britain and Denmark and the different dynamics and histories of citizenship. I conclude by discussing the implications for feminist theory and research, linking results from the case studies with feminist paradigms, with the new problems of citizenship in modern democracies connected with formal gender equality, and with new differences in and between women.

CHAPTER 1

Towards a Gender-sensitive Framework of Citizenship

On the comparative level, the object of this book is twofold: to analyse the different assumptions about gender and citizenship in France, Britain and Denmark; and to analyse the interaction between women's agency, political discourse and political institutions and the implications for social policies and democracy in all three cases. The basic assumption is that there is indeed room for women's agency to influence political discourse, political institutions and public policies depending on the national contexts.

The Heritage from Marshall

T. H. Marshall's model is contested. Sociologists have used his framework when analysing the institutionalisation of social *rights* (Turner 1992), whereas political scientists have emphasised the *participatory* aspect and the need to integrate social groups not just because of their socio-economic status but also because of their socio-cultural 'difference' (Young 1990a).

Today, Marshall is used as the inspiration behind rethinking the framework of citizenship and as a critical measure in our evaluating the extent to which modern democracies live up to the ideals of freedom and equality. The British sociologist Nira Yuval-Davis (1997: 49) has recently suggested that Marshall's definition enables us to discuss citizenship as a multi-tier construct, a construct that applies to people's membership in a variety of collectivities – local, ethnic, national and transnational.

Marshall's model was based on the development of the rights of *men* and thus failed to notice that the development of women's rights and other subordinated groups has had its own history and logic. Yuval-Davis

(1997: 49) has argued that a comparative study of citizenship should consider the issue of women's citizenship not only in relation to men but also in relation to women's affiliation to dominant and subordinated groups, their ethnicity, origin, and rural or urban residence.

Feminist scholarship has noticed that women in many countries gained social rights as mothers or workers before they got the vote, and before they even got civil rights in marriage (Bock 1992). The point is that rights often mean one thing for women and another for men, for instance the right to contraception and abortion, because men and women have different lives and different bodies (Orloff 1993; Pateman 1992). Marshall's framework is based on class and on the interplay between the market and the state, and it neglects the role of family and civil society. The inclusion of women in the framework of citizenship thus poses new questions about the interconnection of civil society, family and the state, and indeed the gendered division of family life.

Marshall's model has been criticised from a comparative perspective. It is based on the political history of Britain, and this chronology of rights does not fit other European welfare states, for example France, Germany or Scandinavia (Rosanvallon 1992; Turner 1992). This point also has implications for the development of a comparative framework for understanding women's citizenship. Not only is the evolution of women's rights and the dynamic of women's citizenship different from men's, but citizenship also has different histories and patterns depending on national configurations (Bock 1992; Sineau 1992b; Pedersen 1993b; Siim 1998a).

The Male-breadwinner Model

During the last ten years the work of the Danish-Swedish sociologist Gøsta Esping-Andersen has been an important inspiration for reinventing the framework of citizenship among sociologists, political scientists and feminists. This framework has categorised welfare states within three welfare regimes: the institutional social democratic model, built on universal citizen rights; the corporatist-conservative model, built on the insurance principle; and the liberal model, built on residual needs (Esping-Andersen 1985, 1990, 1996). The key concept in his model is power resources based on class, and the differences between the regimes are explained by the different dynamics between economy and state. Esping-Andersen's framework (1985) is more dynamic than Marshall's and was originally constructed with Sweden as the ideal model – that is, close to the vision of a universal welfare state based on citizenship.

Esping-Andersen's approach has been an important inspiration for feminist scholarship (Sainsbury 1994), but it has been noticed that gender relations cut across the three systems of welfare because the state–family nexus is different from the state–market nexus. As Lewis (1992: 161) has noticed, 'the worker he has in mind is male, and women only enter the analysis when they enter the labour market'.

The alternative feminist frameworks have emphasised the inter-dependence between wage work and caring work. In their pioneering work the British historian Jane Lewis and the German sociologist Ilona Ostner discussed the categorisation of European welfare regimes from the perspective of the gender division of work. The argument is that the norm about a male breadwinner represents a crucial principle that 'in its ideal form prescribes bread-winning for men and homemaking/caring for women'. According to Lewis and Ostner the principle cuts across the different welfare regimes and has only recently been challenged. In their analysis of the male breadwinner as norm and reality in the development of European social policies, they differentiate between strong, medium and weak breadwinner states (1994: 17–19). The argument is that the strength or weakness of the male-breadwinner model 'serves as a pre-dictor of the way in which women are treated in social security systems; the level of social service provisions, particularly in regard to childcare; and the nature of married women's participation in the labour market' (1994: 19).

The male-breadwinner model is attractive because it gives an ex-planation of women's second-rate citizenship, and it has been influential in comparative feminist research about the welfare state (Sainsbury 1994). It is a useful model that pinpoints a missing factor in Marshall's framework, that is, women's relation to wage work. The model is under-developed, and Lewis and Ostner have acknowledged the need to take the differentiation further because, as they have observed, 'too many and too diverse countries fall into the "strong male breadwinner" model' (1994: 11).

The model tends to reduce both the development of social policies and women's wage work to a single universal logic. The problem with the framework is thus a tendency to explain women's second-rate citizen-ship by one factor – the male-breadwinner norm. I suggest that there is no underlying logic determining gender relations. Neither the patri-archal logic nor macro-economics has the ability to explain the male-breadwinner model. There is a need to discuss the structural forces behind the model as well as the role of actors such as employers, trade unions, political parties and women's organisations in the formation of the welfare state (Pedersen 1993b). The alternative is to develop a more dynamic framework within which we can analyse the different social policy logic and the different interplay between women's civil, social and political rights (Siim 1999a).

Historical studies indicate that social policies towards mothers have often been connected with concerns about women's wage work (Pedersen 1993a). They also indicate that generous social policies towards mothers and children in the French case contrasted with feminist demands to increase women's civil, social and political rights (Bock 1992; Pedersen 1993a). The implication is that neither woman's role in the development of the welfare state nor her political presence can be deduced from the strength or weakness of the male-breadwinner model. Research indicates that there are different meanings and implications attached to the emphasis on women's motherly roles. In countries like France women have high activity rates on the labour market and low representation in politics. In other countries women have a relatively high representation in politics, as in Norway in the 1970s (and the Netherlands in the 1990s), combined with a relatively low activity rate of married women on the labour market (Leira 1992). In sum, the male-breadwinner model captures a crucial feature of the British (and German) case in particular. It is problematic as a general model, however, because it does not explain the variation in or the different logic connected with social policies and women's citizenship in national configurations (Pedersen 1993b).

An important feminist point is that gender systems cut across the existing models of welfare and citizenship. And the attempt to gender welfare regimes by differentiating between strong, medium and weak regimes on the basis of the male-breadwinner norm has been an important step towards a comparative framework sensitive to gender (Lewis and Ostner 1994: 17). Feminist scholarship has increasingly analysed the gender-specific policy logic and dynamic of citizenship from different contexts (Koven and Michel 1993; Orloff 1993). Historical scholarship has documented the different logic and chronology of women's rights as well as the different role of women's agency in the development of welfare states (Bock and Thane 1991; Bock and James 1992; Koven and Michels 1993). It has been argued that women have had a greater influence on the construction of social policies in 'weak' states like Britain and the USA than in 'strong' states like France and Germany (see Koven and Michel 1993). This is difficult to prove and has indeed been challenged by a number of scholars (see Lewis 1994).[1]

The debate about the role of women in the formation of welfare states has raised the question of the definitions of the notions of paternalism and maternalism (Bock 1992). The notion of *paternalism* is usually defined as men's political power over women. There is no consensus about how to define *maternalism*. It has recently been defined as 'ideologies, and discourses that exalted women's capacities to mother and applied to society as a whole the values that they attached to that role: care nurturance and morality' (Koven and Michel 1993: 6). This definition does not include women's active agency and thus makes it difficult to distinguish from paternalism, which may also be combined with a positive assessment of motherhood and women's capacity to mother (for example in the French and Danish cases before World War II).

The French case shows that maternalist ideologies were often shared by women's organisations as well as by policy-makers (Bock 1992; Pedersen 1993b). From this perspective, maternalist policies are those favourable to women in their roles as mothers. The problem is that maternalism is an ideological concept which in theory and research has many different meanings. First, the term tends to obscure the difference between the motivation behind policies, policy logic, and the effect of policies. Overlapping paternalist, pronatalist and maternalist arguments have motivated social policies towards women and children. Second, the use of 'maternalism' as a blanket term does not differentiate between its different forms: what is crucial from a feminist perspective is the extent to which public policies were hostile or favourable to women as workers. Finally, it is important to be able to distinguish maternalist policies from 'women-friendly' policies, defined as policies favourable to women in their multiple roles as parents, workers and citizens and that do not subsume women under their roles as mothers (Hernes 1987).

The debate about the role of women's agency indicates that the male-breadwinner model is not universal logic. I suggest that a gender-sensitive framework of citizenship should therefore be able to conceptualise three relatively independent dimensions and the relations between them: civil rights; social welfare rights, including economic rights on the labour market; and democratic rights.

To sum up, the advantage of the framework of citizenship is the ability to conceptualise women's rights as embedded in different national social policies and democratic politics. Women and men have had different *access* to citizenship, and, at a political-institutional level, the different 'models' of citizenship express different gender systems, that is, specific ways of organising gender relations that have implications for women's agency. Contextualising the framework of citizenship is important for analysing the political discourses, institutions and forces that have each influenced the nature and chronology of women's civil, social and political rights. The implication is that the Danish, French and British cases are expected to express different discourses about gender and citizenship and different social policy logic, which have implications for women's citizenship and the possibilities for and constraints on women's full and equal citizenship.

The Inclusion of Gender in a Comparative Framework of Citizenship

The universal model of citizenship has been connected with the building of the European national states during the last 200 years. Recent attempts to transcend the ethnocentric and androcentric framework of citizenship have come from research about national variations in the formation of citizenship (Turner 1992) as well as from reflections on the struggle of women and ethnic groups to obtain civil, political and social rights (Yuval-Davis 1997).

The following discussion about a comparative framework of citizenship is inspired by the typology of citizenship introduced by the British sociologist Brian Turner (1992). Turner's typology, based on national histories, has two axes or dimensions that describe the interplay between citizens and political institutions, and between the public and private arena (1992: 52–6).

One is the *active/passive dimension,* which expresses how the rights of citizens were historically institutionalised in modern democracies, for example 'from below' through revolutionary movements against the absolutist state, or 'from above' with the active support of the state. The other, the *public/private dimension,* expresses whether the key to citizenship is connected with the public or the private sphere, with public or private virtues.

Turner's model is based on the different histories of citizenship in Europe and the USA. The German case, combining an emphasis on the private sphere (i.e. the family and religion) with a view of the state as the only source of public authority, is taken as a point of departure. On this basis Turner develops an ideal-typical construct with four different cases. On one axis, the passive German tradition with an emphasis on *private* virtues is contrasted with the passive British tradition, where rights were handed down from above by the constitutional settlement of 1688, which at the same time created British citizens as legal personalities. On another axis, the active revolutionary American tradition is combined with the private virtues of citizenship and is contrasted with the active revolutionary French tradition, which is combined with an emphasis on the public virtues of citizenship. The object of his typology is twofold:

> The point of this historical sketch has been partly to provide a critique of the monolithic and unified conception of citizenship in Marshall and partly to offer a sociological model of citizenship along two axes, namely public and private definitions of moral activity in terms of the creation of a public space of political activity, and active and passive forms of citizenship in terms of whether the citizen is conceptualised merely as a subject of an absolute authority or as an active political agent. (Turner 1992: 55)

According to Turner, the structural relationship between the private and public arenas and their cultural meanings are both essential components of any understanding of the relationship between totalitarianism and democracy.

Turner's typology is both ethnocentric and gender-blind because he does not observe that the structural relationship between the private and the public, as well as their meanings, is also an essential component of the understanding of gender differences in modern democracies. The point is that the discourse of the family needs to be analysed from a gender perspective. Sylvia Walby (1994) has noticed that there is a difficulty in Turner's understanding of the private arena, which has two different meanings in the model: individual autonomy in the family, and freedom from state intervention. Yuval-Davis (1997: 57) has constructed an alternative based on Turner's two axes that incorporates the notion of difference for analysing gendered citizenship. She proposes abandoning the public/private distinction and instead differentiating between the state, civil society, and the domain of the family, kinship and other primary relations (1997: 57).

From a gender perspective it is a problem that the liberal model based on individual autonomy did not apply to women. During the 18th and 19th centuries married women had no autonomy in the family, where in both theory and practice they were subordinated as dependent wives (Pateman 1988; Mills 1989). In practice and in theory the 'private' arena of the family is a contradiction in terms – the feminist point being that power relations operate in the family as well as in the social relations of the market and civil society (Walby 1994). There are different perceptions of the private, as well as of the public, arena in political philosophy, and construction of the border between the public and private arena has gendered implications (Lister 1995). Feminist scholars have noted that the private sphere is often contradictory for women because it is both a site of caring and mothering and a site of oppression and dependency (Yuval-Davis 1997).

Historically, women have never been considered to be autonomous individuals, and from a gender perspective there is therefore a need for state regulation of families with the object of transforming the private sphere of the family, civil society and the market. I suggest that gender relations and the perception of caring work is a crucial aspect of social citizenship as well as of the development of the welfare state. The public/private dimension will therefore be redefined to include perceptions about gender as well as the relation between wage work and care work (see Knijn and Kremer 1997).

The gendered perception of the private arena is one problem for Turner's model. Another is the historical exclusion of women and minority groups from an active citizenship. I suggest that gender systems cross Turner's typology of citizenship because the active notion of citizenship does not include women and marginalised social groups. Feminist scholarship has made visible how even the active, republican model of citizenship, like France, where women participated in the revolutionary movement in 1789, was premised on women's expulsion from the public domain (Landes 1988). A problem noted by Yuval-Davis is how the language of active and passive citizenship in effect has many different meanings. The differentiation into active or passive citizens may refer to the division between formal as against substantive rights, to active groups in the *formation* as against the *evolution* of democracy, and to ruling as against being ruled (Yuval-Davis 1997: 59; see also Lister 1998a).

In modern democracies active citizenship has many different meanings, and access to democratic citizenship has been unequal in terms of rights, power and influence. Women were historically excluded from formal political rights even though they were often active, along with men, in voluntary organisations in civil society before they got the vote. I suggest that the inclusion or exclusion of women and marginalised social groups from the public sphere is crucial to the formation and evolution of democracy. The passive/active axis will therefore be re-defined to include activities of social groups and of formal and informal organisations in civil society, as well as their inclusion and exclusion from the public arena (Young 1990a; Phillips 1995; Yuval-Davis 1997).

The Vocabulary of Gender and Citizenship in France, Britain and Denmark

I suggest that a gender perspective on citizenship can bring about a new understanding of the dynamic of citizenship. In Turner's model, France is an example of a revolutionary conception of citizenship 'from below' (1992). From a gender perspective it becomes visible that the republican discourse was based on a specific conception of women's rights and of the family, which feminist scholars have called 'republican maternalism' (Bock 1992). This explains why the republican model has in general supported interventionist family policies, what Susan Pedersen (1993b) has called 'parental policies'. Parental policies were built on a double assumption that women are both workers and mothers – and that subsequently public policies ought to support women in their dual role.

The republican discourse has defended an active family policy, but the hypothesis is that it has at the same time served as an influential insti-tutional and cultural barrier to women's equal integration as citizens. The discourse combines the notion of active citizenship built on the male norm with a notion of the common good that subordinates private values to public virtues (Sineau 1992b). During the last thirty years there has been an integration of women in the labour market and an expansion of childcare centres, but the expansion of social rights has not been followed by an inclusion of women in politics (Jenson and Sineau 1995).

Britain has been characterised as a 'passive' democracy with a strong emphasis on private liberty (Turner 1992). The gender perspective has thrown new light on the social liberal discourse about the private/public divide, which in Britain, in contrast to France, has supported individual rights against the state. The British idea of 'the private' implies that women's needs must be met either through the market or within the family. A strong male-breadwinner model based on the assumptions that women are either workers or mothers has dominated British social policies (Lewis 1994).

It is hypothesised that the social liberal discourse and nature of the public/private divide in Britain has served as an influential institutional and cultural barrier preventing the adoption of public policies supporting the 'working mother'. Women's active citizenship in voluntary organisations has historically been strong, but opposition from the trade unions and conservative forces has prevented the adoption of social policies to support working mothers in the interwar period (Pedersen 1993b). During the last thirty years women have been integrated into the labour market, and it is remarkable that this expansion of women as wage workers has not been followed by a change in social policies to support the role of women as working mothers (Lovenduski and Randall 1993).

The Scandinavian conception of citizenship does not fit into Turner's model. In Denmark, absolute monarchy ended peacefully when the King handed power over to the new democratic constitution of 1849 (Ross 1997: 58). This constitution was ahead of its time and introduced free and equal elections for all citizens, with the exception of women, servants and paupers. Political and social rights developed gradually during the 19th and 20th centuries, and Denmark developed a universal welfare state and a participatory perception of citizenship that incorporated social groups 'from below' (Andersen et al. 1993; Andersen and Torpe 1994; Kolstrup 1996). The modern Danish political culture has been described as a mix of the continental and the Anglo-Saxon tradition that idealised neither the state, like the French, nor the private sphere, like the British (Nielsen 1991: 81).

The Danish political discourse expresses a 'balance' between the public and private arena and between citizens and the state that has enabled social and political forces to influence social politics 'from below' through the cooperation between social democracy, the trade union movement, and voluntary organisations (Kolstrup 1996). It is hypothesised that this may also in some cases have given women's organisations a space to influence social policies (Siim 1999b). During the last thirty years, democratic citizenship has changed to include women's integration into the public, political arena. This has given women new potential to influence public policies through political institutions and organisations. During the same time new problems related to the gender-segregated labour market have become visible as well as new differences 'in and between women' based on education, employment and ethnicity. At issue is the extent to which and on what ground women today can be mobilised around common interests, and in what way women's inclusion makes a difference to social policies and democratic politics.

To sum up, from a gender perspective it is important to analyse the structural relations and discursive meanings of the notions of public and private as well as different meanings of key concepts like civil society, the market and the family. The argument is that women's agency in a broad sense is a key concept that, on both the theoretical and the empirical level, is able to establish a link between the social and political aspects of citizenship as well as between the arenas of market, state and civil society.

In the following chapters, Turner's two dimensions are used as inspiration for developing a comparative framework of citizenship from a feminist perspective. These are the main issues in the analysis of gender and citizenship in France, Britain and Denmark:

- A comparison of the vocabulary of citizenship and gender in the three cases, especially the discursive meanings of the family, civil society and the public arena, and the nature of women's exclusion from the public arena and their inclusion as mothers, workers and citizens in civil society.
- A comparison of women's demands for civil, political and social rights in crucial periods of welfare state formation and the role of women's agency – women's organisations, women's activities in voluntary organisations, political parties and social movements – in influencing politics.
- A comparison of the shifts in the language of citizenship and gender equality and in the policies towards working mothers during the last thirty years.
- A comparison of the shifts in the language of women's active democratic citizenship during the last thirty years and of the implications of women's political mobilisation for the political meaning of gender and for women's inclusion in politics.

The book ends with a discussion about the implications of globalisation and the present restructuring of the European democracies and welfare states for gender and citizenship. Is there a tendency towards a convergence of women's social and political citizenship in the European welfare states towards a dual-breadwinner model and towards women's inclusion in politics? Does women's inclusion in the political elite in Scandinavia express a general tendency toward democratisation, or does Scandinavia represent the exception to the rule?

CHAPTER 2

Theories about Citizenship

The Classical Traditions: Liberalism, Republicanism and Socialism

Citizenship is contested, and the dominant frameworks of citizenship in social and political theory have been inspired by liberal, socialist or republican traditions. During the last ten years there has been renewed interest in rethinking the theories of citizenship and in developing a new synthesis between civic republicanism, liberalism, socialism and feminism (Mouffe 1992a; Phillips 1992; Lister 1997a). New research has examined the tensions and dilemmas in the general principles of freedom, equality and fraternity in the classical traditions on the basis of new problems with exclusion and inclusion in modern democracies (Held 1987; Kymlicka 1990; Mouffe 1992a).

Studying citizenship can thus throw light on some of the major issues about relations between individuals, political communities and the state (Yuval-Davis 1997: 50). The concept of citizenship has laid out a common ground for discussions around the key questions and central dilemmas of modern democracies: the contrast between individual liberty and the equality of citizens; the contrast between the rights and duties of individuals and public virtues of citizenship; and the contrast between the unity of political communities and the right to cultural diversity and difference (Kymlicka and Norman 1994; Mouffe 1994; Touraine 1994).

Rethinking Democratic and Social Citizenship

The key concepts in modern democracies have their roots in the Enlightenment philosophers and in the declaration of the Rights of Man, but there are different interpretations of the basic ideas. *Classical liberalism* has emphasised the rights of the individual and the freedom of the individual citizen from the constraints of the state; the ideal citizen is the 'autonomous' individual. *Social liberalism* (and social democracy) has emphasised the need for social rights as a precondition for political equality and democracy. Socialism has emphasised the need for social equality, and the ideal citizen in social democracy is the citizen-worker. *Civic republicanism* has focused on the need to create a political community, a common bond between citizens, which bridges differences of class, religion and culture. The ideal citizen is the political animal who participates on the public arena with the purpose of serving the common good, and who is abstracted from the individual business of the private world.

The emphasis in civic republicanism on the common interests that tie citizens to the state has been an important inspiration for theories of citizenship. Republicanism can be traced back to the different political philosophies of Aristotle, Niccolò Machiavelli, Alexis de Tocqueville, Jean Jacques Rousseau and, more recently, to Hannah Arendt. Modern republicanism has its roots in the Enlightenment and in the ideas of the French Revolution, which introduced the new ideal of political equality as well as the bonds of fraternity and solidarity between citizens and the state (Rosanvallon 1992).

Modern republicanism has been criticised by liberals for abandoning individual freedom and choice, for giving priority to the 'common good' and for subsuming the interests of the individual under the 'general will'. It has also been criticised by socialists and feminists for underestimating the social inequalities of class and gender that tend to reproduce power hierarchies and inequalities in politics. The ideal citizen in republican thinking is the soldier. This has made republicanism appear to be diametrically opposed to feminism, whereas liberalism and socialism, with the emphasis on individual autonomy and social equality, seems to have more to offer women (Phillips 1992: 49–53).

The new interest in civic republicanism is a reaction to the dominant influence of the political discourses of neo-liberalism and new conservatism during the last twenty-five years. Neo-republican thinkers have expanded the concept of civic duty and have encouraged increased citizen participation in the political process as a way to increase both individual liberty and political equality (Held 1987). One problem with neo-republicanism is its tendency to idealise the public, political sphere and to denigrate both the market and the private sphere of the family (Walzer 1992).

In contrast to liberal individualism, communitarianism has emphasised the shared ideas and solidarities in specific communities (Phillips 1992: 14), and it has been interpreted as either a separate tradition or as another version of republicanism (Bussemaker and Voet 1998). The critique of communitarianism is that its vision is based on a notion of culture that tends to limit the freedom of the individual and the plurality of lifestyles within the community (Bauman 1997: 186–98). Today, there is an increasing tension between the old republican ideals of civic virtues and the growth of cultural pluralism, heterogeneity and difference. There is also tension between the notions of communitarianism and feminism, as well as a certain affinity, because both tend to criticise liberal individualism and to value caring and compassion (Young 1990b; Phillips 1992).

The Framework of Social Rights

T. H. Marshall's work on social citizenship has inspired new theory and research about citizenship locally, nationally and globally (Petersson et al. 1989; Andersen et al. 1993; Rosanvallon 1995; Benhabib 1999). He introduced a comprehensive theory of democratic citizenship in modern societies based on the evolution of rights in British society from the 18th to the 20th century.

On the basis of British history, Marshall (1992: 18) differentiated between three types of rights: the *civil* element that includes individual rights of freedom such as freedom of speech; the *political* element that includes the right to self-determination and to participate in the exercise of political power; and the *social* element that includes the right to a guaranteed minimum of social and economic welfare. During the 20th century the main idea was the expansion of the principle of universal rights, that is, the equal right of all citizens to the same benefit. The conclusion of the analysis of British society was that universal social rights in relation to education and health care were the most important means of integrating the working class into society during the 20th century. The question is the extent to which this model is still useful for understanding the exclusion and inclusion of other oppressed groups and for understanding cross-national differences (Bottomore 1992; Yuval-Davis 1997).

Marshall (1950: 6) understands citizenship as the equal rights of all members of a society to be accepted 'as full members of the community, that is, as citizens'. This understanding focuses on the qualitative aspects of equality and on the right of the individual to enjoy a certain standard of civilised life and to be admitted to a share in the social heritage.

Citizenship in Marshall's understanding is both a normative and a critical concept:

> Citizenship is the status bestowed on those who are full members of a community. All who possess the standards are equal with respect to the rights and duties with which the status is endowed. There is no universal principle

that determines what those rights and duties shall be, but societies in which citizenship is a developing institution create an image of an ideal citizenship against which achievement can be measured and towards which aspiration can be directed. (1992: 18)

Marshall has a vision about a just society based on all citizens' equal participation in social and political communities where social inequalities connected with class will not be passed on from one generation to the next. The main emphasis is on the rights (and duties) of citizens, but he also describes the importance of the common culture and common experiences as an expression of the citizen's membership in and belonging to a political community.

One crucial question in Marshall's tradition is the impact of citizenship on social class. It is his main conclusion that the evolution of modern citizenship has significantly diminished social and economic inequalities under capitalism. The more recent analyses of citizenship in Britain, however, have turned the question around by focusing on the impact of social class on citizenship (Bottomore 1992).

Another key question is the interrelation of civil, political and social rights. In the historical sketch of the evolution of citizenship in Britain, the last 250 years is interpreted as a period of constant drive towards an evolution of citizen rights, especially towards an extension of social rights. This evolutionary model has been criticised for its tendency to determinism (Turner 1992; Giddens 1994).

The recent discussion of Marshall's work has concentrated on the new questions of citizenship in modern welfare states, especially those of immigration, ethnic and gender inequalities, and of new forms of exclusion and poverty (Bottomore 1992; Lister 1995). One of the main points of criticism of Marshall's work has been the tendency towards ethnocentrism and Anglocentrism because he takes the British case as a 'model' for the evolution of citizenship (Rosanvallon 1992).

From a feminist perspective, Marshall's model of citizenship has been criticised for being androcentric because his framework was built on an underlying male norm: the citizen was a man, and wage work was implicitly the basis for citizen rights (Pateman 1992). Feminist scholarship has shown that the welfare systems in most European welfare states have been based on gendered principles of division between wage work and unpaid care work, with men as breadwinners and women as economically dependent (Lewis and Ostner 1994). This has raised the question of the gender-specific meaning and chronology of civil, political and social rights (Orloff 1993). Citizen rights were in general accorded to women later than to men; women were generally regarded as second-class citizens, and often gained social rights as mothers before they obtained the right to vote (Bock 1992).

Visions of Democratic Citizenship

Marshall's classical model has been one inspiration for the recent re-thinking of citizenship. His conception of citizenship has been criticised as a 'citizenship-as-rights' expressing a 'private' or 'passive' understanding of citizenship (Kymlicka and Gordon 1994). The New Right has claimed that the language of rights must be supplemented by a language of responsibilities, whereas the New Left and civic republicanism have claimed the need for a new model of *participatory democracy* that can engage citizens actively in public life (Mouffe 1992a; Phillips 1992).

The underlying questions behind the different models and visions of citizenship concern how politics should be defined and what the social conditions have to be if we are to influence political decisions. A related question is how citizens learn civic virtues. The answers have varied, from civic republicanism emphasising participation in public life, and communitarianism emphasising the value of social practices in the community, to feminist communitarians valuing the 'ethics of care' in the family. All solutions raise the dilemma between the autonomy/freedom of individual citizens, associations and political communities and the need to promote 'responsible' citizenship in accordance with the 'general will'.

Another set of questions relates to citizenship as 'an identity, an expression of one's membership in a community' (Kymlicka and Gordon 1994). How can the new socio-cultural emphasis on 'differences' be integrated into the universal conception of citizenship? The dilemma this time is between the freedom and autonomy of groups and the interests of the (national) political community. Should ethnic groups give up their specific experiences and identities, or is the goal rather to create a pluralist and 'differentiated citizenship' based on heterogeneity and difference (Young 1990b; Phillips 1993)? The present emphases on universalism in the republican (French) culture and on multiculturalism in the liberal democratic culture can be seen as two solutions to the dilemmas of modern citizenship.

The French sociologist Alain Touraine (1994: 176) has criticised both civic republicanism and liberalism by arguing that there is an irrevocable tension between the dimensions of freedom and equality that cannot be removed by a new synthesis or a new 'principle of justice' à la John Rawls. The principle of an active subject that creates itself through a double struggle against the domination (and rationality) of the state and the market is at the centre of Touraine's theory of democracy, which is based on an ideal of individual independence and responsibility. 'Democracy cannot reduce the human being to a citizen; it recognises her as a free individual who also belongs to the economic and cultural community'

(Touraine 1994: 29, my translation). The implication is that if there are no 'models' (male or female), citizens must find new combinations of their public and private lives (1994: 196).

The British political scientist David Held (1987: 24–5) calls his vision the 'double democratisation' of state and civil society. His position combines the principles of liberalism with republicanism and socialism, and he makes 'participation' in a broad sense the central aspect of democratic life. The 'active citizen' could once again return to the centre of public life, involving him or herself in the realms of both state and society.

Chantal Mouffe's (1992a: 4) vision of a radical democratic citizenship also has participation at the centre as well as the need to re-establish the link between social and political citizenship. According to Mouffe there is a need to place the individual bearer of right in a political community based on new political identities, and she defines citizenship as 'the political identity that is created with identification with respublica'. In contrast to liberalism, citizenship is not just one identity next to others, and in contrast to civic republicanism, citizenship is not a dominant identity that overrides all others (ibid.: 235). The aim is to create a new radical democratic identity, a collective 'we' that allows for pluralism, because this is an expression of many collective forms of demands. Mouffe, like Touraine, argues that the tension between liberty and freedom in modern democracies cannot be resolved. She goes one step further and suggests that the tension between private (individual liberty) and public (respublica) is also tension on the individual level between the freedom as individuals and the duties as citizens (ibid.: 238).

The Canadian philosopher Will Kymlicka (1990: 1–8) has evaluated the competing political philosophies, including feminism, by assessing the strength and coherence of their arguments for the rightness of their views. He suggests that there is a common idea in political theory – the idea of treating people 'as equals'. According to Kymlicka, the potential of republicanism is in its emphasis on the civic responsibilities of citizens and political participation, but citizens have to be free if a just society is to be created. The potential of liberalism is in its emphasis on individual liberty and on the freedom of citizens, but there is the need for a political community to defend the principles of individual liberty. The potential of socialism is in its emphasis on social equality among citizens, but there is a need for both autonomous individuals and associations if an egalitarian and just society is to be created.

How does feminism fit into this picture? On the most general theoretical level, the two central feminist criticisms are first the critique of the belief in abstract universalism of civic republicanism, and second the liberal belief in the separation between the public and the private sphere (Pateman 1988; Young 1989; Phillips 1992). Both traditions have been the basis for the exclusion of women from the public, political sphere and their inclusion as mothers. The critique has opened up a fruitful dialogue between political theories and feminism about how to integrate principles of diversity and difference based on gender, race, ethnicity, and about the need to rethink the public/private divide in ways that reintegrate the family within public life (Kymlicka 1990: Ch. 7).

On the comparative political-institutional and political-cultural level, the critique of the ethnocentrism and androcentrism of Marshall's theories has been followed by analyses of different models of citizenship, welfare and gender systems in different national contexts (Bock and Thane 1991; Bock and James 1992). Results from comparative research have highlighted the variations in national political cultures, institutions and discourses that have shaped the different relations between the civil, political and social aspects of citizenship. I agree with Ruth Lister (1997a: 33–41) that the notion of agency can link theory and research and contribute to creating a new synthesis between the historical tradition of participatory republicanism and the liberal social rights tradition. To this I would add the notions of social equality, justice and solidarity from the socialist traditions. The synthesis between the three different dimensions of citizenship can re-establish the dynamic understanding between the empowerment of citizens and the structural constraints on the actions of citizens.

The feminist critique of liberalism, civic republicanism and communitarianism has opened up a discussion about women's active citizenship as well as about the role of women's agency in the formation and evolution of welfare states (Koven and Michel 1993; Lewis 1994). Comparative political history indicates that women's organisations have been active in the fight for civil, political and social rights. It has also shown that there have been different models of mobilisation for women in France, Britain and Denmark and different impacts of women's agency on the formation of the welfare state and the development of social policies (Bock 1992; Pedersen 1993b).

CHAPTER 3

Feminist Approaches to Citizenship

The notion of citizenship as well as the meaning of citizenship for women is contested. Carole Pateman's paradigmatic work was the starting point for the feminist rethinking of citizenship based on a critique of the public/private divide (1985, 1988, 1989). During the past ten years the feminist debate about citizenship has highlighted the contradictions between the general principles of freedom, equality and fraternity/solidarity in the public, political sphere and the continuing fact of sexual inequality. Feminist scholarship claims that women's exclusion from the public, political sphere is to some extent 'determined' by structural inequalities in the family and in the labour market. Feminist scholars disagree about definitions of power and about the meaning of the public and the private sphere as well as about visions for a full citizenship for women.

The feminist debate about 'equality and difference' is connected with the question of citizenship because they both refer to ideas of justice, political participation, power and equality of rights (Bussemaker and Voet 1998: 283). There is a tension in feminist scholarship between visions based on gender equality and visions based on sexual difference. The feminist approaches to citizenship have been inspired by the great philosophical traditions, although at the same time they transcend them. The diversity within feminism is great because the major philosophies are represented within it (Kymlicka 1990: 238).

In what follows I have summed up important differences between the feminist approaches to citizenship in three models: Pateman's patriarchal hypothesis; the maternal-communitarian model; and the pluralist participatory model. I conclude by discussing the challenge from postmodern feminism to the framework of citizenship.

71709

Key Notions in the Feminist Vocabulary
of Citizenship

What I have called the *maternalist-communitarian* model has affinities with the ideas of Jean Jacques Rousseau because it values women's social and cultural difference from men (Elshtain 1993). Historically, sexual difference has been associated with inequality in power and influence, and the problem is whether and to what extent women can be at the same time different and equal.

The *pluralist-participatory* model is rooted in republican ideals of active citizenship as well as in the social liberalism of John Stuart Mills (Phillips 1992, 1993). The focus on political equality between women and men is the basis for a critique of policies reproducing sexual differences between the two. The problem is how to integrate demands for political equality with a defence of bodily rights based on women's difference, for example the right (or freedom) of women to choose whether or not to have children.

Finally, the recent feminist emphasis on difference based on ethnicity and diversity among women is connected with the post-structural and postmodern critique[1] of essentialism and universalism (Fraser and Nicholson 1994; Yuval-Davis 1997). Postmodernism is critical of strategies of gender equality, and postmodern feminists emphasise women's autonomy or freedom as different from that of men. One of the problems is how to reconcile women's individual autonomy with power differences between women and men at the structural level (Nicholson and Fraser 1994).

Feminist scholarship has examined the roots of women's exclusion from politics as well as the conditions for their inclusion in the public, political arena. The critique is that the notion of the *universal* citizen in the liberal (Pateman 1988), classical socialist (or social democratic) (Lister 1993; Orloff 1993) and republican tradition (Phillips 1992, 1993) was based on a male norm.

The feminist critique has shown that the division between the public, political sphere and the domestic sphere is a gendered one because in the liberal, socialist and republican traditions 'men' have been associated with politics and 'women' with the family. The point is that women's exclusion from the public, political arena is in some way determined by structural inequalities in the family and the labour market and by the public/private divide. The recent feminist debate is about the potential of women's agency and the value of motherhood and caring, as well as about the visions of full citizenship for women.

The Patriarchal Figure

Carole Pateman's work (1985, 1988, 1989) has formulated one of the most radical critiques of the concept of 'universal citizenship' in classical political theory. She suggests that the gendered division between the 'private' and 'public' sphere, which is premised on the male norm, explains women's exclusion from politics. In liberal theory the social contract rests on a hidden 'sexual contract' expressed in women's subordination through the marriage contract.

Pateman has explored the construction of motherhood in political theory (1988). According to her, the marriage contract is the root of women's oppression because it makes women dependent on the individual husband's control over their sexuality and work, in the family and in the labour market. She claims that in modern democracies the old patriarchal rule of the fathers has been abolished but that it has been replaced by a new fraternal rule, where men as 'brothers' exclude women from the public sphere.

Pateman has reformulated what she calls the paradox of Mary Wollstonecraft – the claim that women cannot obtain full citizenship 'as women', that is, as autonomous individuals sexually different from men, and that to achieve full citizenship women must become 'like men' and give up their experiences, needs and interests 'as women' (1989: 14).

Pateman's analysis is a powerful critique of liberal political philosophy that has raised crucial questions about the roots of women's exclusion from citizenship in modern democracies and about the political meaning of motherhood (Siim 1988, 1994a). One of the analytical challenges for feminist theory and politics is how to transform citizenship in a way that uncouples the division between the public/private spaces from the gendered division between man and woman.

Pateman's normative ideal is a 'sexually differentiated' citizenship that enables a distinction between men and women as different but equal individuals. In the Jefferson Papers, Pateman reflects on this question, wondering what would happen if the political meaning of motherhood changed: 'If caring for and educating the young were to become part of political life, and not the work of individual women as private individuals, then the practice of motherhood and the capacities it requires could begin to transform citizenship and the meaning of community' (1985: 13).

Scandinavian development in relation to caring work during the last twenty years can illuminate this question. In Scandinavia, the political meaning of motherhood has changed, and women (and gender) today are playing a new role in politics. Women have become integrated into the political elite, although there is no gender equality in political power and there is still a high degree of sex segregation in the labour market (see Chapter 4). Feminist researchers have noticed that political developments in Scandinavia challenge the determination between the socio-economic factors and political equality and tend to support the pluralist thesis about the relative autonomy of politics (Phillips 1992; Skjeie 1992; Siim 1994a).

On the basis of research from Scandinavia I suggest that the politics of motherhood and women's inclusion in politics as citizens are two analytically separate processes that need to be analysed in greater detail from a comparative perspective. In Scandinavia, the expansion in child-care is related to the development of the universal welfare state and to women's participation in the labour market. This has created a new public/private mix that, in turn, has diminished the classical gender segregation (Siim 1988). Research from Scandinavia indicates that women's inclusion in the political elite is closely related to political factors such as the growth of the new women's movement and state feminism. The point is that the politics of motherhood has a very different meaning in different national and historical contexts. The French case (Chapter 4) shows that the inclusion of women in the labour market and the expansion of childcare centres do not by themselves lead to the inclusion of women as citizens. Research indicates that there is a connection but no determination between women's roles as mothers, workers and citizens.

The Maternalist-communitarian Model

One group of feminist scholars has focused explicitly on the positive implications of motherhood and caring for women's political roles, for example the American political scientist Jean Bethke Elshtain (1983, 1990, 1993). In this understanding the 'male' world is often contrasted with the 'female' world, and the dominant language of 'rights' built on public values of 'justice' with a new 'ethic of care' based on the values of the family (Kymlicka 1990: Ch. 7). Elshtain has given a good illustration of this approach, arguing that a restructuring of the private and public worlds must be based on a new moral vision of the private-familial sphere: 'A moral and political imperative that would unite rather than divide women ... would be a feminist commitment to a mode of public discourse imbedded with the values and ways of seeing that comprise what Sara Ruddick has called "maternal thinking"' (1993: 33ff.). Elshtain's understanding interprets the family, women's responsibility 'as mothers' and their preoccupation with 'immediate concerns' as the basis for women's political roles and not as a barrier to their political participation.

This approach rests on a belief in the importance of the family and of women's experiences in everyday life. The sexual division of work thus becomes the positive basis for women's integration into politics and for women's political identities and values. For Elshtain the objective is to humanise bureaucratic politics and create an 'ethical polity' based on a 'politics of compassion' (ibid.: 350–1). The ideal citizen is portrayed as the non-violent, participatory citizen engaged in social movements such as the handicapped and consumer movements.

Elşhtain's ideal is inspired by communitarianism, with an emphasis on the family and community that seems to acknowledge and even to endorse sexual (as well as other) differences (Dietz 1992; Mouffe 1992b). The empirical basis for the maternal model is sociological and historical research. According to Elshtain (1990), studies of everyday life confirm the importance of family values for women's political identities, and historical studies indicate the importance of 'maternal feminism', which struggled to expand the welfare of mothers and children in the early reform movements (see also Bock 1992; Koven and Michels 1993).

The 'maternalist model' has raised important questions about the relations between an 'ethic of care', based on private values, and an 'ethic of justice', based on public values (Kymlicka 1990: Ch.7). Women's responsibility for caring work has undoubtedly had implications for women's political practice. However, Scandinavian research has indicated that maternalism does not have a general explanatory power in relation to women's political participation in modern democracies (Siim 1988, 1994a; A. Christensen 1991).

From a feminist perspective it is difficult to idealise women's experiences 'as mothers' and to reduce women's political participation to their maternal roles. From a democratic perspective it is a problem to equalise the 'mother–child relation' with 'relations as citizens'. I agree with Mary Dietz (1992) that there is a difference between the mother–child relation, which rests on intimacy, inequality and exclusivity, and the relation towards fellow citizens, which rests on equality, distance and inclusivity. From a normative point of view it can be argued that the 'mother point of view' is a necessary but not sufficient condition for citizenship (Kymlicka 1990: 19). It has the potential to develop into 'solidarity with the other' and 'civic-minded world protection', but private and public virtues cannot be reduced to one dimension (Jones 1990). It is a problem that both maternalism and communitarianism tend to reduce the individual woman's freedom to be different from other women and to reduce solidarity to those who are 'like you'. The implication is that the ideal about care tends to suppress differences 'in and between women' (Young 1990a: 307). Maternalist-communitarianism can therefore be combined with direct hostility towards 'the other' who is not like you, and it may be the basis for ethnocentrism and racism (Siim 1999b).

The Pluralist Participatory Model

The third approach is inspired by civic republicanism as well as by participatory democracy. It values political equality and strategies that increase women's political participation and presence in the public, political arena – what I have called a new kind of (feminist) pluralism (Dietz 1992; Mouffe 1992a; Phillips 1992, 1993). The argument is that women's political mobilisation and participation represent a challenge to the theory and practice of universal citizenship and also has the ability to improve the quality of citizenship not only for women but also for other oppressed groups (Sarvasy and Siim 1994).

The ideal is to create a pluralist and differentiated citizenship that uncouples political roles from the division in men and women, and to endorse women's multiple political roles as 'parents, workers and citizens'. According to the British political scientist Anne Phillips (1993: 142–5), the new feminist pluralism has three elements: a *moral* element that recognises differences in women's political values and identities; a *political* element that recognises the plurality of political arenas; and a *social* element that recognises the political meaning of subgroups defined on the basis of race, ethnicity and gender. In contrast to maternalist thinking, based on an affirmation of women's traditional values, the pluralist understanding represents an affirmation of feminist values premised on a break with traditional motherhood. The political objective is to democratise both the family and public political life while at the same time maintaining an analytical difference between the intimacy of the private family and public politics (Phillips 1992, 1993).

The advocates for the pluralist participatory model agree about the goal, but there is no agreement about how to reach a non-gendered citizenship based on political equality between women and men. Phillips (1992: 184) has proposed the adoption of a politics of affirmative action based on gender, ethnicity and race as a way of reaching full equality for these groups in political life. The American political scientist Iris Young (1990a: 184) goes one step further and proposes a group-differentiated citizenship for all oppressed and disadvantaged social groups as a way of empowering these groups.

Phillips (1992) suggests that the solution to the gendered division between the private, domestic sphere and the public, political sphere is not to dissolve all distinctions but to redefine the two domains. The aim is to *ungender* the public/private divide by means of a double democratisation of the family and of public life (see also Mouffe 1992b).

The common political goal is to create a new form of pluralism that includes a plurality of political arenas, political roles and identities for women. This endorses a new form of equality[2] that transcends the 'difference versus equality' distinction and recognises the diversity of social groups and social goods (Young 1990a; Mouffe 1992b; Phillips 1993).

I find that the pluralist vision has many advantages, and it has also raised new questions (Siim 1994a). One is how to link the empowerment of women with the aim of degendering politics – how to connect the long-term ideal of non-gendered citizenship and the immediate concerns about existing asymmetries of power between women and men. What are the social and political changes necessary to reach this ideal, and what kind of reforms can address existing gender inequalities in politics? Can women's political participation be relied on to secure full citizenship for women? And if not, what other measures need to be adopted if women are to obtain full citizenship?

Another key question is how to connect women's liberation struggle with other liberation movements. Phillips (1995) has recently proposed a 'politics of presence' based on the adoption of affirmative action, itself based on gender, ethnicity and race as the means of ensuring full equality for marginalised groups in public life. Young (1990a: 184) has proposed a 'politics of difference' based on a 'group-differentiated' citizenship for all oppressed and marginalised social groups as a way of securing a heterogeneous public. Phillips (1993: 161) is concerned with developing a politics of solidarity between groups, one that implies confrontations, challenges and changes of group identities. Young is concerned with securing the autonomy and empowering of the oppressed social groups rather than with changing group identities.

Mouffe (1993: 86) is negative towards both quota systems for women and group representation. She fears that quota systems is a way of (re)institutionalising gender differences in politics, and that a group-based citizenship represents an essentialist view of 'group', with given interests and identities. Her argument is that the radical democratic project rests on an articulation and creation of new identities of all groups.

The new 'feminist pluralists' share a positive evaluation of the notion of difference in political life and of the self-organisation of oppressed groups, but only Young advocates a politics of group representation, including veto-power in policies that regard the group directly. The alternative visions of Phillips and Mouffe emphasise the transformative aspect of politics based on the interaction between social groups that aims to create new identities and a wider sense of solidarity.

These reflections touch on real dilemmas for a democratic feminist theory and politics. One of the questions is how to secure pluralism and diversity in politics as well as the creation of new political identities and solidarities. I agree that the quota system can be one way to secure a politics of presence for women and marginal groups, although it is not a general means that can be employed in all contexts. I am critical of 'group representation' with veto-power because it represents a static vision of politics. The quota system secures an equal representation of women, but it does not address the question of how to change the asymmetrical power relations between men and women or the need to create new political identities and new solidarities (Yuval-Davis 1997).

Social Constructivism and the Postmodern Challenge

A number of feminist scholars have recently been inspired by the writings of the New French philosophers Michel Foucault, Jean Baudrillard, Jean-François Lyotard and Jacques Derrida (Scott 1988; Flax 1990; Butler 1992). The argument is that there is an affinity between the feminist and the postmodern (or post-structuralist) project because both represent a critique of existing forms of knowledge and power rooted in the Enlightenment. Postmodern scholarship is critical of the key concepts in feminist theorising, such as 'equality' and 'difference', and the aim is to deconstruct fundamental categories like 'subject', 'women' and 'sex' (Butler 1992: 19).

The American political theorist Jane Flax (1992b) has introduced a positive feminist-postmodernist theory of justice. She argues that justice is more potentially useful for feminists than the concept of equality because it leaves room for differences: 'Feminists should seek to end domination, not gender, not difference, and certainly not the feminine' (ibid.: 194). She claims that justice can only be exercised in public, intersubjective spaces and must necessarily be connected with an active notion of citizenship (ibid.: 206).

Postmodern feminism is a contested approach that has been the basis of intensive feminist debates (see Fraser and Nicholson 1990; Nicholson 1990; Benhabib et al. 1995). Feminist scholars have been sceptical of postmodernism because it tends to neglect feminist agency. The American political theorist Seyla Benhabib (1995: 20) has claimed that 'the postmodernist position(s) contributes to eliminate not only the specificity of feminist theory but place in question the very emancipatory ideals of the women's movement altogether'. Postmodern feminists like Judith Butler (1995: 136–7) suggest that there are indeed different views about agency and that the 'emancipation model' has been questioned by a (postmodern) model where agency is the effect of discursive conditions, 'a contingent and fragile possibility opened up in the midst of constituting relations'.

Feminist scholarship is both inspired by the Enlightenment and is at the same time part of the critique of Enlightenment thinking. Feminism has offered its own critique of modernity and during the last thirty years feminist theory has developed its own understanding of diversity between women, sexual difference, and women as agents for construction of commonalities and divisions between women. The British sociologist Fiona Williams (1996: 71) has engaged in a dialogue with postmodernism, and she has noticed that *difference* can be constructed and used in various ways, positively to claim a shared collective experience as a basis for resistance or as a basis for discrimination. According to Iris Young (1994: 733) the feminist dilemma between recognition and deconstruction of gender difference can be resolved by distinguishing between three positions: women as a serial collectivity; women as a group that recognise a certain active commonality; and women organised in feminist groups.

I suggest that the emphasis on women's agency needs to be combined with an analytical distinction between women as a social and political group, and between women as individual citizens and as collectivities. The feminist-pluralist approach is interested in the connection between gender and marginalised social groups and in the often conflictual construction of women's citizenship practice by building bridges across the differences among women and by combining overlapping identities and sometimes contrasting roles of individual women (Sarvasy and Siim 1994: 253).

According to the American philosopher Nancy Fraser (1995), many of the ideas of postmodernism are potentially fruitful for feminism. In a response to the challenge from postmodernism, she has recently tried to develop an approach that is inspired by the different paradigms of Habermas, Foucault, Lacan and Derrida. Fraser (1995: 157) defines postmodernism as 'an epochal shift in philosophy and social theory from an epistemological problematic, in which mind is conceived as reflecting or mirroring reality, to a discursive problematic, in which culturally constructed meanings are accorded density and weight'.

The shift expresses a problematisation of language as well as a conceptualising of meaning. For Fraser (ibid.: 166), the objective for feminism is to develop a plurality of different angles from which to theorise the intersection of gender, race/ethnicity, sexuality, nationality and class in every socio-cultural arena. I am inspired by social constructivism and by Fraser's approach to social analyses, which differentiates between discourse and practice as two analytical dimensions of the social. The claim that the forms used to describe social life are also active forces shaping it is an important methodological point as well as being a useful point of departure in empirical research (Fraser 1988: 146).

In this book the emphasis is on the interaction of discourse and institutions, with agency at the centre. I find that the dialogue between feminism and postmodernism is fruitful, especially the postmodern challenge to feminist essentialism. The postmodern emphasis on discourse and difference is also methodologically important. One of the implications is that feminism, including postmodernism, is not one theory but an eclectic approach that allows for mutual differences and many types of feminism. Another implication is the acknowledgement that research is contextual and that different questions, problems and arenas can be illuminated by a combination of several theoretical and methodological approaches (Lykke, Ravn and Siim 1994).

Feminist Visions of Equality, Difference, and Social Change

Today, key concepts of citizenship such as women's agency and gender equality are contested in feminist theory. Pateman's conception of a patriarchal figure tends to focus on women's powerlessness in relation to public institutions. This is problematic because it rests on a 'structural determination' between the gendered division of work and the political arena, which underestimates the significance of politics and women's potential empowering as political agents. It is difficult to understand how public patriarchy can be changed in modern democracies, or by whom (Siim 1988).

Pateman's vision of a sexually differentiated citizenship is also problematic because it recognises sex as a basis for citizenship but ignores differences based on ethnicity and race. Mouffe (1993: 80–2) has recently claimed that a 'sexually differentiated citizenship' is ambiguous because the solution does not deconstruct but rather reconstructs the essentialist opposition of men/women. Her critique points out that the aim of strengthening women's political roles as mothers can have the unintentional effect of perpetuating sex segregation in the political sphere (Mouffe 1992b; Siim 1994a). The ambiguity of Pateman's vision can be illustrated in a Scandinavian context. There it has been argued that the integration of 'caring and educating the young' in political life has had the unintentional effect of institutionalising the gender difference between 'male' and 'female' citizen roles and of strengthening the sexual division of work in the labour market (Åström 1992; Siim 1994a).

Pateman has conceptualised the role of the family in liberal contract theory, her approach indicating the limits of the liberal approach, which neglects the family for sexual equality. Her work shows how sexual difference built on male domination and the subordination of women is an integrated aspect of modern political thought. Kymlicka (1990: 257) argues that modern liberalism and feminism can be reconciled. And feminist scholars have attempted to integrate the unequal gender roles in modern liberal contract theory represented for example by John Rawls. It is, however, a real problem how to integrate the body, emotions and feelings in the liberal, republican and Habermas-inspired political discourses built on reason and rationality (Mouffe 1992a).

Jean B. Elshtain's 'maternalist-communitarian model' is a conscious effort to (re)institutionalise sexual difference in politics. The model is problematic because in presuming that women 'as women' have sub-stantial interests it suppresses differences among women (Jonásdóttir 1991; Pringle and Watson 1992: 68; Fraser 1995). Scandinavian research indicates that women today have a plurality of political roles and iden-tities and that women's politics are not and should not be based primarily on their experiences as mothers (Christensen 1991; Siim 1994a).

The maternalist-communitarian model is based on women's caring responsibilities in the family. Iris Young (1990b) has argued that there is an affinity between the maternalist model based on the realities of everyday life and the ideas of modern communitarianism emphasising the 'embedded self' situated in existing social practices. In a com-munitarian society the 'common good' is conceived as a substantive conception of the good life that defines the community's 'way of life'. The idea rests on the belief that women have substantive interests 'as women' based on their obligation to care for dependants. This is challenged by the argument that women have a common discursive marginality but that women's interests, like men's, are constructed rather than pre-given (Pringle and Watson 1992: 68).

I am sympathetic to the idea of 'differentiated and pluralist' citizen-ship, which I find expresses a need to deconstruct the gender difference in politics.[3] The pluralist vision can be illuminated by developments in Scandinavia indicating that women and men have a plurality of roles as citizens and that the division between the public and private spheres has lost some of its gendered effects (Siim 1994a). The pluralist focus on women's agency is a key element in rethinking citizenship, although it tends to exaggerate the potential of women's agency to change public institutions and to underestimate the structural barriers to women's full citizenship. The focus on participation tends to assume that participation and mobilisation will 'by themselves" create gender equality.

Research from Scandinavia indicates that this is not always the case (Andersen et al. 1993: Chs 7, 8) and that there is a real danger of women being 'added to' the participatory project without the male norm being challenged (Sarvasy 1994; Siim 1994a). Feminist research indicates that the question of whether women's political presence will change the form or content of politics is an open one that needs to be studied from a comparative perspective (Skjeie 1992). I suggest that the growing social inequalities on the global and national levels have created a need for a transformative politics premised on a synthesis between social and political equality and on the creation of new solidarities between women and marginalised social groups (Dean 1995; Fraser 1995; Lister 1997a).

The strength of the postmodern approach is the attempt to deconstruct essentialist categories like 'woman' and 'man'. This is an important perspective, but the danger is that 'deconstruction' becomes the dominant approach and that women's agency disappears, with the result that feminism becomes subsumed under postmodernism and that the theoretical (and political) problem – how to end gender domination – disappears from the analysis (see Flax 1992). Therefore the emphasis on discourse and language needs to be combined with a new understanding of gender based on historical and comparative research of the interaction of discourse, agency and political institutions.

Each of the three approaches thus illuminates different aspects of women's citizenship in modern societies. Gender inequalities in political power are still to some extent structured by the gendered division of work and male domination in society. I suggest, however, that there is indeed a 'relative autonomy of politics',[4] including discourses, institutions, laws and culture. One of the implications is that the potential for and limits to women's equal citizenship on the political level need to be explored in further detail through comparative studies. Cross-national studies indicate that there is a complex relationship between the state, the market and civil society. They show that the connection between women's inclusion/exclusion in politics and the sexual division of work in the family and society is contextual and that politics can be both the cause and the effect of the sexual division of work (Koven and Michel 1993).

The preliminary conclusion is that political participation and representation is a necessary, though not sufficient, element in a multiple strategy to include women in the political process. Strategies to secure women's access to full citizenship need to address questions such as equal social and political rights for women and men, as well as differences among citizens in terms of colour and ethnicity. The asymmetry of power between social groups is one of the crucial challenges for feminist theory and politics that needs to be addressed both on a structural, institutional and symbolic level.[5]

In the following chapters I take the feminist-pluralist approach as the basis for a dialogue between liberalism, socialism and civic republicanism about the need to create political communities and identities and new solidarities among women citizens through public dialogues between different social groups. The main argument is that feminists need to deconstruct the old paradigms as well as to construct new understandings of democratic citizenship.

CHAPTER 4

Gender and Citizenship: The French Case

Assumptions about Gender in the Republican Discourse

In this chapter I analyse the logic of the exclusion and inclusion of women in citizenship in France and discuss the key element in the French discourses about citizenship and the implications for women's political, civil and social rights. My objective is to illuminate the republican discourse about women's democratic and social rights in crucial periods of the formation of the welfare state and democracy. The focus is on the shifts in the discourses and politics of gender and citizenship and on the changing role of women's agency. The research interest is to understand the political meaning of gender in contemporary debates about citizenship

The French political scientist Pierre Rosanvallon (1992: 16) has noticed that Marshall's model of citizenship does not apply in the case of Germany, where the welfare state was developed before universal suffrage, and even less to France, where the three aspects of citizenship coalesced during the Revolution of 1789. Rosanvallon has criticised. Marshall's model of citizenship for being too narrowly linked to the institutional development of political ideas and therefore tending to underestimate the uneven development between institutions and ideas. Democratic citizenship is one of the key elements in the political culture and political history of France (Rosanvallon 1992; Touraine 1994), and in contrast to social liberalism there is no tradition for analysing social rights as part of the theoretical framework of citizenship (Rosanvallon 1995).

France is one of the four cases in Turner's typology of citizenship, and his framework has inspired me to think about the specificity of the French case from a comparative and gendered perspective. Turner

(1992: 52–6) uses the revolutionary French tradition as an example of active citizenship 'from below' giving emphasis to the public arena. He contrasts the French conception of citizenship with the German and British cases, and uses Rousseau's political theories to illustrate the radical break with the old social and political order:

> Revolutionary political theories, acting against the absolutist conception of sovereignty, followed Rousseau in conceptualizing society as a collection of individuals whose existence would be represented through the general will in popular parliamentary institutions. What bound Frenchmen together into a common nation was again the concept of citizenship. Frenchmen had ceased to be merely subjects of the sovereign and had become instead common citizens of a national entity ... The differences between the French and English revolutionary tradition can be summarized in two contrasting views of citizenship by Rousseau and Burke. For Rousseau in *The Social Contract* the viability of citizenship required the destruction of all particular intervening institutions which separated the citizen from the state. By contrast Burke in *Reflections on the Revolution in France* in 1790 argued that the essence of citizenship was the continuity of local groups, particular institutions and regional associations between the sovereign power of the general will and the individual. (Turner 1992: 54)

This quotation illustrates some of the ambiguities of the French republican heritage. On the one hand the public activities of the individual citizens are valued and the citizen is the hero; on the other there is a negative perception of intermediary organisations and institutions that separate the individual from the sovereign power. Rosanvallon (1992) has described the essence of the French republican view of citizenship as a type of universalism that creates a radical conception of political equality between citizens and at the same time establishes a direct link between the individual and the state. In French republican thinking the dominant language is thus about an active democratic citizenship, and there is no tradition for including individual social rights in the framework of citizenship (Jenson and Sineau 1995).

In terms of the *active/passive dimension*, the French case is portrayed as the classic example of an active revolutionary citizenship model where popular movements overthrew the absolute monarchy 'from below'. French republicanism was inspired by the classical ideals of the city-state as well as by the ideas of the Enlightenment. Compared to the American Revolution of 1776, which proclaimed a new republic of free and equal individuals, the French Revolution and French political history constructed a different kind of republicanism with solidarity as one of the key notions.

French political scientists have stressed that French political and intellectual history transcends the liberal language of abstract individualism by placing the individual as part of the national political community. And historians and political scientists have recently suggested that there is a specific French conception of citizenship, a 'singularité française' with implications for women's citizenship (Rosanvallon 1992; Jenson and Sineau 1995; Ozouf 1995).

Feminist scholars have also started to analyse the interconnection between political and social rights within the framework of citizenship and to question the meaning of citizenship from the perspective of women (Jenson and Sineau 1995; Frader 1996). This chapter builds on this new body of scholarship and discusses the meaning of the French specificity for gender relations and for the links between women's civil, political and social rights from a comparative perspective (Del Re and Heinen 1996).

The active citizenship model has been challenged from a feminist perspective because women were not included in the vote. A key issue in the connection between republicanism and women's citizenship has been women's lack of formal political rights. The French Revolution, based on the principle of universal political rights, nevertheless excluded women from the city by denying them the right to vote for more than a hundred years (Landes 1988; Rosanvallon 1992; Scott 1997a). Feminist scholarship has suggested that this exclusion has had far-reaching implications for the notion of citizenship, creating as it has a gendered political subject and political institutions based on a radical separation between women and men's citizenship (Sineau 1992b). First, universal suffrage gave men formal political rights in 1848 about a hundred years ahead of women, who were not allowed to vote until 1944. Second, social policies with the object of protecting women as workers and mothers came *before* the right to vote (Sineau 1992b; Frader 1996). Third, one of the key issues about republicanism and women's citizenship has been married women's lack of fundamental civil and social rights (Pedersen 1993a,b).

In terms of the *private/public dimension*, Turner (1992: 55) suggests that the French case has combined the principle of active citizenship with an attack on the family, religion and privacy. The republican discourse has valued the public arena and public virtues and has been hostile to religion and the family, as well as towards intermediary voluntary associations in civil society. The key to citizenship is the vote, and there is no theoretical tradition for integrating the notion of individual social rights into the framework of citizenship, except in the new body of feminist scholarship. In the French intellectual tradition the concept of citizenship is predominantly attached to the language of democracy and political rights and separated from the language of social policies and social rights. Feminist scholarship has recently attempted to analyse the interrelation of the French notions of social rights and political citizenship from a comparative and gendered perspective (Jenson and Sineau 1995; Del Re and Heinen 1996).

In the republican vision of the good life, the state is the expression of society and the organiser of solidarity. Contrary to the liberal understanding, the rational state is portrayed as a neutral administrator of civil society and freedom is associated with the public, political sphere. Contrary to the Danish/Scandinavian notion of citizenship, the emphasis on the political community and the public good in French political culture is followed by a tendency to subsume private concerns under the public good: 'French political life has until now been dominated by a perception of democracy that subordinates political actors to the needs, collective consciousness and interests of society/the nation/the people' (Touraine 1994: 118, my translation).

One of the implications is that the public/private divide is in reality a hierarchy in the political culture between public and private spaces: between public civic virtues ('le sens civique') and the private relations between citizens ('les relations civiles'). Another implication is a gap between the political discourse about active citizenship and the actual history of French political institutions.

There is also a curious gap between the political radicalism of the early Revolution and the late formation of the French welfare state 'from above' during the Third Republic (1872–1944). The French welfare system has been inspired by Bismarckian principles of social insurance, but in terms of social policies Rosanvallon (1981) has noticed that France at the beginning of the century lagged behind Germany and Britain. Furthermore, there is an interesting contrast between the formation of the French welfare state 'from above' and the parallel formation of the Scandinavian welfare states by social movements 'from below' between 1880 and 1920 (Schmied 1995: 40). This late development of the French welfare state has had far-reaching implications for women's social and political citizenship.

From a feminist perspective the republican hostility to the private family is ambiguous, because the republican discourse was premised on a language of familialism that places the family at the heart of social policy.[1] The French sociologist Michel Messu (1998: 2) has noticed that familialism is an ideology that distrusts intermediary structures between the family and the state and emphasised women's (public) roles as mothers. Feminist scholarship has noticed that in terms of the *family* the republican discourse has been contradictory. The Revolution of 1789 gave women new civil rights, including the right to divorce, but since the adoption of the Code Napoléon in 1804 husbands were given juridical power or *patria potestas* ('the father's power [over his family]'), premised on married women's lack of civil rights (Sineau 1992b; Knibielher 1993).

The late formation of the French welfare state contrasts with its pioneering role in relation to family policy. Feminist scholarship has shown that the French state actively promoted a system of state-regulated family allowances that were first adopted in 1932 (Pedersen 1993a). Susan Pedersen (1993b: 357) has recently suggested that the 'politics of the family', governed by a policy logic which she has called the 'parental welfare state', aimed to redistribute to wage earners with children from those without. Since World War II, family policies have been at the heart of the French welfare state and were formally embedded in the foundation of the welfare state (Offen 1991: 140–1; Pedersen 1993b; Hantrais and Letablier 1996).

During the 1930s the politics of the family was supported by strong interest groups which, with different arguments, advocated family policy: business organisations, pronatalist groups, Catholic women's organisations, and feminist groups. The new family politics is an expression of familialism and was adopted in the interwar period at a time when women did not have the formal right to vote and according to the Code Napoléon lacked basic civil rights in marriage (Sineau 1992b).

French family policy is ambiguous and highly contested. The French tradition of family policy has fluctuated between redistributive, familialist and pronatalist objectives that transcended the deep division between Left and Right in French political life (Hantrais 1996: 64). Feminist scholarship has different interpretation of French family politics in the interwar period (Offen 1991; Koven and Michel 1993). Some use family policies to illustrate the positive aspects of state support for the role of women as mothers in the republican nation-state, while at the same time defending women's right to work (Offen 1991: 152); others use family politics to illustrate the oppressive aspects of the republican discourse towards married women under the Code Napoléon (Sineau 1992b).

The new Constitution of the Fourth French Republic after World War II marked a radical shift from the perspective of women citizens. Women finally gained the right to vote,[2] and the preamble to the Constitution also opened up a new discourse about women's equal rights that included the right to work (Offen 1991: 152). The Fourth Republic marked a formal shift in the discourse of gender and democratic citizenship, but married women still lacked fundamental civil and social rights. The modernisation of French family politics started under President Giscard d'Estaing, and the new discourse about gender equality was introduced during the 1970s (Hantrais 1992, 1996). The old family law, the Code Napoléon, was gradually modernised and married women finally gained full equality with their husbands in 1983 (Offen 1991; Sineau 1992b).

François Mitterrand's presidency (1981–93) represented a new discourse about state feminism and gender equality. Mitterrand and the Socialist Party developed a veritable program for gender equality, which was followed by new initiatives and legislation towards equality (Jenson and Sineau 1995). In spite of the setbacks caused by economic crises, it has been noticed that since the 1980s French family policies have been forced to recognise the need for the state to support both family diversity and the relationship between the family and employment (Hantrais 1996: 64).

The contradiction between women's relatively high activity rates on the labour market coupled with their lack of political power, influence and visibility in the public sphere has become one of the main barriers to the further improvement of women's citizenship (Sineau 1992b). During the last thirty years women's political mobilisation in the new women's liberation movement (le Mouvement Liberation des Femmes – MLF) has changed women's democratic citizenship, but women have remained marginal in relation to political institutions. The low representation of women in parliament, less than 6 per cent up to the last general election in June 1997, has recently provoked an intense feminist debate about strategies for including women in political life. One strategy *for* parity aims to get an equal number of representatives of women and men in all political bodies. The other strategy *against* parity aims to develop other forms of *mixité* that combine the political integration of women with other excluded groups (see Scott 1997b; *Nouvelles questions feministes* no. 4, 1994 and no. 2, 1995).

In what follows I look first at the republican discourse about citizenship which excludes women from active citizenship but indirectly includes them as 'republican mothers'. Then I discuss the meaning of the ambiguous family policies for women introduced in the interwar period. Third, I focus on the shifts in the discourse about women's civil, political and social rights after World War II, on women's new political roles and on the new discourse about gender equality introduced by Mitterrand and the Socialist Party in 1981. Finally, I look at changes in the democratic citizenship of women and men and discuss the recent feminist discourses and strategies aimed at developing a more inclusive political citizenship for women.

Democratic Citizenship and Women's Exclusion from Political Rights

French scholars have recently analysed the contradiction between universalism in the political culture and the de facto exclusion of women from the vote until the Fourth Republic (Rosanvallon 1992; Touraine 1994). Pierre Rosanvallon (1992: 452) has identified two models of access to political rights for women: the French model based on radical individualisation, hostile to women's vote, and the utilitarian and gradualist British model based on interest representation and incorporating the principle of women's vote.

Rosanvallon has questioned the conventional explanations of French opposition to women's suffrage – Catholic culture, the republican fear of women's vote, and institutional blockage in the Senate. His argument is more philosophical: in France the right to vote is an individual one, whereas in Britain women got the right 'as women' with special functions and special interests. He suggests that the republican opposition to women's vote was based on the (anthropological) claim about women's dependency, as well as on the sociological claim about women's social functions as mothers. The argument is that there was a gap in French political culture between radical individualism and the ideas of ordinary people (1993: 137–8). Rosanvallon's approach points to a contradiction in republican thought between egalitarian principles and the prevailing gender roles based on inequality. Feminist scholarship has suggested that the 1789 Revolution constructed new gender roles (Fraisse 1989; Varikas 1994). The American historian Joan Landes (1988: 10) has claimed that the *ancien régime* was in fact more democratic from the point of view of women than the new republic, because at least elite women had public influence as part of the aristocracy before 1789.

The constraints and promises of republicanism

French philosophers and historians have recently discussed the contradiction between the radical concept of individual equality in the public sphere and gender inequality based on the ideology of women's sexual difference (Duby and Perrot 1992a). Feminist scholarship has noticed that the emphasis of the French language of citizenship on the concept of fraternity/solidarity in the public sphere is combined with an ideology that celebrates the family and the public function of motherhood, often called 'republican motherhood' (Knibielher 1993: 37). One group of scholars suggests that the importance of the public function of the family and of women's cultural roles has given women compensatory powers as mothers (Offen 1991; Ozouf 1995). Another has stressed the negative impacts of the republican ideology of the family, which has also contributed to perpetuating women's marginal political roles and lack of political power (Sineau 1992b; Riot-Sarcey 1993).

Feminist scholarship has criticised the concept of democracy that, in practice, has excluded women from political rights, although there are different interpretations of why women were excluded from citizenship in France. Some have emphasised the negative aspect of universalism, which is based on a separation between the 'public' and the 'private' arena, that is, on sexual difference (Fraisse 1989; Varikas 1994). More recently Mona Ozouf (1995) has focused on the promises of republicanism and on the potential it offers women.

Joan Landes' historical work is a critical analysis of the paradoxical relationship between feminism and republicanism. She has suggested that the fall of the older patriarchy gave way to a more pervasive gendering of the public sphere because gender became a socially relevant category in post-revolutionary life (1988: 13). The implication is that both republican motherhood and feminism can be seen as two variant but related outcomes of the transformation of the absolutist public sphere. Landes concludes: 'The universal bourgeois subject was at the outset a gendered subject. Only male rights to full individuality were protected. The revolt against the father was also a revolt against women as free and equal public and private beings. Undeniably then liberty and equality came to be overshadowed by fraternity [the brotherhood of men] in the new order produced by the revolution' (1988: 158).

Landes' point is that the claim to universal brotherhood hides the particular behind a veil of universalism. The paradox is that the representation of women in the public sphere seems to require their exclusion. In this interpretation the reconstructed post-absolutist public sphere is not socially determined but was constructed during the historical struggles. From this perspective, the contradictions in the political system can at the same time be interpreted as the cause of new gender relations and as the effect of the prevailing social relations of gender.

The philosopher Geneviève Fraisse (1989, 1995) has also referred to the internal tensions in republican thought between universalism and particularism as the basis for the political exclusion of women. She suggests that there have been, and still are, two movements for democracy. One hides the sexual difference behind the idea about the universal, or the general, and thus makes a *particularity* of women. The other wants to change the world with the participation of both men and women, but has until recently always stopped halfway. She has observed that the ideas about equality and freedom 'for women' came not from republicanism but from utopian and revolutionary socialists like Charles Fourier and Henry Saint-Simon.

Mona Ozouf's interpretation can illustrate the positive perception of republicanism. Her argument is that the Revolution of 1789 on a number of issues questioned 'paternal power', through the right to divorce and a new law that equalised daughter and son in relation to heritage, and also touched 'the power of the husband' (1995: 341). According to Ozouf the Code Napoléon of 1804 was a setback which does not compromise the egalitarian republican heritage. From this perspective, the Revolution represents a new powerful figure that has at least the potential to change gender relations:

> In relation to gender equality, or simply gender relations, the Revolution of 1789 changed everything. It made all inequality illegal, and any pre-established distribution of roles precarious. It emphasised that human activity forms a sufficient basis for the political order. And it is possible to claim that it made women's subordination extra painful because it was wrapped in a discourse that contradicted it. It made it more visible, more disturbing, less tolerable, and promised them at least in the long run the abolition of all inequality ... In reality it made women's political exclusion much more problematic. Therefore, even if it temporarily gains a new power after the revolutionary transformation, the natural determination cannot last long in a world where everything is constructed. (Ozouf 1995: 351–2, my translation).

Ozouf's interpretation thus focuses on the egalitarian promises made by the Revolution. Consequently she takes issue with the (feminist) argument that the French Revolution left women's oppression untouched, or even exacerbated it. Her explanation of women's exclusion from the public sphere combines Rosanvallon's argument about the importance of abstract individualism in the political culture with arguments about women's relative power in the family. Ozouf suggests that in a model where equality is the key notion it is possible for women to celebrate 'difference' with humour and irony and without essentialism (ibid.: 381–3).

Ozouf has pointed out that there is indeed a French model that is built on republican equality. From this perspective, the aim of the Revolution and the vision for the new republican woman ('la femme republicaine') were not to separate the public and private spheres but rather to integrate women into the public sphere. This point is illustrated by the expansion of a girl's right to education in a secular school of the Third Republic with la Loi de Camille Sée (in 1880) (Ozouf 1995: 365–74). The law also illustrates the ambiguities of republicanism to women. On the one hand it opened new possibilities for girls to secondary education but on the other it was based on a philosophy of gender segregation.

The two different interpretations illustrate that the heritage of the republican discourse and the French exceptionalism ('la singularité française') is contested. Feminist scholarship and political scientists agree that the exclusion of women from the public arena was not determined solely by prevailing gender relations but was also constructed through the political discourses, policies and the political history of republican institutions. The egalitarian promises of the Revolution about an active citizenship were not fulfilled during the First and Second Republics. The conclusion is that the language of universalism and radical individualism has been contradictory for women, because it was premised on a notion of the family and women's social role as mothers which has contributed to the reproduction of women's exclusion from democratic citizenship.

Feminist arguments about women's civil, political and social rights

The philosophical debate about gender and citizenship in France has raised important questions about the implications of the French model for the struggle for women's rights. Feminist scholarship has stressed that women's fight for political rights has been closely related to the struggle for the social rights and social protection of mothers, and feminist activists have linked arguments for civil, political and social rights (Bock 1992: 382). The German historian Gisela Bock suggests that feminists were united by an interest in mothers and motherhood, which she has called 'feminist maternalism', which wanted the state to recognise the rights and needs not only of workers but also of mothers. Yvonne Knibielher (1992: 37) indicates that there was an active 'maternal feminism' ('un feminisme promaternel') in France during the 19th century with a language that spoke in favour of the civil and social rights of mothers.

Ozouf (1995: 383) suggests in a recent essay about 'la singularité française' that French feminism often combined universalism with particularism. One implication of universalism is that it has not been legitimate to make demands as a particular group, because in French political culture the opposite of exclusion can only be complete assimilation. Another implication is that women have been less militant because they have obtained a different supplementary power as mothers (Ozouf 1995: 380–1). Joan Landes (1988: 129) suggests that early feminists like Mary Wollstonecraft have endorsed what she calls 'republican motherhood'. This is based on the idea that women should participate in politics by being mothers and by raising future (male) children to the republic, and that women's civil and political status as mothers should be raised through education.

Historically, the republican discourse has inspired the feminist struggle for social justice and equal rights. One example is the liberal French aristocrat Marquis Condorcet, who gave the first and the most eloquent defence of women's political rights based on the principle of equality in the essay 'On the admission of women to the Rights of citizenship', published in 1790 (Badinter and Badinter 1988: 296; Landes 1988: 113). Another example is Olympe de Gouges (1748–93), who published the 'Declaration of the Rights of Women' in 1791 and became the first republican woman to take the promises of the French Revolution seriously. In her first article, de Gouges demanded equal political rights for women and men by boldly declaring: 'Woman born free remains equal with man in terms of rights. The social distinctions can only be based on the common good' (in Gouges 1988: 103, my translation).

De Gouges' declaration of rights expressed a radical version of republican equality, arguing that in the republic the laws ought to be an expression of the general will and that consequently all citizens should contribute to the formation of the laws either personally or through their representatives. Her declaration is inspired by Rousseau and is an example of a language of citizenship linking demands for political, civil and social rights. In the preamble she formulated a veritable strategy of empowerment for a mobilisation of women to fight for their own rights. The key to her strategy was *political* rights, but she included the demand for civil and social rights such as that to education and divorce, and for the equality of children, including illegitimate children, in the right to inheritance (Gouges 1988: 69–129). Except for the right to divorce adopted by the republican convention in 1793 (Scott 1997a), the declaration of women's rights was too advanced for the time.

Condorcet's position was the exception among the French revolutionaries. He represented a small minority among the revolutionary men attached to the Girondins who supported women's rights in education and politics. Condorcet belonged to the Conféderation des Amis de la Vérité formed in 1790 and was particularly devoted to improving the situation of women (Landes 1988: 119). The women's section was a lobby for justice for women; its leader, Etta Palm, had a vision of welfare work in which the children of poor women would be cared for and educated. In 1792, with the establishment of the first republic, all males with a few exceptions were granted universal suffrage (Rosanvallon 1992). Divorce was seen as a crucial feminist issue, and women benefited from changes in their legal status, with marriage and divorce now governed by civil statutes.

Women's political influence reached a climax during the six months of 1793 with the formation of radical groups exclusively for women. One of these was the Society of Revolutionary Republican Women, which attempted to impose a female version of militant republicanism on women. The Jacobins gradually gained control of the Convention, and in October all women's political clubs were dissolved. In the same year, Olympe de Gouges died on the scaffold, accused of treason against the republic because of her affiliation with the Girondins. Landes (1988: 143) has suggested that the defeat of the Society marked an important turning point in the revolution, with a growing centralisation of power under Jacobin rule and the subsequent period of reaction.

During the 19th century, the egalitarian challenge from Olympe de Gouges was taken up by Hubertine Auclert (1848–1914),[3] who Offen (1992) has described as the first self-proclaimed feminist. Auclert's history is closely connected with the development of republican feminism. She is interesting because she was one of the few French feminists at the time to give precedence to political rights over civil (and social) rights (Offen 1992: 72). Auclert demanded political equality in her electoral program for women from 1885: 'The political assembly must be composed of an equal number of men and women' (Gaspard et al. 1992: 126, my translation). Auclert was an exception, because French feminism in the 19th century in general was pro-maternal, giving mothers priority over social and civil rights, demanding parental authority, giving married women the right to work and to dispose of their wages and working mothers the right to maternity leave (Knibielher 1993). Auclert argued that the vote was the cause, not the effect, of civil rights and of women's emancipation (Ozouf 1995: 217). She hoped that the political effects of the women's vote would be to replace the 'État minotaure' with a Mother State, 'un État maternel', which would give social and civil rights to women (Rosanvallon 1992: 401). During the parliamentary election of 1910, along with other feminists, she put forward a political program describing maternity as the greatest of all social functions and demanding that the state meet the needs of mothers and children no less than those of soldiers (Cova 1991: 123).

These examples show that the meanings of the French model as well as of the implications for feminism are contested. Some, like Ozouf, have focused on the promises of the Revolution. Others, like Landes, have noticed the tension between the ideology of protection of women as mothers and workers, supported by the republican discourse as well as by social Catholicism, and the vision of gender equality expressed by republican feminists (Pedersen 1993a; Del Re 1994: 96–110; Frader 1996). Auclert's argument illustrates the potential tension in the feminist discourse between demands for political rights based on equality and demands for social rights based on the needs of mothers and children (Scott 1997). This tension can be illuminated by the debate about French family politics in the interwar period.

The Politics of the Family and Women's Agency in the Interwar Period

Feminist scholarship has raised the question of the logic of the French family model as well as its implications for women. Lewis and Ostner (1994: 25) have placed France as a moderate male-breadwinner regime because women have gained entitlements as citizen mothers as well as citizen workers and have historically been able to combine the roles of mothers and workers. There is a common belief in the republican discourse and in social Catholicism that the welfare of families and children is a public, not a private, concern. This has been expressed in a political consensus about a tradition of active family policies with state intervention to support families with children, including lone mothers (Bock 1992; Frader 1996).

A number of feminist scholars have stressed the negative heritage of the French family model for women, which was based on a contradiction between women's lack of civil rights in marriage and protective social policies supporting mothers and children (Sineau 1992a; Frader 1996). France was known as one of the most familist and pronatalist countries in Europe in the interwar period, and in 1920 the state introduced a 'Mother's Day' ('fête des Mères'), as well as a model for mothers with five or more children (Bock 1992: 404). Mariette Sineau (1992b: 479) has observed that the Latin model, based on the Code Napoléon, has been a constraint on the development of women's civil and political rights compared to the Anglo-Saxon and Nordic models. In France, the Code Napoléon from 1804 gave husbands the juridical power over their wives within the family, and the status of women as legal minors without responsibilities in law lasted until after World War II (ibid.: 474; Knibielher 1993). The lack of civil rights in marriage included the right of married women to work outside the home without the consent of their husbands, to dispose of their own wages, and to share paternal authority over children.

Laura Frader (1996: 116) observes that the 1913 law granting maternity leave was the first step towards recognising working women's rights to protection as mothers. She found that working women in the post-World War I period increasingly claimed social protection on the basis of their status as both mothers and workers and demanded a system of family allowances regulated by the state (ibid.: 120–1). She concludes that there were two positions on how to protect women that dominated organised women's discourses on social provision before World War II. One minority position defended the right of women to work while simultaneously providing support for maternity by women organised in the communist-affiliated trade unions Confédération Génerale de Travail Unitaire (CGTU). The other, based on women's withdrawal from wage labour, compensated women for their motherly duties through the unwaged mother's allowance defended by women organised in the big trade union movement Confédération Génerale de Travail (CGT) (Frader 1996: 124).

Frader has examined the debates among working women organised in women's commissions in the CGT and CGTU, which did give working women a political voice within the labour confederation at the national level in the interwar period. She shows that CGT women largely followed the pronatalist and natalist position of the CGT, which privileged maternity as a social function whose collective benefits and costs should therefore be borne collectively. These women tended to privilege motherhood over work. Women in the communist-affiliated CGTU took a different approach, defending women's right to work (Frader 1996: 120–1). According to Frader the feminist voices that defended the right of women to work as well as demanding gender equality in the family represented only a small minority before World War II.

During the interwar period the French state began to support a new system of allowances to working families. In 1932 it adopted a Family Allowance Law ('allocation familiale') that gave benefits to working families tied to wages and financed by employers. It was followed by a new law in 1939 that improved allowances and included an unwaged mother's allowance ('allocation pour les mères au foyer'), which became part of the reformed Family Code of 1939.

Susan Pedersen (1993a: 14), comparing the contrasting logic of French and British family models in the interwar period, suggests that the French welfare state has been both 'understudied and much misunderstood' because it has been governed by a policy logic very different from the dominant British norm. She describes French family policies as parental, directed to the redistribution of resources to wage earners with children from those without children, in contrast to British social policies, which are an articulation of a male-breadwinner logic (1993a,b): 'Parental policies do not assume that women are necessarily dependent, nor that men always have "families to keep"; rather they presume the dependence of children alone and hence redistribute income primarily across family types and not along gender lines' (1993a: 17).

The point is that the Family Allowance Law of 1932 targeted *children* rather than prescribing a particular role to mothers as full-time homemakers. One of the implications is that family policies actually did improve the welfare of women and children at a time when French women did not yet have the right to vote and women's organisations were weak and divided. Pedersen's study (1993a) indicates that the chief agency of family politics in France was not the Left or women's organisations but industrialists who created a financial system that made a comprehensive national policy possible. Family allowances were tied to wages and were financed by employers in the form of direct levies. The conclusion is that the implications for women of what Pedersen has called the 'politics of the family' supporting women in their roles as 'working mothers' have been ambiguous.

Another controversial issue is what has been the role of women's agency in the development of French family politics. Feminist scholars have shown that there was an alliance in France between state policies to protect mothers and motherhood and feminist demands on the part of mothers (Bock 1992: 398). Research has indicated that women's organisations were not the passive objects of social policies in this period, although they lacked the right to vote. Women's organisations were active as pressure groups in support of social policies on the family and children, but according to Pedersen they did not play a major role in the formulation of French family policy. Women's organisations were divided into two major groups: social Catholicism, organised in Union Feminine Civile et Sociale (UFCS), and Republican Feminism, organised in Union Française pour le Suffrage en France (UFSF). One wanted to revolutionise motherhood, and the other defended individual liberty and married women's right to work, but both supported the Family Allowance Act of 1932.

Feminist research indicates that the French case is contradictory from the perspective of women's citizenship. On the one hand the system of family allowances, including the unwaged mothers' allowance of 1939, supported working families without directly restricting women's wage work. On the other hand, the dominant political discourse of the Third Republic was pronatalist and policies were motivated by the need to raise the birthrate rather than by women's rights. More importantly, the Family Code explicitly denied women equal civil rights in marriage (Del Re 1994: 137; Frader 1996: 119).

The large number of women in the French workforce compared to other European countries (between 1856 and 1961 more than 30 per cent of the economically active population were women) was one reason for the exclusion of married women from employment (Offen 1992: 142). During the 1930s there were campaigns directed at working mothers, but there were no legal restrictions on married women's wage work until the Vichy government in 1941 (Pedersen 1993a). Pedersen's study illustrates the contradictory logic of French social provision before World War II: women could claim new rights but in a context of paternalist control that limited their choice both publicly and privately. 'Motherhood was to be "endowed" through family policies, but women's choice to participate in this new state project was to be simultaneously curtailed', for example through the Family Code, which included harsh laws punishing abortion (Pedersen 1993b: 265).

Recently the positive impact of French social policies on women's welfare has been noted in comparative feminist scholarship, because these were premised on married women's wage work and not on a male-breadwinner model, as in countries such as Britain (Offen 1991;

Koven and Michel 1993). From a comparative perspective, Koven and Michel (1993: 22) find it puzzling that 'maternal' feminism succeeded in interwar France, where women did not have the vote, but not in Britain and Germany where they did. Offen has also stressed the positive implications of family policies for mothers during the interwar period. There is a specific French feminism which she has named 'relational' feminism and which she defines as 'an egalitarian but gender-based vision of social organisation emphasising women's rights as women'. This included republican feminism and social Catholicism, both of which aimed to improve women's social rights as mothers (Offen 1991: 135).

The conflicting feminist interpretations illustrate the contradictory aspects of French family politics in the interwar period. Some favour parental policies because they improved the welfare of working mothers and children without having normative implications for women's wage work. Others suggest that the adoption of the unwaged mothers' allowance, which privileged families with a male wage earner and dependent wife in the context of the Family Code of 1939, illustrates the negative aspects of pronatalist French family policies (Pedersen 1993a). The legacy of French family policies is problematic from a feminist perspective because policies were premised not just on women's lack of political rights but also on married women's lack of fundamental civil rights. I therefore tend to agree with Pedersen's conclusion (1993b: 406) that the 'pronatalist rhetoric of childbearing as a patriotic duty and Catholic doctrines of the unity of the family were so powerful, so verbose, as to limit the liberating potential of any family policy'. The French case thus illustrates the need to distinguish between types of family policies with different policy logic: maternalist policies directed exclusively at supporting women in their roles as mothers, and parental policies directed at supporting families, irrespective of women's wage work. It also illustrates the need to distinguish between policies that increase women's economic dependence and policies that increase women's individual civil and political rights (see Sineau 1992).

Shifts in the Discourse and Politics of Women's Rights

The French Liberation Movement gave women the right to vote in 1944, and the principle of equal rights was institutionalised in the preamble to the constitution of the Fourth Republic. The constitution of 1946 introduced a new discourse about women's citizenship and gender equality, but family policies were slow to change. In 1965 the law on marriage was reformed and married women gained control over their own property and legal affairs, but they did not gain full civil rights in marriage until after 1970[4] (Sineau 1992b: 474; Hantrais 1993: 122–3; Knibielher 1993).

The politics of the family became embedded in the foundation of the French welfare state after World War II. In 1946 the government extended family benefits by increasing the rates of both children's allowances and the single wage-earner allowance, and during the next three decades French family policies privileged families with a male wage-earner and dependent wife, or a wife employed part-time (Pedersen 1993b: 409).

In France, social protection is based on corporatism and social insurance, and the area of family policy is the only one where the state has guaranteed comprehensive and uniform treatment (Hantrais 1996). Unlike other benefits, family benefits were universal, not means-tested, and although they were still partly financed by contributions, it has been noted that family benefits are more akin to a universal (or targeted) social welfare system than to an insurance-based one (Palier 1998: 25).

Feminist scholars have noticed that a fundamental shift took place in French social policies between 1965 and 1985, when women received equal civil and social rights and 'every policy affecting women, from reproduction to retirement, was rewritten' (Offen 1991: 152). Women gained new reproductive rights to contraception (1967); the pill was covered by medical insurance in 1974; and abortion finally became legal in 1979, although it was not reimbursed by medical insurance until 1982 (Mossuz-Lavau 1992). From 1970, reference to the head of household disappeared and both parents shared parental authority; the same law gave single mothers parental authority and the right to pass their name on to their children. Finally, in 1975, divorce by mutual consent was recognised.

One of the hallmarks of social welfare in postwar France has been the shifting between policies supporting motherhood as a recognised social function and measures designed to integrate women into the labour force (Hantrais 1993: 116; Hantrais et al. 1996). The postwar social welfare system introduced in 1945 reflects a Bismarckian tradition and is made up of a large contributory domain and a narrow non-contributory one (Bouget 1998: 156). Most benefits are earnings-related and entitlements are conditional on the contribution record gradually extending to cover all sectors of the population and all risks (Palier 1998). The social insurance system is funded primarily by employers' and employees' contributions rather than by taxation, and implementation is controlled by the elected representatives of employers, unions and the insured (Hantrais 1996: 52).[5]

Since the 1970s, public policy measures in the form of generous family-centred state provisions have helped women to combine employment and family life, and the MLF has helped to place an expansion of childcare institutions high on the political agenda (Hantrais et al. 1996). During the 1980s the difference between Left and Right became less clear-cut, as both groups were forced by changing family and employment structures to recognise the need for the state to support family diversity and the family–employment relationship (Hantrais 1996: 64).

During the 1970s there was increasing feminist agitation on the Left, and the different groups of the MLF were mobilised around the struggle to change the abortion and marriage laws. According to Sineau, women developed a 'protest electorate' that put pressure on the dominant political institutions. In 1975 parliament responded by adopting a new divorce law, allowing divorce by mutual consent, and a new more liberal abortion law initiated by President Giscard D'Estaing (Sineau 1990: 97). The MLF was demobilised during the 1980s, and during the 1990s French feminism became fragmented into different ideological fractions, as in other European welfare states (Jenson 1993). MLF ideology to a certain extent transcended both egalitarian feminism and feminism based on sexual difference.[6]

Feminism and political institutions

Feminism as a political movement began from the promises of egalitarian republicanism, but in France women's organisations have been divided between republican feminism and social Catholicism, with different strategies about how to improve the position of women (Bock 1992; Pedersen 1993b). According to Sineau (1990) most women's organisations were until 1968 linked to parties and organisations that were part of the ideological battles between Left and Right.

The birth of the women's liberation movement, which was part of the political and cultural revolution following the student revolt of May 1968, marked a new stage for French feminism (Sineau 1990). The MLF was a heterogeneous movement with many ideological tendencies (Trat 1992: 20).[7] The principal goal of the MLF was the liberation of women through the creation of a new feminist consciousness and a new anti-authoritarian organisation of women fighting the patriarchal society. The MLF was critical of parliamentary politics and did not have voting guidelines, with the exception of the organisation Choisir la Cause des Femmes headed by the lawyer Giséla Halimi.

The election of the first Socialist president, François Mitterrand, and the formation of the Socialist government in 1981 marked a shift in the relation between feminism and political institutions. Jenson and Sineau (1995) have analysed the new alliance between the Socialist Party and the feminist movement, focusing on Mitterrand's discourse and politics towards women. Their study indicates that there have been both continuities and breaks in the objectives of family politics during the last twenty years. The new positive action program launched by Mitterrand in 1981 opened a radical new discourse about gender equality with the object of creating a new historical alliance between feminism and socialism. In what follows, the implications and limitations of state feminism in France are discussed on the basis of Jenson and Sineau's analysis.

The republican notions of fraternity and solidarity express recognition of a national community and the legitimacy to act in its name with the purpose of achieving social justice, which is a very different philosophy from liberalism (ibid.: 13–14). French family policies have traditionally been guided by a familist and pronatalist logic with the object of protecting motherhood and supporting families. To some extent this transcended the cleavage Left/Right. Historically, however, the Left has generally been supportive of equal rights for women, including political rights, while the Right has opposed women's individual rights (del Re 1994: 108–10). The new aspect of the political culture after 1960 was a growing split between the Left – Mitterrandism – and the Right – Gaullism – in relation to family policies and women's rights.

In 1978 the Socialist Party adopted a new document about women's rights: 'Le manifeste du Parti socialiste sur les droits des femmes'. This was followed by the presidential program '110 propositions pour la France' adopted by the Socialist Party in 1981, which included important statements about equal rights for women. These proposals make a number of promises to women in three key areas:

1. In the area of democratic rights the object was to increase gender equality by proportional representation, with a minimum 30 per cent women on the party lists to national, regional and local assemblies.
2. In the area of equal rights for women the object was to create equality in the work place and in relation to pay, the right to information about contraception and the right to reimbursement of abortion, and respect for women's dignity – against sexual discrimination and harassment.
3. In the area of family politics the object was to improve parental leave for mothers and fathers and to create 300 000 places in public daycare institutions for children under 3 years of age as a means of helping women achieve equality at work (see Jenson and Sineau 1995: Annexe 2).

On the basis of these proposals, Mitterrand became directly engaged in a debate with feminist organisations during the presidential campaign in 1981. As a result of the program the attitudes of the feminist organisations towards Mitterrand (and towards party politics) changed. Feminist organisations like Choisir, la Ligue des Droits des Femmes (from 1882), the MLF, and even Simone de Beauvoir, for the first time recommended voting for a specific political candidate, the Socialist candidate François Mitterrand (ibid.: 136).

After being elected president in 1981, Mitterrand started a fairly ambitious program of state feminism. Following the policies of Giscard d'Estaing, who in 1974 appointed the first junior minister, Secretariat d'Etat, in charge of the position of women (Françoise Giroud), Mitterrand appointed Yvette Roudy as the first Minister for Women's Rights. During the first presidential period, 1981–86, Roudy was directly answerable to the Prime Minister, while the responsibility for family politics was placed in the secretariat for 'State and Family', headed by Georgina Dufoix, in 1988. During the second presidential term the balance between the two positions shifted. The Secretariat for Women's Rights lost power and Mitterrand appointed Dufoix as the new Family Minister (Jenson and Sineau 1994–95).

In terms of *democratic* rights, the universal political culture of France has been hostile to women's representation in politics and to the inclusion of women in the political elite. The new discourse of state feminism can be seen as an attempt to introduce a new vocabulary of gender and democratic citizenship, but it did not succeed in integrating women into the political elite or in increasing the number of women in political institutions. In 1982 the Socialists tried to live up to their promises by adopting a law securing about a 25 per cent quota for women in municipal elections, but in 1983 the French Constitutional Council declared quotas to political elections unconstitutional. In 1993 the Socialist leader, Michel Rocard, took the initiative to reserve half the places on the ballot in the European elections to women, which increased the number of elected women to 29.8 per cent. In the national elections the number of women in parliament up to 1997 remained under 10 per cent, with the result that France and Greece had the lowest percentage of women representatives in the EU (Jenson and Sineau 1999: Annexes 9 and 10; and see Table 5 in the Appendix).

Equality at work was a key question for the feminist movement and was also at the centre of Mitterrand's political program. *The right to work –* equality in work, promotion and pay – became one of the priority areas for Socialist governments. The action program was ambitious, but according to Jenson and Sineau it was premised on an equality discourse focusing on the training and education of women and tending to hide the structural constraints to equality. The 'Loi Roudy' was based on a legal strategy against sexual discrimination inspired by American legislation, and official evaluations indicate that measures to increase equality in women's entrance to higher positions have not been successful (Jenson and Sineau 1995: 223).

Feminist scholars have discussed why policies of equality in relation to work, which was a priority area for the Socialist government, have been difficult to implement. One explanation is economics. The action program was carried out during the economic crisis and the growing economic problems of the Socialist government, and this has no doubt restricted the political choices of Socialist governments (Trat 1992: 14; Jenson and Sineau 1994–95). Another explanation is the nature of the trade union and feminist movements. Trade unions played an important part in the implementation of the legislation, and sexism as well as Stalinism in the trade union movement has made it difficult for women to influence union policies (Trat 1992: 15–17). Trat mentions that sectarianism in the French feminist movement towards the unions has made alliances between feminism and the unions difficult, with the result that a relatively low number of women are organised within trade unions. Instead, many working women, like nurses, chose to fight through co-ordinating committees without active support of the unions. The division between the unions and the political parties has finally made the implementation of gender equality difficult.

Social rights to kindergartens and day-care institutions have been important feminist demands in France, where the number of women who work full-time is higher than in most European countries, with the exception of Scandinavia (Hantrais 1993). Mitterrand promised to create 300 000 day-care places, but the economic crisis as well as the logic of natalist policies prevented him from carrying out this policy. During Left governments the emphasis in family policy shifted from a horizontal to a vertical distribution that focused on the child, and after 1985 family policies again privileged large families as well as single mothers. During the 1980s, family allowances for the second child increased, while they were reduced for the third, and extended benefits for children up to the age of 3 were introduced ('allocation jeune enfant'), but in 1994 there was still no support for the first child. According to Hantrais (1996: 63), 38 per cent of family benefits were distributed on a means-tested basis by the end of the 1980s.

In French family politics the object is for single mothers to be economically active, and so the benefit is paid for a limited period only (from one to three years), and today only poorly educated, unqualified mothers with many children are totally dependent on welfare. Since 1976 single parents have received a benefit ('allocation de parents isolé') that guarantees a minimum income on the basis of the number of children (Hantrais 1993: 133). In 1996 single parents represented 13 per cent of households with children.

Anti-sexist legislation includes the right to information about contraception, the right to reimbursement of abortion expenses, and respect
for women's dignity – a move against sexual discrimination and harassment. The demand for abortion has been important for the feminist
movement because of the strength of Catholicism in France. Attitudes
towards abortion have followed the division Right/Left, and many
Catholic groups are still against it. The Right is opposed to treating
abortion as a social right that includes the right to reimbursement of all
expenses (Mossuz-Lavau 1992). During Mitterrand's presidency, the proposed anti-sexist legislation making sexism illegal, like racism, was never
passed because of opposition from both Left and Right. It was claimed
that the proposal hindered freedom of expression, and it was seen as a
moralistic law. This contrasts with the proposal against sexual harassment, which was passed unanimously because it was interpreted as the
protection of women against superiors in the labour market and
included in labour legislation (Jenson and Sineau 1995: ch. 9). The
difficulties of implementing the EC legislation against sexual harassment (adopted in 1988) in France can be linked to the weak role of the
trade unions.

Mitterrand has been portrayed as a supporter of the egalitarian
feminism that started a democratisation of the family, but according
to Jenson and Sineau (1994–95: 51) the vision of egalitarian family
politics did not last long. They suggest that the reason why family politics
changed was related not primarily to the economy but to politics. There
were two conflicting objectives that lay behind the family policies of
the socialists and Mitterrand: securing equality between women and
men, and securing a large number of children (pronatalism). They
indicate that after 1983 family politics became increasingly pronatalist
and that the expansion of day-care institutions was blocked. Georgina
Dufoix introduced a new family benefit in 1986 ('Allocation Parentale
d'Education': APE), which represented about 1000 francs per month
to parents who interrupted their work after the third child. According to
Jenson and Sineau (1994–95: 50–2), APE became a veritable mother's
wage that encouraged women to leave the labour market, and after 1986
various Socialist governments continued to support the familist policies
of the Right by targeting young families and families with many children.

Jenson and Sineau have summarised the balance after fourteen years
of Mitterrand's presidency. They stress that women have gained new
formal rights on the labour market, although no real equality has been
achieved in relation to work. As a result of the economic crisis, neo-
liberal economic policies pursued by the socialists and the lack of
alliances between trade unions and the feminist movement, women
today have become vulnerable in the labour market, with a higher

unemployment rate than men. They give a relatively negative assessment of the effect of Socialist policies on women. This may be attributed in part to the high expectations in France attached to the Socialist discourse of gender equality.

Comparative scholarship has generally evaluated the impact of French family policies on women more favourably than Jenson and Sineau. Hantrais and Letablier (1996: 128–30) suggest that the 'family-centred' French policies increasingly resemble what they call the 'family-friendly' policies of the Scandinavian welfare states, because both emphasise the family–employment relationship. The point is that the different policy logics – the egalitarian principles of Scandinavian social policies and the family-centred French state provisions – have increasingly produced similar outcomes.

In terms of gender equality in politics, there is no doubt that the Socialist attempt to change political institutions failed. I therefore agree with Jenson and Sineau's (1995) conclusion that the political lesson to be learnt for women after fourteen years of Mitterrand's presidency is the need to strengthen women's political rights and political power. Evaluations of the policies of the different Socialist governments have shown that gender equality in the labour market is not enough. There is also a need for equality policies in relation to politics as well as 'body politics', for example the right to abortion.

During the 1990s it has become clear that macro-economic developments and labour market policies affect equality among men and women, and French feminist scholars argue that women need to be present in politics to influence political decisions – to gain power in society and to feminise institutions, including parliament. In France at present there is intense feminist debate about different strategies for integrating women in politics: whether women should demand representation as a social group through the demand for parity in parliament or through quotas in the political parties (Fraisse 1989; Young 1990a; Varikas 1994; Phillips 1995).

The Transformation of Women's Democratic Citizenship

Universalism is a key notion in republican discourse, and French political culture has given priority to the national political community over local communities, and has feared particularism and autonomous organisations. Political institutions have traditionally been negative towards women's autonomous organisations and towards gender quota and gender equity ('mixité'). The position of women is still marginal in political and administrative institutions, and feminist scholars have suggested that political power is one of the main bastions of male power (Sineau 1988).

Disillusionment with the policies of Socialist governments has been followed by a new feminist mobilisation for political rights. A number of feminist groups from different political observances are agreed about the demand for parity or 'mixité' in politics. In the French debate the notion of parity is defined as *complete* equality between women and men in relation to political representation (Gaspard et al. 1992). The demand for parity as a political objective is proposed as a means by which to increase gender equality in politics after forty years of formal political rights and fourteen years of Socialist rule. The number of women in parliament during the last twenty years has been extremely small, and in the last general election (June 1997) for the first time rose from 6 per cent to slightly above the symbolic 10 per cent (Sineau 1999).

Strategies for political equality: 'démocratie paritaire'

One response to the political exclusion of women has been the demand for parity, which means a legal right to the equal representation of men and women in politics with the object of replacing the 'rule of brothers' with a real democracy. Parity is defined as 'perfect equality' in politics, inscribing the right to 50 per cent women in all political bodies in law. Gender equity in politics can be interpreted as a simple and at the same time very radical demand (Gaspard et al. 1992: 129). This new politics is supported by arguments about *equality* as well as by arguments from the perspective of *sexual difference*, and parity has been defended as a way of transcending the old tension between equality and difference (Gaspard 1994).

Parity is an indication of a new orientation of women towards institutional politics, and the idea has raised intense debate among feminists about the philosophical roots as well as the political implications of an increase in their political representation (Gaspard et al. 1992).

The organisation for parity, 'Reseau Femmes pour la Parité', was founded in January 1993, and one of the founders, Françoise Gaspard, argues: 'Women have been collectively excluded from politics because of their sex. It is therefore "as women" that they should claim to be integrated as equal citizens in the city, all the more so since the political institutions bear witness to a special opposition to women's equal access from political institutions' (1994: 41, my translation).

This principle challenges both republican universalism and feminist egalitarianism, which has criticised all conceptions of sexual differences rooted in biology as essentialism. According to Gaspard (1994: 42), the novel aspect of the debate is the fact that feminists who have always fought essentialism see the concept of parity as 'a road to equality' for women in politics. The argument is that the debate about parity has mobilised part of the French feminist movement and has raised new questions about the different roads to equality for women in politics.

Geneviève Fraisse (1995) interprets the present feminist demand for parity by law as an example of a radical form of equality. The purpose is to realise a 'perfect equality' in the political sphere between women and men. It is presented as a utopian idea – a way to conciliate the universality of the laws with the irreducible difference between women and men. Fraisse's perspective is predominantly philosophical: as utopia is negative, the present cannot be taken as a model. The philosophical basis for parity is the idea that the world is composed of two sexes, two principles: men and women – the masculine and the feminine. In this understanding, the idea of parity has been interpreted as a way of ending the false universal and the false particular and of creating a new universal that is not gender-neutral.

Many feminists share Fraisse's thesis about women's different relation to politics and their different expectations of men, although the position is motivated by different philosophical and theoretical arguments. Fraisse refers the idea that woman is 'the other' ('alterité') to the philosophical ideas of the Frankfurt school, while Gaspard has referred directly to Pateman's thesis that in political theory there is a 'sexual' contract behind the 'social contract' (Gaspard et al. 1992: 64–8).

On the philosophical level, the potential of Fraisse's analysis is to combine demands for *equality* between women and men with the claim to *freedom/autonomy* for women. The new demand for equality can be combined with new ideas of women's difference. On the basis of equality, women today can choose to be different from men and likewise to be different from other women. The problem with the analysis is a certain ambiguity with the theoretical position and with the strategy of parity. To the extent that this figure rests on the philosophical base of women as 'the other' – 'the second sex' – it tends to perpetuate the segregation of women from men. The position has different philosophical roots, but 'parity' is connected with the same ambiguity as Pateman's utopian ideal of a 'sexually differentiated citizenship', one that would enable the two sexes to be 'equal and different'. Like the figure of 'the other', this ideal can be interpreted as a way of perpetuating sexual segregation and hierarchy. A further problem with a vision of democracy that divides the universal into two sexes is the tendency to obscure differences of race, ethnicity and class.

A second group of feminist scholars, such as Eleni Varikas, is critical of the idea of parity because it implies that women should be represented 'as women'. Varikas (1994) is generally against group representation, and, more specifically, has questioned whether women as a group have common interests that can be the basis for representation. The argument is that it is problematic to institutionalise gender differences in politics through legislation because it is not possible to describe positively what a woman is or what a man is. Dividing humanity and the 'universal' into two sexes leaves the problem of the underrepresentation of other social (and ethnic) groups and the need to rethink democracy in terms of multiplicities that would fulfil the political aspirations of all citizens. Varikas's solution is therefore to propose new forms and processes of equity that can integrate not only women but all excluded groups in politics.

The feminist debate about parity is based on different interpretations of the meaning of gender differences in politics. Studies of women's political attitudes are used as confirmation of the idea that women have a different relation to politics than men (Sineau 1988; Mossuz-Lavau 1994c). Investigations indicate that the excluded (women) are more ready to act, and have a more concrete relation to reality and are more sensitive to the link between 'private' and 'public' than men (Mossuz-Lavau 1994c). This is taken as support for the argument that women have common interests in relation to politics 'as women' (Gaspard 1994). The counter-argument employed by feminist scholars like Varikas (1994: 5–6) is that women must be mobilised politically on the basis of a concrete program that can create a link between 'le politique' (the political arena) and 'la politique' (political values), not on the basis of their sex.

The debate about parity ('une démocratie paritaire'), adopted either by legislation or by referendum as part of a constitutional reform, has today become a rallying point for French feminists on the political-institutional level. The idea of parity of women and men in political bodies has different philosophical roots and different practical implications from the quota systems practised in the Nordic countries. First, the philosophical argument for parity is often 'the biological difference' and not, as in the quota system, 'women's historical marginality in politics' (Fraisse 1989). Second, the demand for parity is not, like the quota system, interpreted as a transitory measure but as a question of inscribing political equality as a permanent right within law, or even in the constitution (Sineau 1994). The quota system is a means of integrating minority groups in politics and has been criticised by advocates of parity for treating women as a minority group. Finally, the demand for parity privileges a *legal* strategy, while the Scandinavian quota system has been a result of *political* processes. In Denmark, quotas have been part of voluntary politics, adopted by the Social Democratic Party and the Socialist People's Party, and later abandoned (see Chapter 6).

I conclude that the demand for parity is an ambiguous one. It opens up an important discussion about the meaning of women's political interests and about the relation between women's political presence and their political identities. Parity is a demand for political rights for women rooted in the universalist political culture, but the arguments are at the same time framed in the language of sexual difference between women and men. The demand for parity can be interpreted as the fulfilment of Pateman's vision about full and equal citizenship for women, but it is open to the objection that it may also contribute to the reconstruction of segregation between women and men in politics. The quota system has a different logic because it expresses a form of equity that links political representation of women with marginalised social groups. It can therefore be interpreted as an alternative strategy more closely related to the demand for a pluralist and differentiated citizenship.

The demand for equal representation and power is an important feminist demand, although there are different strategies for reaching this. I find that the advocates for parity tend to confuse theoretical and empirical arguments. The theoretical framework does not distinguish between women as a social and political group. One of the key arguments for parity is women's different relation to politics from men. This is not a theoretical argument but an empirical question that needs to be explored through comparative and historical research. This study indicates the historical and national variations in women's relation to politics and in the extent to which, and on what issues, women express common political interests and identities. Empirical observations about differences in the relations of women and men to politics must be interpreted and cannot in themselves be taken as support for the theoretical position of parity. The argument is that gender differences in politics may have different implications for women depending on their social class, ethnicity and race, and on different policy contexts.

Changes in women's and men's political participation and identities

Mariette Sineau (1988) has asked women in the French political elite about their experiences in politics. Her investigation indicates that there are gender differences in relation to the political arena. Women politicians have a *negative* identity in relation to political forms, that is, the rituals, language and norms that constitute political life, but this is not followed by a *positive* identity as feminists (ibid.: 45). Women on the Right argue that women in politics will create a new equilibrium because women have different (complementary) political values from men, while women on the Left argue that women in politics will create a more just society (1988: 206). The results of the investigation of women politicians indicate that more women in politics may change the forms of political life, increasing the focus on concrete political problems related to everyday life, but women cannot be expected to agree on the solutions to these problems.

Janine Mossuz-Lavau (1993a,b) has analysed changes in gender differences in political values, interests and participation from 1945 to 1993 through quantitative and qualitative investigations. She interprets the changes in women's voting pattern since 1944 as a development from *apprenticeship* to *autonomy*. In the first stage, women were more conservative and had a higher abstention rate than men, but today there is a small gender gap in favour of the Left: women on the Left (socialists and ecologists) vote a little more than men and on the extreme Right a little less. The question is what is the implication for their political identities of the changes in women's voting patterns.

Reversion of the gender gap from right to left

The investigation of the developments in women's political participation and attitudes since World War II indicates that one of the results of the changes in the women's vote in France is a reversal of the gender gap from Right to Left. During the first period, from 1944 to 1970, women had a higher abstention than men and a higher degree of the vote for the Right than men. In the presidential election in 1965 there was a 12 per cent gender gap in the second round, where women tended to vote more to the Right (De Gaulle) than men.

During the second period, 1970–88, the gender gap narrowed from about 12 per cent to about 5 per cent, and there was an equalisation between men and women in abstention. Mossuz-Lavau describes the third period as one of women's autonomy. There is a tendency for women to vote more to the Left than men, more for the ecologists, less for the extreme Right, and to be more negative towards the Maastricht Treaty than men. In the presidential election of 1988 there was a small gender gap, with more women than men in favour of Mitterrand. The investigation concludes that the equalisation of the voting patterns for men and women in politics hides potential differences in political priorities between women and men. In the elections of 1993, the gender gap in favour of the Socialist Party disappeared as a result of women neglecting the Socialist Party because of its policies (Jenson and Sineau 1995).

One question is why women have changed their vote. Another is the meaning of the recent vote for the Socialists. Mossuz-Lavau's investigation indicates that it is the Left that has responded to the social changes in women's situation by voting for women's reproductive rights – legalisation of contraception and abortion – whereas the Right is often more ambiguous and has sometimes directly opposed these rights. This is supported by Jenson and Sineau's (1994–95, 1995) findings that the Left under Mitterrand's presidency have introduced a new discourse favourable to expanding the rights of working women, through a veritable 'feminisme d'État', although there was a return to more traditional family policies after 1983.

The results of empirical research indicate that gender is still an important variable in politics in France in terms of political interests, political information and political alienation. There is a difference in interests (–6%), information (–11%) and alienation that can no longer be interpreted as an expression of political passivity, because today women vote to the same extent as men. The meaning of the gender difference can only be explored through qualitative investigation.

What explains the changes in women's vote in France from Right to Left? Mossuz-Lavau has pointed towards a combination of three factors: women's increased education; their growing labour market employment; and the decrease in women's religious practice. The tendency for working women to be both politicised and radicalised compared to women without wage work seems to be a general tendency in all European countries and one that is usually explained by the contradictions women experience as working mothers. In France, Catholicism has been an independent cultural factor, and Mossuz-Lavau has illustrated the strong trend towards an equalisation between men and women in relation to the practice of Catholicism. In 1952, 52 per cent of women and 29 per cent of men went to Mass every Sunday, whereas in 1991, 11 per cent of women and 9 per cent of men went to Mass once a week.

Results from the Danish Investigation of Citizenship indicate that changes in the socio-economic situation of women and their cultural ideology do not in themselves explain the changes in women's relation to politics. The conclusion is that political-cultural and institutional factors have played a relatively autonomous role in the changes in the relation of Danish women to politics. The Danish study indicates that higher education may stimulate women's interest in politics, but it does not *per se* make women inclined to vote Socialist. The study by Jenson and Sineau further illustrates the dynamic interplay between women and political institutions and the ability of political organisations to draw women into politics by raising new issues on the political agenda that concern women, because they are related to women's daily life.

The meaning of politics: differences in women's and men's conception of politics

The difference between how women and men relate to politics has been illuminated by Mossuz-Lavau (1994b) in her qualitative investigation of the relationship of French citizens to politics. Nine hundred and ninety-two men and women were interviewed and asked: what does politics mean to you? The results indicate that there are still gender differences in how women perceive politics across all political divisions in both Left and Right. The political discourse of women tends to be about *human needs*, while for men it is about the *constraints of politics*. And women tend to be interested in political *goals*, men in the *means* (Mossuz-Lavau 1994b: 36). She concludes that the potential of women's political culture is a focus on the concrete problems of daily life that does not separate private needs from public concerns, but it is an open question to what extent the gender difference can be the basis for collective political action.

The investigation indicates that women and men occupy the same political space but have different relationships to it. Women's space is described as less 'rich and diversified' than men's, but it is not clear what the implications of this gender difference are – whether women have less information about politics than men, or are active in less diversified political forms than men. Mossuz-Lavau stresses that women's difference cannot be explained by a 'time-lag' or by a 'lack of information' because women tend to have their own political discourse. This interpretation of how women perceive politics begs the question of how politics should be defined. In France there is an important distinction between policies ('la politique'), that is, political issues, values and problems, and politics ('le politique'), that is, the political arena with specific rules, institutions and organisations. The results indicate that women tend to be more hostile to 'le politique' – 'the political game' – than men, and also to be more interested in the substance of politics than men.

The investigation addresses the meaning and implications of women's specific concept of politics – 'la politique au feminine'. Women's vision indicates that politics ought to be about people not about power, about daily life and not about abstract political programs. One reason for this difference is probably the sexual division of work – in the sense that women's caring responsibilities render them receptive to the human problems of daily life. They develop a sense of social needs ('le capacité d'autre'), whereas men tend to focus on the constraints of politics. Men look at the means, women at the goals. Mossuz-Lavau (1994b: 36) concludes that the political culture of women, in contrast to that of men, does not separate the 'private' from the 'public' world. This understanding of politics transcends the division among women into Right and Left.

A brief comparison of key notions in the political, institutional and cultural context in Denmark and France may illustrate the similarities as well as the differences between women's political values, identities and practice. The comparison concerns results from the Danish Investigation of Citizenship from 1990 based on a representative survey of 2000 people (Andersen et al. 1993; Andersen and Torpe 1994).

One similarity between the two countries is related to the fact that women in both countries are less interested in politics than men and feel that they are more alienated from politics than men. In both countries women more so than men believe that 'politics is too complicated'. Another similarity is the notion women have of politics that tends to link 'social' and 'political' issues. Women have been more interested than men in dealing with the problems of daily life, and they are more positive than men about preserving and expanding social policies to protect disadvantaged groups, for example children, the handicapped, the sick and the elderly.

The point is that similar interests, for example in the well-being of children, must be represented and translated into political programs and projects, the implication being that there are different interpretations and representations of similar values. It is possible to interpret women's concern with social issues as an expression of both feminist and anti-feminist values, with values of the Right as well as of the Left. Women have historically been concerned with reproduction, children and sexuality, but they have disagreed about the concrete content of family policies. Today, women often disagree about the meaning of solidarity, about who should be included in and excluded from national solidarity and social rights. It is disputed whether solidarity should be expanded to immigrant groups, or should only concern solidarity with citizens within the nation-state (Dean 1995).

One important difference is the position of women as 'newcomers' in French politics. This contrasts with Denmark, where, since 1970, women have gradually become integrated within the political process and the political elite. On the formal political level, women gained the right to vote late in France (in 1944), while in Denmark women gained the right to vote relatively early (in 1915). What is more important is the fact that on the level of *practice*, Danish women have achieved a 'presence' in politics, and research indicates that they participate in a plurality of political arenas (Andersen et al. 1993), for example in the trade union movement, schools and day-care institutions, political parties, social movements and political organisations as well as in parliament. Danish research gives no indication that women have a 'more restricted and less rich political universe' (in terms of information and knowledge) than men. I conclude that in France women are regarded, and still regard themselves, as *outsiders* in relation to both political organisations and political institutions. This shows that in contrast to Denmark the republican French model has been a constraint rather than a potential for women's integration into politics. The implication is that there is a growing gap between women's high level of labour market participation and their marginalisation in politics. This is the basis for the feminist demand for parity.

Conclusion: Promises and Constraints on Equal Citizenship

There is no doubt that the political history of citizenship in France has followed a different logic from Marshall's model. France is an example of an active model of citizenship where the people destroyed established social and political institutions 'from below' in 1789. From a feminist perspective there are many paradoxes here. First, the new republic challenged all aspects of absolutist rule and at the same time excluded women from democratic citizenship. Second, the republican discourse valued women as mothers of citizens, and although the family was at first violently attacked it came to be perceived as an institution with important public functions. The republican discourse introduced a radical new language about individual equality, one that also had positive impacts on women's citizenship, especially in relation to education and the labour market.

In terms of *democratic citizenship*, the promise of French republicanism has been a vision of political equality. Political scientists have analysed the contradictions in the political discourse of radical individualism, which did not include women as persons or citizens. And feminist scholars have suggested that the universal bourgeois subject constructed by the Revolution was at the same time a gendered subject, and the body politic a gendered body that excluded women citizens (Landes 1988; Scott 1997a). The republican discourse excluded women because they were not perceived as equal individuals but as different in nature from men and with social functions in the family (Rosanvallon 1992).

In terms of the *public/private divide*, there has been a strong emphasis on the public sphere and on public virtues in the republican discourse. The formation of the French welfare state was a political project 'from above' during the Third Republic, and since the interwar period the 'politics of the family' has been at the centre of the French welfare state. The discourse about the family has been ambiguous, and state support to families with children has traditionally combined maternalist arguments for protecting working mothers with paternalist arguments attempting to return married women to the family. Historically, women did enjoy certain rights as workers and mothers before they obtained formal political and civil rights. World War II represented a radical break. Women finally gained the vote, gender equality was inscribed in the constitution of the Fourth Republic, and pro-active family policies were institutionalised in the postwar social security system. Between 1965 and 1985 family policies were gradually modernised and married women gained full civil rights. There is, however, a strong continuity in the logic of family politics, which became visible under the Socialist regime, and family politics has oscillated between pronatalist and redistributive objectives.

The shift in political institutions after 1981 influenced women's social and political rights as well as the discourse about gender equality. During Mitterrand's presidency a new vocabulary of gender equality was adopted, directed towards improving the position of women as workers and mothers, and a program for gender equality in politics was introduced for the first time. In spite of setbacks caused by the economic crises and high levels of unemployment for women, the objective of gender equality has been most successful in the areas of education and the labour market. The shift of regime did not fundamentally change the pro-natalist objective of family politics as the state has always protected women's reproductive function and to some extent also the economic activities of women. Family policies became increasingly motivated by pronatalist ambitions under Mitterrand and less by gender equality. Women and working mothers still have among the highest activity rates in Europe after Scandinavia, however, and the highest number of places in childcare institutions for children over 3 years old (see Figures 1 and 2 and Table 4 in the Appendix).

From a perspective of citizenship, the gap between the republican promises of equality and de facto gender inequality is presently most acute on the political arena. The object of Mitterrand's state feminism, to integrate women into parliament 'from above' through a system of proportional representation, represented a real break with the republican past. The initiative was unfortunately blocked by the Constitutional Council, with the result that women remained marginal in parliament. In this context the radical demand for parity between women and men in political institutions has captured the imagination of many feminist groups across the political spectrum as the road to political equality.

I have suggested that the demand for parity is ambiguous from a feminist perspective. First, it is an elite strategy that depends on political initiatives imposed by law and not on a mass mobilisation of women in society. The strategy also rests on a problematic separation of the discourse about social justice from that about political rights. The demand for gender equality is presented as a goal 'in itself' and not, like the quota system, a means of transforming the political agenda and political institutions to make them more democratic and responsive to everyday problems. In French political culture, parity has gradually gained support as a pragmatic strategy to increase gender equality in political institutions. The recent surveys have indicated that there is a majority of citizens who support measures that will increase women's presence in politics. There is, however, no agreement about whether to increase women's representation by a progressive quota system, by the adoption of a law based on strict parity, or by voluntary means (*Le Monde*, 31 October 1998). In June 1999 the French constitution finally introduced the principle of equal access of men and women to political office and legislative functions ('l'égal access des femmes et des hommes aux mandats electoraux et aux fonctions éléctives'). This text does not satisfy the advocates for strict parity but it can be interpreted as one step towards the inclusion of women in political institutions (Halimi in *Le Monde Diplomatique*, September 1999: 7)

Feminist research has shown that in France women are, and still regard themselves as, outsiders in politics and that they have a different relation to politics from men, in relation to both political institutions and political issues. Women tend to be more critical of the political game than men, and more inclined to combine politics with social questions related to daily life. There are crucial differences in the notion of politics in Denmark and France in relation to political institutions as well as to political issues, which are both an expression of and the cause of Danish women's presence in political institutions. In terms of political issues, high politics connected with foreign politics and 'the common good' is separated from the daily lives of people. In terms of political institutions, politics in France is closely linked to classical political institutions such as the presidency, the government, the parliament. This contrasts with the Danish case, where politics has increasingly become related to social services and associated with problems in people's daily lives, and where political participation includes participation of parents in social service institutions, for example in relation to childcare and schools. The perception of politics 'as high politics' removed from the problems of daily life can be seen as both the cause and the effect of women's exclusion from politics.

One interesting question is whether the present coalition government of Socialists, Communists and Greens, in power after the last general election of June 1997, will be able to fulfil the promises of a more

egalitarian and democratic public, one that includes the political participation of women and marginalised groups in the governing of society.
Among other things, this would imply challenging the perception of
universalism embedded in republican institutions and discourses and
moving towards an acceptance of the ethos of pluralism of political
representation and ideas. It would also imply challenging the strict
distinction between social and political aspects of citizenship towards
recognition of the connection between politics and social problems.

CHAPTER 5

Gender and Citizenship: The British Case

Assumptions about Gender in Liberal Discourse

In this chapter I analyse the logic of the exclusion and inclusion of women in citizenship in Britain. What has been the perception of women's civil, political and social rights, and how has women's agency influenced the formulation of social policies? I explore the changing nature of gender and citizenship in the crucial periods of welfare state developments, and look at the changes in the discourse of citizenship in periods when gender and citizenship has been an issue in political discourse and social policy. The focus is on the shifts in the discourses and politics of gender and citizenship and on the changing role of women's agency. The research interest is to understand the political meaning of gender in contemporary debates about citizenship.

Britain has a unique status in the development of the framework of citizenship because T. H. Marshall's paradigmatic model of citizenship was based on the political development of Britain and the integration of the British working class. Marshall (1992: 10) described the gradual evolution of civil, political and social rights, and he stressed that the three elements of citizenship were originally blended, later to be divorced. He traced the formative period of each aspect of citizenship to a different century. The 18th century was the period for civil rights, the 19th century for political rights, and the 20th century for social rights. He claimed that by the 19th century civil rights were universal, and that in economic life the basic right was the right to work.

Carole Pateman was the first to challenge the universalism in Marshall's model from the point of view of women's citizenship. Pateman (1989: 185) pointed out that married women in the 19th century lacked fundamental civil rights, and she questioned 'independence' as the central criterion for citizenship because it is based on masculine attributes and abilities. The point is that women lack the three elements of 'independence': the capacity to bear arms, to own property, and for self-government.

Brian Turner is also critical of Marshall's model and tells a different story about the evolution of citizenship based on a comparative framework. Britain is one of the four ideal types in Turner's typology for the formation of citizenship rights rooted in the national political histories of Britain, France, Germany and the USA (see Chapters 1 and 2). In terms of the active/passive dimension, Turner contrasts the active revolutionary French model that defeated absolutism from below with the passive English model where rights were handed down 'from above', and where citizens are subjects with rights. In the English legal tradition, gradualism is connected with the common-law tradition that created a common basis for individual rights. Turner suggests that in the liberal democratic solution positive democracy emphasises participation, although democracy is often contained by a continuing emphasis on privacy and the sacredness of individual opinion (1992: 55).

In terms of the public/private dimension, the British notion of citizen-as-subject, according to Turner, indicates a relatively extensive notion of social rights but also the passive character of British civil institutions. Turner (1992: 53) has stressed the importance of the class structure in the British case, because effective social rights resided in individual rights to property, the majority of the population thereby being excluded from social and political participation.

According to Turner, the differences between French and English revolutionary traditions can be summarised in two contrasting views of citizenship, one by Jean Jacques Rousseau, the other by Edmund Burke:

> For Rousseau in *The Social Contract* the viability of citizenship required the destruction of all particular intervening institutions which separated the citizen from the state. By contrast, Burke in *Reflections on the Revolution in France* in 1790 argued that the essence of citizenship was the continuity of local groups, particular institutions and regional associations between the sovereign power and the general will and the individual. For Burke an organised civil society must have hierarchy, order, regulation and constraint; Its hierarchical character precluded the very 'rights of man'. (Ibid.: 54)

From a perspective of democracy the emphasis in the quotation above is on the positive perception of voluntary organisations in civil society as key elements in the British pluralist political culture, which is a key element in the ideology and discourse of both liberalism and conservatism. According to Turner, the British model of liberalism was based on a positive perception of citizens as bearers of rights, and the common-law tradition has provided a common basis for rights. Liberal democracy also has a positive perception of participation, although it is contained by the passive character of the civil institutions and by the priority given to private virtues.

Feminist scholarship has criticised the liberal discourse because the strong emphasis on individual rights has not applied in the case of women. Feminist scholars have observed that the division between the public and the private arena has at the same time been interpreted as the freedom of the family from state intervention (Walby 1994). Women did gain civil rights in marriage earlier than in continental countries like France and Italy, but formal civil rights were contrasted with the economic dependency of married women on their husbands. Two examples show that the gradual evolution of political and social rights did not apply to women. One is the fight about married women's right to work, the other is the violent opposition to women's suffrage by powerful forces on the Right (Pateman 1994).

The discourse about citizenship and the assumptions about gender have changed during the last hundred years. According to the British sociologist Ruth Lister (1998a: 310), three waves of citizenship have been identified in British political thought. The first was the three decades before World War I; the second the period after World War II and the 1960s; and the third the last two decades of the twentieth century. New liberalism[1] changed the meaning of British liberalism and influenced the formation of the welfare state from the beginning of the twentieth century.

According to Bill Jordan (1989: 78), new liberalism in Britain introduced a more positive role for the state, which paved the way for social democracy and social democratic ideas of social rights that were later incorporated in the British welfare system. The Beveridge reform of 1942 appealed to the value of social citizenship, and the social democratic principle of universalism was incorporated in the British welfare state after World War II, especially in the National Health Service (Thane 1991, 1993; Pedersen 1993a).

Feminist scholarship has brought out how the principle of universality in British social policy was based on the male worker and the exclusion of married women from social insurance (Pateman 1989; Lewis 1992, 1994; Lister 1993). Historians have traced how women organised in the labour movement and in women's organisations were actively developing alternative conceptions of citizenship that would reflect the experience of women (Thane 1991; Lewis 1994). One of the most controversial issues was the proposal to expand welfare rights for mothers and children in the form of family allowances. According to Susan Pedersen (1993b), the attempt to create a system of family allowances was defeated during the interwar period by three powerful forces: social scientists, Labour Party men, and male trade unionists and civil servants.

Feminist scholarship has portrayed the role of the state as predominantly passive in relation to the family, because the 'social question' has been interpreted as a problem of class. The social democratic vision of an active state is contrasted with the Labour Party's perception of the family as part of the private sphere. The principle of universalism in social policy has thus been premised on a strong male-breadwinner model that excluded married women from many social rights (Lewis 1992; Lister 1998a). The objective of the British Labour Party was to redistribute resources to the working class, not to families with children within the working class (Pedersen 1993a,b). From a gender perspective the emphasis on class has been a problem, because the Labour Party and the trade union movement have been dominated by a masculine ethos that has subsumed women's interests under the interests of the working class (Lewis 1992).

Recent feminist scholarship has compared the role of women's agency in the origins of the welfare state. These indicate that although women's voluntary organisations were strong during the interwar period, they had only small impact on the formation of social policies in Britain (Lewis 1994). Women were already well organised before World War II in relation to the political parties, but it was difficult for women's organisations to influence the formulation of social policies (Thane 1992; Lewis 1994). Feminist scholars have observed that at this time women played an important role at the local level and within the party organisations, but they were not the main actors in national social policy (Thane 1991; Pedersen 1993a). As a result, since World War II social rights have been conditioned on (male) employment, and children have been seen as private problems, not as a social responsibility. Class has been a dominant force in welfare state developments, and the Labour Party and the trade union movement actively supported the male-breadwinner model as the dominant norm in postwar social policy (Lewis 1992; Pedersen 1993a). Despite the relative strength of the feminist movement, democratisation was until recently identified with the problem of integrating the working class in society.

The expansion of social policies after World War II under Labour governments created a new framework for social citizenship rights during the 1960s and 1970s. The war opened up a new debate about the proper welfare settlements between individuals and the state (Lister 1998a). Reconstruction of the welfare state after the war marked a shift in the discourse about citizenship and introduced an element of social citizenship built on universal rights to health care, education and work. Feminist scholarship has pointed out that the new discourse was deeply

gendered and that the notion of the male breadwinner was a corner-
stone in the National Insurance Scheme adopted by the Labour
government (Lewis 1992; Pedersen 1993a). The implication is that up to
the mid-1970s social policy in Britain was premised on the normative
value that men were the sole breadwinners and that a woman's role as a
mother was private (Lewis 1992).

The last two decades of the twentieth century have been identified
as the third wave of citizenship, opening up a new debate between the
New Right and Centre Left about the nature of citizenship and about
the rights and obligations of citizens. According to Lister (1998a: 314),
the third wave represents a shift of language from a focus on citizen
rights to a focus on citizen obligations. The third wave of citizenship was
sparked by ideological attack on the postwar social democratic conception of social rights following the conservative/neo-liberal takeover
of government by Mrs Thatcher in 1979 (Lister 1998a). Thatcherism
represented an ideological shift in the discourse about citizenship, but
her discourse about the family and her social policy principles were
ambiguous towards women. At the same time they threatened women's
social rights and maternity rights and encouraged their obligation to
work (Lewis 1992). According to Lovenduski and Randall, Thatcherism
also opened up a new space for feminist interventions in political
institutions by stimulating a Centre Left debate about married women's
economic dependence on men, and about the role of the state in
relation to equality policies and public childcare (Lovenduski and
Randall 1993). Political developments during the last two decades have
attacked the 'politics of dutiless rights', but at the same time they have
opened a new debate among the Left activists and academics about the
rights and obligations of citizens and about the gendered nature of
citizenship rights (Lister 1998a).

Recently the Labour Party introduced new discourses of state–family
relations that signal a shift in the discourse of social citizenship. The
election victory of the Labour Party in May 1997 opened up the possibility of an alliance between New Labour and feminism. The implications
of the New Labour government for gender relations are contested.
According to the British historian Donald Sassoon (1997), there is the
possibility of a new gender contract based on an intelligent social welfare state, a new model of women's socio-economic role and women's
political inclusion. Lister (1998b: 313–16) is more critical of the new
language of citizenship, because she believes it expresses a shift from
rights to obligations and a new emphasis on work and family obligations
that creates problems for unemployed women and lone mothers. From a
feminist perspective, New Labour's strategy – recently labelled the 'Third
Way' – has both positive and negative elements. The key criticism of the

'work ethic' has been that it does not take account of the value of the unpaid work of reproduction and care carried out by women. The introduction of the new childcare strategy as part of economic policy, comprising both childcare provision and family-friendly employment policies, however, is a positive support for working women.

In what follows I look at the shifts in the paradigms of citizenship, focusing on the connection between gender and citizenship in three periods where citizenship has been an issue in social and political thought (Lister 1998a). First I look at new liberalism and democratic citizenship around the turn of the century and discuss the discourse about the family and the role of women's agency in the interwar period. Second, I look at the new framework for social citizenship after World War II and discuss the relationship between the labour movement and feminism. Third, I look at the recent shifts in the discourse and politics of citizenship during the last thirty years and the changes in women's democratic citizenship with the growth of the new feminist liberation movement

New Liberalism, Democratic Citizenship and Family Politics

According to Turner, Britain is an example of a passive democracy in which there is an emphasis on the freedom of the individual from the oppression of the state. According to feminist scholarship the gender dimension takes a particular form in liberal ideology, where the division between the public and private arena is accompanied by women's economic dependency on their husbands (Pateman 1988; Fraser and Gordon 1995; Shaver 1997). From a comparative perspective, it has been observed that in Britain women gained civil rights in marriage as well as political rights relatively early, compared with Latin countries like France and Italy (Sineau 1992b: 475). The implication is that during the 20th century there was a growing contradiction in Britain between married women's civil rights and their economic dependency in the family (Pateman 1989).

The passive role of the central state in social policy was questioned by the first wave of citizenship before World War I (Lister 1998a). New liberalism represents a shift in the language of citizenship. According to Bill Jordan (1989: 78), new liberalism was a philosophical attempt to remedy the shortcomings of liberalism by introducing the concept of the 'common good' in an attempt to transcend individualism and appeal to a collective notion of citizenship. The common good required a social minimum standard of living for all, underpinned by welfare reforms.

Liberal governments between 1906 and 1914 introduced a number of social reforms in the area of progressive taxation, the old-age pension (1908), and unemployment and national health insurance (1911) (Lewis 1994: 40). According to Lewis, this political development at the same time represented a shift towards a centralised welfare state that was accompanied by a decrease in the active role of women on welfare policies.

The vocabulary of citizenship and women's suffrage

According to Marshall's framework, political rights were gained in the 19th century, with the 20th century marking the start of the expansion of social rights (1992: 13). Historical research indicates that the timing and dynamic of the struggle for citizenship were different for women and men. The first wave of citizenship opened up a debate about social rights at the beginning of the century, but it did not address the issue of women's rights (Jordan 1989; Lister 1998a). Although women's suffrage was the key issue for feminist organisations at the turn of the century, women's political and social rights were not part of the debate about citizenship.

The prevailing consensus in social theory and research about the gradual extension of rights in Britain has been challenged from the perspective of women citizens. Pateman (1994) has observed that women's struggle for suffrage in Britain was a long and violent process that did not follow logically from the extension of the franchise to all men, but was met with fierce resistance from many men and some women.

The question of women's suffrage was raised in 1832 following the First Reform Act that granted the vote to all men. It was later taken up by the liberal thinker John Stuart Mill in his attempt to extend the arguments for suffrage to include women by amending the Second Reform Act in 1867. Mill has been described as the only major liberal thinker who explicitly applied the principle of liberalism to women. In the classic work *On Liberty*, from 1859, he contrasts the value of individual freedom with the patriarchal institution of marriage and the legal and social position of women (Okin 1989: 211). Female equality was based on the universal principle of just treatment that would at the same time contribute to the general welfare of society. In *The Subjection of Women*, Mill's argument for women's vote was based on his belief in the principle of perfect equality that gave 'a voice in choosing those by whom one is to be governed' to all citizens as a means of self-protection (Collini 1989: 168). Women finally gained the vote in general elections in 1928 after a prolonged and dramatic struggle between pro- and anti-suffrage activists.

Pateman (1994: 336) has recently asked three important questions about women's suffrage in Britain (and the USA). Why did it take women so much longer than men to gain the vote? Why did some women organise against their own enfranchisement? How did women gain the vote in the end? She has suggested that the separation of the public and private spheres explains why suffrage at the national level was so vehemently opposed: 'The reason for the length of the struggle for womanhood suffrage was, then, that it was not merely participation in government of the state that was seen to be at issue but the patriarchal structure of relations between the sexes and conceptions of masculinity and femininity' (ibid.: 339). According to Pateman, women organised within the anti-suffrage movement argued along the same lines in both Britain and the USA. They wanted the protection of women, which they believed could be secured through the separation of the private and public spheres. Many women as well as men opposed suffrage because the vote was seen as a threat to the family.

One prevalent explanation for granting the vote to women was that it was a reward for the work of women during the war. Pateman finds that the reference to women's agency – their determined efforts in organised labour and feminist movements demanding the vote for women – is a more plausible argument. She writes that the fear of an electorate that included women had abated considerably by the end of World War I, with the growth of the party system still dominated by men (ibid.: 343). In the British context, the reference to women's agency seems convincing because the suffragist movement was strong and women were well organised inside and outside the political parties.

Pateman's thesis that the (liberal) separation of the public and private spheres can explain why suffrage was so vehemently opposed at the national level is interesting from a comparative perspective. The thesis is at odds with the recent argument by Rosanvallon that it was easier to integrate women in politics in Britain than in France. According to Rosanvallon (1992: 395–6), France and Britain represent two different roads to political modernity, with diverse philosophical discourses that have implications for women's suffrage. In the French case, women gained the right to vote 'as individuals', whereas in Britain women gained the right to vote 'as women' because of their difference from men. The point is that arguments about women's 'difference' from men in the French case was used to keep women out of politics, but in the British case it was possible for J. S. Mill to use the same arguments from a utilitarian perspective to include women in politics. This illustrates how key notions in feminist thinking, such as 'equality and difference', are embedded and derive their meanings from the national, historical, political-cultural and institutional contexts.

Women's agency and the formation of the welfare state

The story about the incorporation of married women's economic dependency on their husbands into British social policy is well known, and the implications of the principles behind it have been widely discussed in feminist scholarship on the welfare state. In the following, I discuss the main theories of why Britain developed a male-breadwinner model and the role of women's agency for the development of social policy (Pedersen 1993a; Lewis 1994; Sainsbury 1994).

The role of women's agency in the formation of the British welfare state has been examined from the perspective of comparative feminist research (Koven and Michel 1993; Lewis 1994). This has been followed by an interesting debate about the role of women's agency in the building of the British welfare state (Thane 1993; Lewis 1994). Lewis is sceptical about the influence of women's agency, arguing that women have played little part in the construction of the core elements of the British welfare state. Another British historian, Pat Thane, is more positive about the role of women in influencing social policies, stressing that women have a share in the making of the post-World War II British welfare state through their activities in the Labour Party (Thane 1993: 351).

Thane has shown that the division of work between the central and the local level has enabled *voluntary organisations* to play a central role in the administration of welfare in the pre-World War I period. The point is that the state structure, with its reliance on local and private forms of welfare, opened up space for women's political activities at the local level that allowed women's voluntary associations to flourish (Thane 1991, 1993). According to Thane (1993: 343), the state before 1914 had 'a small, but strong and flexible core firmly directing the key activities of state (like war) and supervising the delegation of functions defined as less essential to local authorities and voluntary organisations'. On this basis she suggests that it is a misunderstanding to categorise Britain as a weak state or a minimal state based on the small central bureaucracy that consciously limited the area of government. The functions that were found less important were mostly education and welfare services, areas where women were actively influencing the shaping of the British welfare state.

Thane has shown that there was a strong organisation of women within the British party structure even before they gained the vote. Women were active in the Labour Party from its start in 1906 and played a significant role in it between the wars. The party formed a minority government in 1924 and again in 1929. A handful of women were elected to parliament from 1924 onward, Margaret Bondfield becoming Britain's first female cabinet member as Minister of Labour in 1929. Thane's research (1993: 372) indicates that the influence of Labour women, and indeed of other women, on social politics has to be analysed at both the local and the central level, and that woman in Britain have made a positive contribution to state formation.

Lewis's analysis of the development of British social policy challenges the optimistic interpretation of the role of women's agency. Lewis (1994: 40) has noticed that the gradual centralisation of social policy made it increasingly difficult for women's organisations to influence the central state. She has shown how the balance of the mixed economy shifted in favour of a centralised welfare state after the first decade of the twentieth century as the philosophy of welfare changed. The early foundation for the British welfare state was laid by the Liberal government, which passed a number of welfare measures granting an old-age pension in 1908 and national health and unemployment insurance in 1911. Lewis has found no evidence that women influenced this legislation (ibid.: 42).

Thane and Lewis agree that women's agency was strong in relation to the welfare services provided by the voluntary sector and local government, but Lewis emphasises that British women were not policy-makers at the national level. She writes that British women made the transition from unpaid voluntary visitor to paid health visitor and social worker in the employ of local government, although they very rarely advanced to paid policy-making positions in the civil service (ibid.: 44). The point is that the influence of women decreased with the gradual centralisation of the welfare state and the change in the discourse of welfare from voluntary towards professional work after 1914.

From a comparative perspective Lewis concludes that British women, in contrast to their American counterparts, played little part in the construction of the British welfare state in relation to welfare provided by the central government (ibid.: 40). She suggests that the argument supporting women's agency in building the modern welfare state rests on the idea that the boundaries between the public and private spheres were porous. Lewis's interpretation is supported by Susan Pedersen's work (1993a,b), which claims that British women were only able to domesticate the public within certain rather narrow limits.

Feminism and the campaign for family policy

In her comparative study, Susan Pedersen (1993a: 133) has analysed the conflicts between women and men in the labour movement on the issue of maternal benefits for families with children in Britain in the interwar period: 'Labourism and feminism were poised for a number of bitter quarrels in the post-war era'. According to Pedersen (ibid.: 219–23), women's claim for family allowances was defeated by two powerful discourses: Labour Party men and trade unionists on the one hand, who argued for the family wage to keep up male wages, and civil servants (and social scientists) on the other, who denied that the support of motherhood should be a concern of government.

British women were, like men, politically active before they gained the vote, and the powerful women's organisations attached to the major political parties were an important feature of British politics. Thane (1993: 344) has observed that women traditionally played a major and acknowledged role in the Conservative, Liberal and Labour parties.[2] Women also played an important role in the British Labour Party and the Women's Labour League (WLL), which actively supported the party from 1906, twelve years before women gained the vote. In 1918 women became integrated within the party structure and organised in Women's Sections of party branches. According to Thane, they formed a semi-independent female network within a mixed-sex party. In the interwar period women comprised a majority of the individual members in the party, female membership reaching between 250 000 and 300 000 in the 1930s and rising still higher after 1945 (Thane 1993: 344). In spite of this, the Labour Party was male-dominated in the sense that leadership and members of parliament were overwhelmingly male, with decision-making at the annual conference being dominated by male-controlled trade unions.

British feminism, broadly defined, was relatively strong after World War I, and between 1906 and 1939 the largest feminist organisations campaigned for maternal and child health and for economic assistance to mothers. During the 1920s and 1930s family policy became a women's issue, a way of shifting resources from men to women (Pedersen 1993a). There were a number of feminist organisations, and feminist research has identified different strands of feminism during the first half of the century – liberal feminists and feminists connected with the labour movement (Dale and Foster 1986: 5).[3] According to Jennifer Dale and Peggy Foster (ibid.: 19), class divisions between the different feminist organisations, especially between the mainly middle-class women in the National Union of Societies for Equal Citizenship (NUSEC) and the labour movement women of the Women's Cooperative Guilds, weakened the impact of feminism on the labour movement and hence on social policy.

Liberal feminists, organised since 1897 in the National Union of Women's Suffrage Societies (NUWSS), saw the struggle for the vote as the dominant cause that would give women political influence (ibid.: 6). Attitudes among liberal feminists changed after World War I, when the NUWSS changed its name to the NUSEC and began to campaign for equal rights for women in social and economic matters. From the late

1920s feminists began to talk about the 'new feminism' which, rather than seeking equality with men, was more concerned with women's specific needs and aspirations (ibid.: 7).

Women in the labour movement formed the second strand of British feminism, including women in trade unions, and organisations such as the Women's Cooperative Guild formed in 1883 as an offshoot of the cooperative movement. These feminists gave priority to immediate social reform rather than to socialist transformation, to social needs over and above abstract notions of equal rights, and were less likely to place gender interests over class interests (ibid.). According to Dale and Foster the Women's Cooperative Guild, and later NUSEC, played a central role in the campaigns[4] for economic assistance to mothers and children. Women in NUSEC had moved away from the demand of equal rights in favour of giving priority to the needs of mothers and children.

Pedersen (1993a: 138–77) has also observed that what became known as the 'new' feminists developed a vision of 'separate but equal', campaigning for endowment of motherhood on the road to women's economic independence from men before World War II. The sole result of the campaign was the widow's pension bill in 1925, which was a way to endow some mothers.

During the 1920s the object of the campaign for family allowances was no longer economic independence for married women but a redistribution of income between childless families and those with children. The debate about family endowment took place within the Independent Labour Party and the trade union movement. Labour women represented at the National Conference of Labour Women were in favour of family allowances as a way of rewarding women's unpaid caring work, but the proposal was defeated.

Research has shown that women were active in the debates about social and family policies in the labour movement as well as in women's welfare organisations (Pedersen 1993a). This raises the question of why women's attempts to influence the social policies in the interwar period failed. Feminist scholarship has identified a number of factors that help to explain why the campaign for economic assistance to mothers and children did not succeed.

According to Pedersen (1993a: 219–23), the opposition within the labour movement killed the proposal for family allowances, because the trade unions defended the male wage. According to Thane (1991: 112), the debate in the labour movement was not simply about gender relations but was also located in a wider discourse about the role of the state in relation to the labour market. Thane suggests that the trade union movement has traditionally been against state intervention in the labour market. According to Dale and Foster (1986: 19), the divisions between liberal and 'welfare' feminism weakened the impact of feminism on the Labour Party, especially during and after World War II.

The studies all indicate that the powerful influence the trade unions had on the policies of the labour movement as well as the division among women's organisations along class lines both contribute to explaining why women's organisations did not succeed in influencing social policy. Whatever the explanation for failure to adopt family allowances in the interwar period, the implications for postwar Britain were profound. Pedersen's research has demonstrated that the victory of the male-breadwinner model in the postwar British welfare state was premised on the active support of Labour and the trade union movement and on the defeat of feminism. One of the implications was that women's demands were subsequently subsumed under the presumed interests of the ungendered working class.

The Male-breadwinner Norm in the Postwar British Welfare State

The role of the family in the British welfare regime has been analysed in comparative feminist scholarship by Lewis (1992), Orloff (1993) and Shaver (1997). According to the Australian sociologist Sheila Shaver (1997), the British policy regime operates on the premise of gender difference, but does little to address the consequences of this inequality. It leaves to the family and the market the disadvantage attendant on women's responsibility for care work (ibid.: 25). The liberal character of the welfare regime is reflected in a benefit structure characterised by low levels of benefits, the ready use of means-testing, and policy dualisms that encourage private provisions for all but the lowest income groups (ibid.: 4–5). After World War II, the labour movement's ideology about a family wage and the belief in married women's economic dependency on their husbands were explicitly incorporated in the foundation of the modern British welfare state on the basis of the Beveridge report (Pedersen 1993a).

Comparative feminist scholarship has taken the British model as the point of departure for an alternative categorisation of welfare states as strong, moderate and weak male-breadwinner models (Lewis 1992; Lewis and Ostner 1994). Lewis and Ostner (1994: 17–19) have described Britain as a strong male-breadwinner model which in social policy has perceived married women either as mothers or dependent wives, not as breadwinners. The male-breadwinner model has been a powerful concept in research on the welfare state. It has challenged the hidden assumptions about the relation between paid work and welfare in the dominant paradigm about welfare regimes.[5]

Feminist scholarship has pointed out that one of the key aspects of the British welfare state has been the economic dependence of women on their husbands, based on the normative premise of the exclusion of married women from the labour market. The family wage became an assumption in social insurance (from 1911) that was later made an explicit premise for British social policy after World War II (Lewis 1992, 1994). The Beveridge reform of 1944 introduced new principles of solidarity which from the point of view of class represented a shift towards universalism in social citizenship. According to Jordan (1989: 85), the social democratic principle of citizenship was partial and short-lived compared with the more 'integrated' welfare systems of Scandinavia. From a gender perspective the commitment to ensure full employment through the male wage incorporated the principle of the male breadwinner in social policy (Lewis 1992; Pedersen 1993a; Lewis and Ostner 1994).

The universal character of the male-breadwinner model has been challenged by results from comparative studies questioning the belief in Britain as the paradigmatic case. Pedersen's comparative analysis of Britain and France has shown that France was governed by a different logic, one she has called the 'parental welfare model' aimed at taking from childless workers and giving to working families with children. The counter-hypothesis put forward in this book is that from the point of view of social policies towards women and children, Britain in fact represents an exception to the rule of European social policies. This hypothesis is supported by recent research indicating that the majority of European welfare states, with Britain as an exception, have expanded public childcare services during the last twenty years (Hantrais 1996; Lewis 1997a).

Universalism and married women's economic dependency

It is ironic that the ideal of the male-breadwinner model was explicitly incorporated in social policies after World War II when the Labour government for the first time came to play a major role in the construction of the British welfare state. Beveridge proposed a comprehensive social insurance scheme built on a new vision of the welfare state based on greater state responsibility for the health and welfare of citizens. In the Beveridge report of 1942, the government for the first time accepted the responsibility for maintaining full employment. In terms of family policy, there were three main principles: working men and their wives as a team in the insurance system; a system of national health service; and a system of universal child benefits (Pedersen 1993a; Sainsbury 1994).

The Labour government constructed the welfare state on the basis of the Beveridge principles. Beveridge was aware of the value of married women's unpaid work, and wives and husbands were treated differently under the National Insurance Act of 1946. Single women were treated like men, but married women were normally exempted from the work-related provisions and insured as housewives. A system of universal family allowances did become part of the new welfare system as a payment to mothers, but it was only a supplement — it was never really accepted and it remained small in value (Pedersen 1993a: 354).

Feminist scholarship has asked why the British Labour government, in contrast to the French Conservative governments, failed to develop an active social policy directed towards the family after World War II. The liberal influence on policy-makers that emphasised the private notion of the family and citizenship partly explains the opposition to the state playing an active role in family policy. But this is not the whole explanation. Feminist scholarship has illuminated the key role played by the Labour Party and the trade union movement in the institutional structure for making social policies (Lewis 1992, 1994; Pedersen 1993a: 424). The male domination in the labour movement is therefore an important part of the explanation for the continued strength of the male-breadwinner logic in the British welfare system.

Feminist historians have also wondered why there were no real improvements in women's social citizenship after World War II. Pedersen (1993a) has noticed that women were absent from the policy-making structure. A number of women's organisations did give evidence to the Beveridge Report, but only the National Council of Women (NCW) wanted men and women to be treated equally, paying equal contributions for equal benefits (Dale and Foster 1986: 16). This indicates that women were divided in their attitudes towards the family wage. According to Dale and Foster many women welcomed the report because for the first time the economic status of 'home-makers' was explicitly acknowledged. The only protests against the exemption of married women from compulsory insurance came from egalitarian feminists organised in the NCW, who complained that married women should be insured independently against sickness and incapacity (Pedersen 1993a: 354).

Feminist scholars have emphasised that the male-breadwinner ideology left its impact on all postwar reforms after the National Insurance scheme and the social assistance program. According to Sainsbury (1994: 158), the breadwinner ideology has influenced married women's rights in four ways. First, the National Insurance scheme allowed married women to opt out and rely on their husbands' contributions, thus giving up the right to benefits in their own right. Second, married women who

decided to remain in the National Insurance scheme paid full contributions but received lower benefits than married men and single
persons unless they were the main breadwinners. Third, the adult
dependency allowance provided an incentive for women to stay at home
because it was paid only for dependants without an income or with
earnings less than the allowance. Finally, in the case of married couples,
only the husband could apply for means-tested benefits. This contrasts
with male-breadwinner countries like the Netherlands, where contributions and benefits are tied to individuals (Kremer and Knijn 1997).

Historians remind us that there is an important difference between
assumption and realities about married women's paid work. Feminist
scholarship has observed that working-class women were never excluded
from the labour market and that their participation did in fact rise after
World War II. The breadwinner ideology did have far-reaching effects on
women's social rights, however: women were denied equal rights and
married women were encouraged to renounce their rights in the labour
market. The effect was to enforce married women's economic dependency on their husbands.

Lewis (1997a) points out that it has been a problem to fit lone
mothers into the system of the male-breadwinner model because the
state has had to decide whether to treat them as mothers or breadwinners. Widows were included in social insurance and divorced and
unmarried women in social assistance. Beveridge also tried to include
lone mothers in the social insurance scheme but failed, and they were
instead included in the non-tax-based system of family allowances. The
claims of lone mothers as mothers were explicitly acknowledged under
the National Assistance Act of 1948, by which they were not required to
register for work if they had dependent children under 16 years of age
(ibid.: 7). Lone mothers fared relatively well on social assistance in the
1970s when social assistance was treated as a citizen right, and it had
become less and less worthwhile for lone mothers to enter the labour
market because of low wages and high childcare costs (ibid.: 70). Lewis
has shown that from a comparative international perspective the pattern
of women's labour market participation in Britain, with the high
participation of married women and low participation of lone mothers,
is highly unusual (ibid.: 71).

Development in British social policy after World War II illuminates
the crucial role played by collective actors and discourses – in this case
the labour movement and the belief in the male breadwinner – in
framing new social policies. It also illustrates the institutional hypothesis
that, once chosen, the policy logic – in this case the male-breadwinner
model based on gender difference – has tended to become self-
enforcing. Indeed, social policies until the Thatcher governments have

been remarkably stable and have continued to treat women primarily as mothers or dependent wives who would not normally be wage workers (Lewis 1994). Despite the increase in married women's labour market participation, until recently social policies supporting 'working mothers', for example the expansion of childcare centres, has been met by strong political opposition (Lewis 1992).

From a comparative perspective, there has been a remarkable political-cultural consensus about the necessity of leaving the responsibilities for children to parents, contrasting with the strong ideological struggle between Right and Left about nationalisation of industry (Ruggie 1984). This consensus is now under challenge from changes in the socio-economic roles of women as well as from a new emphasis by the Right and Left on active labour market policy, which includes married women and lone mothers (Lewis 1997a; Lister 1998b).

Shifts and Continuity in the Gender Model

The male-breadwinner logic became dysfunctional as married women increasingly participated in the labour market during the 1960s and 1970s (Ruggie 1984; Sassoon 1987). In the same period the socialist and feminist movements were relatively strong in Britain from a comparative perspective. This raises a question about the influence of the discourse of social democracy and feminism on social policies. Why have British social policies since 1960 towards married women and the family continued to follow the same policy logic? Why has the integration of married women in wage work during the last thirty years not been followed by the expansion of public childcare provisions? Comparative European research indicates that the discourses and policies of non-intervention advocated by different British governments in relation to married women's employment and childcare have been the exception rather than the rule (Ruggie 1984; Hantrais 1996).

Feminist scholarship has questioned why the (social) liberal vision of non-intervention in family affairs was reproduced in the 1960s and 1970s in the face of new discourses about equality and radical changes in state–society relations under different Labour governments (Lovenduski and Randall 1993). The labour market is one of the policy areas marked by a new discourse of gender equality and by many positive forms of state intervention, for example the Equal Pay Act of 1970, the Race Relations Act of 1976 and the Sex Discrimination Act of 1975.

Lovenduski and Randall describe equal opportunities and equality at work as major mobilising issues for women during the 1970s. The Equal Opportunities Commission was founded with the support of organised women who discovered that the equality legislation of the 1970s had taken a new turn, one based on new forms of civil rights with very little British legal tradition behind it. Lovenduski and Randall (1993: 217) have a fairly positive assessment of the effects of equal employment policies. They interpret equal employment policy as an area in which women's movement politics has indeed influenced practices, transformed the agenda, and populated the policy community.

Mary Ruggie has a more negative evaluation of the new policies of gender equality. She observes that state institutions like the Training Services Agency and the Employment Services Agency began targeting women workers. According to Ruggie (1984: 140), the new equality initiatives did not change labour market policies towards women; these remained within the liberal welfare paradigm of state–society relations based on the principle of non-intervention in family affairs.

Childcare provision is an interesting case which has been used by feminist scholars to illustrate a policy area with minimal changes. During World War II there was a conscious integration of women into the British labour market accompanied by an expansion of childcare facilities as part of the war effort, but after the war married women were actively discouraged from wage work (Riley 1983; Ruggie 1984: 204). Despite the increasing labour market participation of married women, childcare provision in the UK has been among the poorest in the EU and in fact declined between 1945 and 1984 at a time when it was expanding in most European countries (Ruggie 1984: 222–3; Hantrais 1996).

The roots of inadequate childcare provision in the UK are deep (Riley 1983). In analysing the dynamic of the British system of day-care provision, Ruggie has suggested that it is related to class. According to Ruggie (1984), the welfare state does intervene to secure public day-care provision but only for working mothers on welfare, and she suggests that in general working women are perceived as within a marginal social class. 'Public day care provision excludes the interests of non-welfare working mothers. By implication the state deems it to be in the public interest not to provide universal day care. The interests of working mothers are thus fragmented from the norm, subordinated to it, and particularised' (ibid.: 248). She interprets this type of intervention in the case of day-care provision as typical of a liberal welfare state that determines how and the extent to which the state intervenes. Yet the particular combination of welfarism and liberalism is peculiar to Britain. The point is that public day-care has been provided in Britain for different groups which supported different principles – health, education and especially children at risk – but it has never been a policy supporting working mothers.

Lovenduski and Randall (1993) and Randall (1996) are dissatisfied with the general reference to the liberal principle of non-intervention in the family. They emphasise that, in practice, the postwar state under different governments intervened in the family on a whole series of grounds – social work, education and medicine. They suggest that the political-ideological climate after World War II strengthened the liberal vision of the family, and especially the role of mothers within it. They add factors such as the lack of a public institution in support of the aim of overviewing childcare. This last point is illustrated by the institutional split between nursery education, which is seen as a matter for the Department of Education, and day-care, which is seen as the responsibility of the Department of Social Security, with no national childcare agency with overall responsibility for childcare. It is part of the strategy of the New Labour government (of June 1997) to expand childcare centres to overcome this institutional split in the public organisation of childcare (Sassoon, pers. comm.).

Finally, Lovenduski and Randall (1993: 286) point to a split in the feminist discourse about the role of the state in childcare in the sense that one group wanted to expand day-care provision, with the other opposing and wanting to develop collectively run, community-based services.[6] According to Lovenduski and Randall, a number of factors help to explain why national campaigns for childcare failed in the 1970s and why childcare campaigning became more visible in the 1980s. Feminist reservations were partly a realistic response to external constraint and partly a consequence of the character of second-class feminism in Britain. They indicate that feminist attitudes to childcare and maternity rights during the 1980s gradually changed with women's increased participation on the labour market, although childcare failed to inspire feminist action. Instead unions started to discuss these issues, and equal employment rights networks campaigned for childcare at the national level (ibid.: 301).

From a comparative perspective, it is surprising that the liberal ideology of non-intervention in family life could survive in the face of profound social and economic change. Feminist research has thus illuminated the gap between the new labour market policies introduced during the 1960s and 1970s and the liberal welfare paradigm towards the family that was reproduced during the same period. The discourse of the Labour Party, the male-dominated trade union movement, and a spilt in feminist discourse all contributed to support the liberal ideology about the private character of the family.

Rights and obligations in the discourse of Thatcherism

According to Lister (1998b: 312), the New Right theory was followed by a revival of the language of citizenship. Margaret Thatcher's victory in 1979 opened an ideological attack on the social democratic welfare state and on the privileges of the trade union movement. Thatcherism fundamentally challenged the postwar social democratic conception of social citizenship with its focus on social rights. The New Right emphasised the obligations of citizenship in the official economy of paid employment (ibid.: 314–18). This in turn led to a reworking of the language of citizenship by the Centre Left in the late 1980s and early 1990s, and citizenship proved to be a key intellectual tool for the defenders of the welfare state (Lister 1998a: 3).

During the Conservative governments, established social rights increasingly came under strong pressure from neo-conservative political forces, especially in relation to education and health care, and neo-liberal economic policies of privatisation substantially weakened the established social rights of citizens. Peter Taylor-Gooby (1996: 104) writes that policy developments in the 1980s and 1990s pursued four main aims: to contain the level of public spending; to expand the role of the private sector; to extend the principles of the markets; and to increase central power over the welfare system. The effects of the policy changes were to increase inequalities and consumerism and to make the UK system more reflective of the structure of class inequality. At the same time mass unemployment increased the general problems of working-class families, children, and indeed lone parents, with resultant marginalisation and poverty.

According to Taylor-Gooby (ibid.: 113), the pattern in relation to gender inequality is more mixed. Cuts in government spending generally affect women more than men because women tend to be more dependent on social assistance, especially the growing group of lone mothers who are dependent on benefits. And social security changes affect women workers, since they are lower paid than men and are more dependent on the redistributive element in state schemes. The conclusion is that gender and class inequality cut across each other and that the changes tend to continue the process of assimilating gender and social class inequality

Lovenduski and Randall (1993) have also discussed the contradictory discourse of family policy under Mrs Thatcher. On the one hand, Thatcher initiated a discourse and politics of intervention in family affairs to support traditional family values. An example is the new Child Support Act of 1991, which sought to compel absent fathers to contribute to the upkeep of their children. On the other hand, the government also formulated policies that were much less dogmatic, such as the 1989 Family Law Reform Act that aimed to eliminate the legal disadvantage associated with illegitimacy and the 1989 Children Act (ibid.: 266–9). Lister (1992: 21) has also observed that the Tory party was ambiguous about the employment of married women, although in practice it concentrated on the maintenance obligations of fathers.

The discourse of Thatcherism opened up a new debate about the nature of citizenship, women's family obligations, and their socio-economic roles during the last twenty years. Feminist research has shown that there is a growing gap between the increase in the labour market participation of married women and changing family forms (Drew et al. 1998: 98) and the policy logic behind social policies. The Beveridge report gave women an indirect social citizenship right through their husbands and attached married women's claim to citizenship to their maternal role. The Family Allowance (today Child Benefit) is the only citizen right paid directly to mothers, and it is a benefit to the child, not the mother. The social insurance scheme excluded lone mothers, who had to rely on means-tested assistance (Lewis 1997a).

Just as in the case of women in France and Denmark, the number of women in paid employment in Britain has gradually increased during the last twenty years, but many British women work part-time and receive low wages, and there has been no substantial improvement of crèche provisions or maternity leave (Drew et al. 1998: 98; Leira 1998: 167; and see Figures 1 and 2 in the Appendix). From a comparative perspective, social welfare programs in Britain have done remarkably little to improve the social and economic situation of working mothers.

The discourse and policies of Thatcherism challenged the old social democratic discourse of rights. There was a move towards individualism, enterprise and consumerism, with Thatcherism emphasising the obligations of citizens, including family obligations. The obligations on fathers to support their children were enforced, and lone mothers were encouraged, but not forced, to take paid employment. The British social policy regime under Thatcher, despite a fundamental change in the discourse of citizenship, continued to reflect the gender logic that favoured a male breadwinner family form. In spite of important changes, social policy under Thatcher thus remained premised on married women's economic dependence on their husbands (Lister 1993).

The Transformation of Women's Democratic Citizenship

Britain has had a long history of feminism and women's social movement activism, but it has been difficult for women to gain national political representation. As recently as 1992 only 9.2 per cent of members of parliament were women. Feminist scholars in Britain have suggested that one of the key factors behind women's underrepresentation in formal politics is that the sexual division of work gives women less time and less mobility to participate in politics. Women's greater preference for participation in voluntary organisations and the local arena has been emphasised as an alternative potential for women's political citizenship (Lister 1993).

Political scientists have pointed out that institutional and discriminatory barriers have been major constraints on the political representation of women in Britain. According to Lovenduski and Randall (1993), the remarkably centralised and unitary character of the British government and voting systems has made it difficult for feminism to influence politics and for women to be represented in parliament. However, they have traced a new productive relationship between feminism and the state during the 1980s as well as a growing presence of feminists in established political organisations (ibid.: 352). They conclude that while the 1980s was a time of contradictions it also led to positive changes, enabling feminism once again to make an impact on Britain.

Historically, the involvement of women in decision-making in Britain has been greater at the local level of politics than at the national level. Feminist scholarship has noticed that local government has again become a major, if not the major, arena of feminist activity in the 1980s (ibid.: 20). Britain had until then no tradition of a regional level of decision-making, and local authorities have been entirely the creation of parliament. Although local authorities do not have much power, they *are* responsible for areas such as housing, social work and childcare. The 1964 London Government Act and the 1974 Local Government Act established new regional authorities for London and six of the major cities. Government under Mrs Thatcher actually reinforced centralisation, especially in central–local relations, and by 1984 all the metropolitan governments had been disbanded.[7]

Lovenduski and Randall (1993: 154) have observed a growth in women's committees during the 1980s. With the establishment of the Women's Committee of the Greater London Council in 1981, women's committees spread to a number of other Labour-controlled authorities in the 1980s. This development has been described as municipal feminism creating a group of professional feminists who have become part of a sex equality network that continues to promote the interests of women even when committees remain few in number (see also Stokes 1998).

The centralised state contrasts with the democratic and egalitarian norms that have favoured women's political participation in voluntary organisations and at the mass level. Geraint Parry and colleagues (1991: 145) have shown that the participation of women in politics has increased since 1960. The result of their comprehensive investigation of political participation in 1984–85 has shown that today there are only minor differences in this regard between women and men at the mass level. The results of the national survey also indicated that men are much more politically active than women in the age group 23–49. This difference is interpreted as a 'life-cycle' effect due to childbearing and child-rearing, because marriage and the presence and absence of children in Britain tends to increase the gender gap (ibid.: 146). This result confirms the feminist claim that, in Britain, family factors like marriage and children are still a major barrier to women participating in politics (Randall 1987; Lister 1993). This claim is not supported by results from the Danish Investigation of Citizenship, which indicate that family and children are no longer such a barrier but tend to draw both mothers and fathers into the politics of everyday life as parent-citizens (Siim 1994a,b).

Results from investigations of political participation at the local level indicate that women in Britain make up 20 per cent of activists and that 20 per cent of local leaders are women compared to about 30 per cent of elected leaders. These results confirm that although women activists have been included in democratic leadership, at the local level also, 'leaders are middle-aged, middle class men' (Parry et al. 1991: 350).

According to Parry and colleagues, the gender gap is basically an expression of differences in resources, especially in individual resources like education and in collective resources like membership of organisations. Feminist scholars usually see the gender gap in political participation mainly as a result of the persisting sexual division of labour. On the basis of the results from the Danish Investigation of Citizenship cited above, I suggest that we need to be cautious about universal explanations of gender differences in political participation (see Chapter 6). The meaning of education, the sexual division of labour, and the relation between local and national politics need to be interpreted from different political, institutional and cultural contexts (Siim 1994a).

The studies of the political participation of women in Britain confirm that women are active around local welfare issues, and they indicate that family factors are still a major constraint on women's inclusion in politics. They also confirm that in Britain there is still a gulf between 'formal' and 'informal' political arenas that makes it difficult to carry over the influence women have at the local level, in voluntary organisations and at the grassroots, to a presence in national politics. This differs from the Danish case, where women's representation in national politics is greater than their local representation, and where women have historically been able to transform their influence in voluntary organisations and social movements to a presence in formal politics.

Feminism and political institutions

Studies of the relation between feminism and political institutions have painted a somewhat more optimistic picture of the influence of women on politics in Britain. According to Lovenduski and Randall

(1993: Ch. 5), the 1980s changed the political opportunity structure in a way that made a feminist infiltration of political institutions possible, especially in the Labour Party, the trade unions and local government. They indicate that in spite of the masculine ethos in the labour movement, feminists have successfully influenced the Labour Party, for example through the Labour Women's Action Committee.

There has been general hostility to quotas in the selection of parliamentary candidates in Britain, with the result that in 1992 only 13.7 per cent of Labour MPs were women. In the same election, the gender gap re-emerged on the agenda among women over 35, who voted Conservative in significantly greater proportions than men (ibid.: 157). One example of feminist interventions is the growing acceptance of quotas for women in the Labour Party during the 1990s, as expressed in the amendment of the party constitution to establish quotas of women on most party councils at the 1991 Labour conference (ibid.: 141–2). Labour Party feminists have been more successful in influencing the policy agenda and in politicising issues of concern to women than in increasing their political representation (ibid.:144).

Results from the last general elections (in May 1997) indicate, however, that Labour is changing its image among the electorate (Sassoon 1996). The quota system was used for the first time in the election of 1997, with the number of women MPs almost doubling. Today, about 25 per cent of the New Labour group in parliament are women, and women comprise about 20 per cent of all ministers – members of the Cabinet and backbenchers alike (Henig 1999; and see Table 6 in the Appendix).

According to Lovenduski and Randall (1993: 148), women also increased their power and presence in the unions throughout the 1980s. Inequality between women and men in the trade unions became an issue, and policies to increase the representation of women on union councils and committees were adopted. In 1988 the trade union movement established an Equal Rights Department, and in so doing enhanced the status of equality issues. The unions committed themselves to fight for classical issues, such as maternity rights and childcare, as well as new gender issues such as sexual harassment at work, positive action in the form of training for women, and job evaluation.

To sum up, the social and political changes of the 1980s and 1990s meant one thing for class and another for gender. The politics of Mrs Thatcher was a direct ideological attack on the socialist perception of social rights which, paradoxically, opened up new political space for feminist intervention. This was especially true in the Labour Party, the trade unions and local government. The aim of feminist intervention has been to change the democratic forms of decisions, to make them less hierarchical and more responsive to the grassroots, as well as to put new issues onto the political agenda such as sexual harassment and positive action.

Feminist scholarship has suggested that the strong masculine culture in the British labour movement has until recently worked against the integration of women within the Labour Party, because women are more concerned with social issues and lean towards consensual rather than combative politics. Although researchers agree that the masculine culture has had negative effects on the promotion of women's interests in the labour movement, Lovenduski and Randall (1993: 157) have indicated that the difference between men has also enabled feminist interventions of various kinds.

The recent changes in the discourse and practice of the labour movement have helped to place new issues that concern women onto the political agenda, for example gender equality on the labour market, maternity rights, and childcare provisions. Feminism has introduced new democratic forms – described as 'a consensual ethos in which all voices are heard, in which doubts are explored' – which have challenged 'the authoritarianism and demagogueries' of the Labour Party of the 1960s and 1970s (ibid.: 158).

One of the questions concerns the extent to which feminist forms of democratic organisation will be used as an inspiration to modernise the discourse and practice of the Labour Party of the 1990s (ibid.: 159). Another key question is the extent to which the new discourse of the labour movement will be transformed into social policies promoting the interests of working women and their children. And, finally, there is the matter of whether the new discourse and policy can combine the promises of universalist social policies with the multidimensional nature of difference (Lister 1998a: 324).

New Labour, the family and the interests of women

The Labour Party gained power in May 1997 after a landslide victory based on a new strategy that included a new role of the state towards working women and their family. According to Lister (1998: 316), the strategy of the New Labour government towards a more intelligent state with active citizens represents both a break and continuity with the discourse of obligation. There is a state commitment to support working mothers through an expansion of day-care centres, but the obligation to take paid work may at the same time create problems for unemployed women and lone mothers because they will have to accept any suitable employment (Lewis 1997a; Lister 1998a: 315).

The reform strategy of New Labour has opened up a debate about the nature of the family and the interests of women created by the prevailing division in social policy between private and public care. According to Jordan (1989: 144), the nature of households in Britain has created a female altruism and common interests between women as primary carers. He suggests that the sexual division of work, the failure to provide state services and the legislation on protection of dependants means that 'the majority of women in Britain have more to lose from sharing with the poor than to gain from challenging patriarchy'.

Feminist scholarship has also addressed the differences between women and their need to form alliances along the lines of class, race and ethnicity. One of the effects of Thatcherism has been to increase the divisions between women; new opportunities for women with education contrasts with increased problems for poor families and lone mothers and their children.

The philosophy and program of New Labour, especially the language of obligation and responsibility, represent both opportunities and problems for women. Sassoon (1996) has pointed towards the positive aspects of Labour's welfare reforms because in them there is an explicit commitment to gender equality, a commitment to break with the passive role of the state and a commitment to expand childcare services.

Lister (1998b: 12) has been more critical of New Labour from the perspective of social rights for women. According to Lister the government does recognise its role in supporting caring responsibilities, in particular through its childcare and family-friendly employment policies, but from the context of strengthening the obligation to paid work. There is a danger that the New Labour program will benefit women with high education as well as two-earner families, but not lone mothers, unemployed women and home-makers. One central issue is therefore the kind of support that should be provided for those unable to undertake paid work for whatever reason. From this perspective, one of the major challenges for New Labour is whether it is a party primarily for the middle classes or whether it will have the courage to address the growing problems of social, economic and political exclusion through a politics of redistribution (ibid.: 20).

Conclusion: Towards a New Paradigm of State– Family Relations?

The relation between liberalism and feminism has been, and still is, ambiguous. The legacy of liberalism is support for individual rights, which has been a major inspiration for feminism. The principle of non-intervention in family matters has, however, been interpreted as one of the major barriers to women's equal citizenship. Since World War II there has been broad political consensus in the British policy regime about the principles of gender difference based on the male-breadwinner norm. This principle was modified by the increasing integration of married women in paid employment as well as by the neo-liberal tendency to treat women as workers. During the 1970s and 1980s there has been a growing contradiction between women's socio-economic roles and the social security system. The different Labour and Conservative governments have, however, until recently followed a similar social policy logic, ignoring the consequence of the sexual division of work for gender inequality and leaving the disadvantage consequent on women's responsibility for care work primarily to the market and the family.

One question is why the state has put the interests of men before those of women. To what extent have state policies been influenced by patri-archy, the interests of employers' organisations, or the labour movement? Feminist scholarship has employed different approaches and vocabu-laries in analysing the British welfare state from a gender perspective. In spite of this, the studies all confirm that the labour movement has indeed favoured a male-breadwinner model premised on married women's economic dependence and has also played a major role in applying this principle to social policy. There has been a contrast between women's civil rights in marriage and their lack of social rights. This is the basis for Lewis's (1992: 159) thought-provoking hypothesis that in Britain patriarchy has been located in collective institutions rather than within the private family.

The centralised state structure has been described as a separate barrier for women's active citizenship, which has put constraints on women's agency. One of the main problems for feminists in Britain has been their lack of influence on national social policy. Although feminism during the 20th century has been relatively strong, it has not trans-formed women's social activism at the local level into an increase in their representation at the national level, or an increase in women's influence on the central state.

On the positive side, feminist scholars have suggested that the prin-ciple of liberal pluralism has been a potential for the self-organisation of citizens which has also encouraged women's involvement in voluntary organisations and strengthened their ability to influence the local welfare state. During the 1980s, local government has again become one of the main arenas of feminist activity, and the women's committees can be seen as positive examples of opening formal to informal politics. During the 1990s, the New Labour government has also for the first time committed itself to increasing the political presence of women in the national arena.

The dominant liberal values of non-intervention in family matters, as well as the New Right family interventionism, came under serious challenge from the Report of the Commission of Social Justice from 1994 and from the philosophy of New Labour (Lister 1998b). The commission was established by the Labour Party and has been followed by major changes in Labour policies.[8] The report introduced a radical program for social and economic reforms that expressed a political alternative to both the passive (welfare) state and to the male-breadwinner model (Sassoon 1996). The reform program was the inspiration for Labour's political debate about a renewal of the British welfare state and about the need for an active welfare state in which individual responsibility was combined with collective solidarity. The vision was to develop an intelligent welfare state that would prevent poverty through public policies that enabled citizens to combine lifelong education with wage work and care for the weakest social groups (Social Justice 1994: 223). The key point from the perspective of gender and citizenship was to accomplish the restructuring of the welfare state, taking into account the independent socio-economic roles of women.

The New Labour principles concerning a more active social state thus represent a conscious break with the past in a number of policy areas. Policies supporting employment of married women, of increasing public provision for childcare as well as of including women in politics challenge the old masculine ethos of the labour movement. The new social programs are designed to help working mothers, but proposals to strengthen the obligation to work in social policy are disputed. They have opened up a debate about the problems concerning the obligation on poor women and lone mothers to engage in paid work and to take any available employment (Lewis 1997a; Lister 1998b).

From a comparative perspective, the social program towards the family and the discourse about gender equality of the new Labour government can be interpreted as a convergence towards the strategies of social democracy of the Nordic countries.[9] From the point of view of the family and gender equality, the Labour Party and the Nordic social democracies have never belonged to the same 'family' of the Left. The new discourse about the inclusion of women in active citizenship as well as the initiatives to integrate married women within the labour force through an expansion of childcare provisions can, however, be interpreted as a step towards 'convergence'.

The New Labour government is committed to promoting the interests of women, and especially to improving the situation of working women. One step has been to increase the number of women Cabinet ministers and other MPs and to establish a Women's Unit as part of the Cabinet Office as well as a Ministry for Women. In relation to social policy, the government has not yet improved childcare provisions or addressed the problem of the growing social and political marginalisation of poor women and children. Another problem is New Labour's emphasis on the moral obligations of the family and of parents in relation to social policy, which is different from the norms, values and policies of Scandinavian/ Danish Social Democrats. For this reason it is too early to conclude that there is in fact a convergence of the visions and policies of New Labour and the Nordic social democracies in relation to social rights and political inclusion of women.

The recent academic debate about the new vocabulary of citizenship has highlighted new problems for women in dealing with the responsibility of citizens in relation to the family and civil society as well as the work obligation (Lister 1998b). One of the challenges for New Labour will be to determine whether or not the new legislation will address social inequalities, increase women's democratic influence, and expand the role of women's agency in both the party and society.

CHAPTER 6

Gender and Citizenship: The Danish Case

Assumptions about Gender in Danish Political Culture

In this chapter I analyse the discourse and politics of gender and citizenship in Denmark. I trace the development of the welfare state and democracy between 1915 and 1995, looking at the dynamic, meaning and implications of shifts in the interplay of gender and citizenship. The focus is on three crucial issues: democratic citizenship and the role of women's agency; the formation of the universal welfare state and the subsequent shift towards a dual-breadwinner norm; and women's inclusion in democratic citizenship during the last thirty years. The emphasis is on understanding the shifts in the discourse and politics of gender and citizenship and on the role of women's agency. The research interest is to understand the political meaning of gender in contemporary debates about citizenship.

In relation to the active/passive dimension, I look at the discourse about gender and the role of women's organisations in the development of democracy and social policy. In relation to the public/private dimension, I look at the discourse about women's wage work and the organisation of care work in the public and the private sector.

The Scandinavian democracies have important commonalties compared with the dominant Anglo-American political culture. They are often portrayed as small, homogeneous and peaceful democracies governed by the political ideas of social democracy, which include 'a passion for equality' (Alestahlo and Kuhnle 1987). Gøsta Esping-Andersen (1985) first described the Scandinavian welfare states as 'social citizenship states' based on universalist social policies directed towards all citizens. He contrasted Scandinavian social policies with residual (and neo-liberal) social policies directed towards the poor and Continental (conservative) social policies based on the insurance principle (1985: 34).

Feminist scholarship has been more critical of social democracy based on class interests and dominated by paternalism, which has made women the objects and not the subjects of public policies (Hernes 1982). Helga Hernes was the first feminist scholar to challenge the negative perception of social democracy. She described the Scandinavian welfare states as potentially women-friendly states 'that would enable women to have a natural relationship with their children, their work and public life' (1987: 15). But during the 1990s this positive image of Scandinavia has been challenged by political and economic developments, especially in Sweden, and social and political differences between Denmark, Norway and Sweden have become increasingly visible. A recent investigation gives an overview of the social and political factors of the Nordic gender model (Bergquist et al. 1999: 253–65), but there are still no systematic analyses of the implications for gender and citizenship.[1]

Academic debate in Denmark has not explicitly been framed in the language of citizenship. The key words in welfare state research have been social equality and universality, and the discourse about democracy is about the political participation of citizens (Siim 1998a). The meaning, formation and evolution of civil, political and social rights in Denmark do not fit within existing models. According to Henrik Kaare Nielsen (1991: 81), Danish political culture is a mix of Continental and Anglo-Saxon traditions. In his framework political culture is defined broadly as the attitudes, values and political participation of citizens in relation to political institutions and procedures as well as to the informal political process. In Nielsen's analysis of the political cultures of Germany and Denmark, there are several key characteristics of the Danish vocabulary of citizenship.

In terms of the active/passive axis, the key element is the peaceful formation of Danish democracy by an alliance between the absolute monarchy and the educated elite. The introduction of democracy in 1849 did represent a radical break with the old monarchy, but like Britain, citizens' rights and democracy were introduced peacefully in 1849, not as in France through violent revolution. In contrast to Britain, women's suffrage was also gained peacefully in 1915. During the 20th century the meaning and practice of citizenship changed from a passive to an active model based on the successful social organisation of peasants' and workers' movements (Nielsen 1991: 63–87).

Historically, the political culture has been influenced by a 'cocktail of bourgeois liberalism and Grundtvigean populism which was a unique Danish phenomenon' (Nielsen 1991: 79). One of the key figures in the Danish farmers' movement was the clergyman N. F. S. Grundtvig

(1783–1892), whose ideas became institutionalised in the Folk High Schools and in the cooperative farmers' movement. Since the beginning of the 20th century the ideology of the United Farmers Party (Det Forenede Venstre, today called the Liberal Left Party) as well as Danish political culture and institutions have been inspired by Grundtvig (Østergård 1992: 77). The egalitarian values and the participatory understanding of democracy in Danish political culture were connected with a differentiated class structure with many independent small-holders, and strong class organisations of small landowners and workers. The economic and social strength of the peasant movement forced the liberal intellectuals, and later the Social Democratic Party, to take the political ideas of the farmers seriously.

In terms of the public/private divide, there is a pragmatic perception of the public arena that has given priority neither to public nor to private virtues, and the state is perceived as a tool for solving social problems. As in Britain, there was a positive perception of voluntary organisations, but in contrast to Britain the high degree of involvement of social groups in voluntary organisations in civil society has created a balance between citizens and the state, between the public and private sphere. The Danish citizenship tradition can thus be described as a combination of the principle of democratic self-organisation 'from below' with an emphasis on public solutions (ibid.).

Danish scholarship has not systematically studied the connection between social and democratic aspects of citizenship (Andersen et al. 1993).[2] Research has tended to focus either on the nature of the democratic political culture (Nielsen 1991) or on the formation and development of the universal welfare state (Kolstrup 1997).

Nielsen's comparative study of social movements in Denmark and West Germany, described above, illustrates the first approach to Danish citizenship from the perspective of the 'democratic self-organisation' of social movements. According to Nielsen (1991: 80), there is a split in Danish political culture between the strong sense of autonomy of citizens in civil society and their perception of the state as the medium for the public good. This culture after 1960 is described as integrative and conflict-solving, where popular experiences have a highly developed competence for democratic self-organisation, based on experiences from the folk high schools and the working-class movement (ibid.: 77). Nielsen's story contrasts the Danish way of defining and 'doing politics', based on an interaction of social movements and the state with elements of politics 'from below', with Continental models of politics that interpret politics mainly 'from above'.

The participation of citizens 'from below' has also been expressed in the Danish vision of democracy as a way of life that concerns individuals in their daily lives (Koch 1961). Nielsen (1991: 82) explains the relatively strong communitarian tradition of self-organisation in Denmark with the agrarian economy, the economic organisation and cultural emancipation of farmers in the 19th century, as well as with the social movement of workers in the 20th century. The differentiated class structure has been followed by a fairly high degree of pluralism in political life. Danish political development has produced a universalist political consensus between the economic and political organisations of farmers and workers about key aspects of the welfare state.

The second approach to Danish citizenship can be illustrated by a recent study by the Danish historian Søren Kolstrup, who has analysed the formation of the Danish welfare state from the perspective of the working class. Kolstrup (1996, 1997) has traced the roots to the universal Danish welfare state in what he calls 'Municipal Socialism' ('kommunesocialisme') between 1900 and 1920. The study indicates that welfare agents in civil society played a crucial role in building up the Danish welfare state.

According to Kolstrup (1996: 455), there were four driving forces in the formation of the welfare state: political parties, especially the Social Democratic Party; voluntary organisations, including a number of women's organisations; local socialist communities; and the central state. The implications are first that the universal welfare state was inspired by philanthropy, liberalism and socialism. I would add feminism. The second point is that the peasants' and workers' movements were able to penetrate the state apparatus by a democratic struggle (Kolstrup 1997: 20).

Kolstrup (1996: 454) observes that there is an ambivalence on the part of citizens towards the state, in the sense that demands for 'more state' in Denmark have come 'from below' from the voluntary organisations and social reform movements. Unfortunately the investigation does not systematically analyse the role of the different women's organisations in the development of municipal socialism. He does, however, mention the importance of women's organisations as agents of local welfare concerning women and children in the 19th and early 20th centuries. Women were active in relation to free school meals and in activities connected with Mothers' Help (Mødrehjælpen), a private organisation helping unmarried pregnant women to give birth.

Kolstrup's story of the formation of the Danish welfare state focuses on the discontinuities and breaks in political development. This challenges the dominant story by Esping-Andersen, where the growth of the universal Scandinavian welfare states is portrayed as a gradual process, with social democracy playing the crucial role. The two interpretations agree that class has been the determining element in the formation of the Danish welfare state, and that the consensus between Left and Right about the universalist welfare state was built on a class compromise between workers and farmers. Kolstrup (1996: 14) suggests that the class compromise between workers and middle-class farmers in 1933 was built not on a stable alliance but rather on a cynical compromise between the Liberal Agrarian Party and the Social Democrats brought about by the economic crisis in agriculture. The new element in Kolstrup's interpretation is the emphasis on cooperation between welfare agents in civil society and the role of the local state and the Radical Liberal Party (Det Radikale Venstre) as agents of social reforms. Basically both interpretations are gender-blind, although Kolstrup does mention the role of women's organisations.

Danish scholarship generally agrees about the key role played by social democracy in the adoption of a welfare strategy based on full employment and social equality, but some interpretations are critical of the effects of social democracy on women and marginalised social groups (Christiansen 1996). Niels Ole Finneman (1985: 252) suggests that the social democratic discourse has been governed by a 'spirit of brotherhood' defined as solidarity among men, which was also a 'patriarchal' spirit that aimed to create social progress and social cohesion through a rational organisation of society. Uffe Østergaard (1991) has noticed that the relatively homogeneous Danish welfare state is based on a high degree of unity between state and society, a unity that has, in practice, made it difficult to integrate minorities such as immigrants and political refugee groups. Nielsen has also noticed that the limit of the universalist political culture was expressed in negative attitudes towards strangers in civil society connected with the petit bourgeois culture of farmers, smallholders and entrepreneurs in the countryside.

I suggest that political developments in Denmark have been marked by a double tendency towards participation 'from below' and regulation 'from above'. Since the 1930s corporatism,[3] based on the gradual incorporation of economic class organisations, has grown, and since World War II centralised, male-dominated economic and political organisations have played a key role in political development. In Denmark social democracy has also been able to combine a paternalist perception of women as objects of social policies with ideals about social equality, workers' participation and the equal worth of women and men (Hernes 1987; Siim 1990); the gendered division between 'citizen-worker' and 'citizen-mother' dominated the political discourse of social democracy until after World War II (Marcussen 1977; Siim 1994a), although it was acknowledged that working-class women in practice often had to rely on wage work for economic reasons (Ravn 1995). The emphasis on social equality and equity in the political culture was thus combined with a belief in the sexual difference between women and men.

In contrast to Norway and Sweden, the Social Democratic Party in Denmark has never been able to govern alone and has never gained political hegemony. The driving force of the universal Danish welfare project was the Social Democratic Party in alliance with the small Radical Liberal Party. The unique Danish mix of liberalism, cultural radicalism and social democracy distinguishes Denmark from Norway and Sweden, and this has also had both positive and negative implications for the discourse about citizenship and gender equality (Siim 1998a; Bergquist et al. 1999).

From the perspective of gender equality the Danish model of citizenship shows a contradiction between the vision of active citizenship and a corporatist and paternalistic political culture that tended to subsume women's interests under class and party interests. The positive perception of voluntary organisations has, however, provided a potential space for women's organisations to influence politics, which has enabled them to campaign for social policies in the interests of women and children (Kolstrup 1996: 454; R. Christensen 1997: 15–16). Feminist scholarship has recently documented that in some cases at least, women's organisations were able to shape national public policies in the interwar period (Ravn 1995; R. Nielsen 1996).

This chapter traces the shifts in the discourse and politics of citizenship, and discusses the possibilities for and limits to women's ability to shape their own lives and influence politics. The focus is on the interconnection of social policies and political equality, with women's organisations at the centre. From a gender perspective, the fundamental shift in the discourse and practice of social and political citizenship happened in Denmark after 1960. First, the institutionalisation of a universal welfare state has been followed by a move towards a dual-breadwinner norm based on a dramatic expansion of the number of publicly funded childcare centres (Siim 1997a). Second, gender equality has during the same time become official policy and women have become included as active citizens and as part of the political elite (Siim 1998a.).

Democratic Citizenship, Social Rights and Women's Agency

Danish democracy, founded in 1849 with the adoption of a free constitution inspired by the French Revolution, represents a radical, albeit peaceful, break with the old monarchy (Ross 1967). The new constitution gave the vote to all citizens 'except women, undeserving poor, servants, criminals and people who were insane' (Koch and Hvidt 1999: 40). Women gained formal political rights early compared to countries like France, and the fight for suffrage was peaceful compared to that in Britain.

In Denmark, women's vote was won gradually, and according to Dahlerup (1977: 166) there was no real opposition to women's suffrage between 1908, when women had gained the right to vote in municipal councils, and 1915, when women finally gained the right to vote in national elections. Compared to France, married women gained formal civil rights in marriage relatively early with the adoption of the 1925 family law, and in 1919 the principle of equal pay with men was adopted in the public sector.

Women did not substantially increase their political representation in parliament until after 1960. During the interwar period the principal actors in the fight for equal rights were women's rights organisations in cooperation with women organised in the Social Democratic and Radical Liberal Parties. After the vote was won, demands for equal rights between women and men on the labour market became the key to gender equality.

The driving forces in the development of the welfare state were the Social Democratic Party and the small Radical Liberal Party, formed in 1905 by a split in the United Farmers Party.[4] The Social Democratic Party was formed in 1871. In 1884 the first two social democrats were elected to parliament and in 1913 it became the biggest party in parliament; the first Social Democratic minister was appointed in 1915. In the interwar period the party developed a popular reformism based on an alliance with the working population. From 1929 until 1940 the Social Democrats formed a majority government along with the small Radical Liberal Party; it was based on a majority in the Lower House (Folketinget) of parliament (Rigsdagen) against a Right majority in the First Chamber (Landstinget) until 1936.

After women gained the municipal vote in 1908 the Social Democratic Party tried actively to recruit women, and from 1915 the number of women organised in the party began to grow. From 1925 until 1965 between 30 and 40 per cent of party members were women (Dahlerup 1979: 24–5). Despite this, the Danish Social Democratic Party was unfavourably disposed to having separate women's organisations within it. From 1929 to 1969 the women's committees met with opposition and never gained a strong position within the party (ibid.: 29–32).[5] The opposition to a separate women's organisation within the Social Democratic Party is difficult to understand because women's organisations in the Swedish and Norwegian Social Democratic parties were fairly strong (ibid.: 11). This Danish specificity may explain why leading Social Democratic women came to play such a major role in the Danish Women's Society with, for example, Edel Saunte being elected as chairman in 1936. It may also help to explain the unique alliance between the party and the Danish Women's Society during the 1930s (R. Christensen 1997). During the interwar period, minority positions within the party as well as in the Danish Federation of Trade Unions (De Samvirkende Fagforbund i Danmark) supported a more democratic, egalitarian and gender-sensitive discourse.

The small Radical Liberal Party has played a key role in Danish politics since 1905, and during the 1930s the Radical Liberal Party was active in advancing social policies that improved the rights of women and children. The ongoing competition about the votes of the small land-owners between the Radical Liberal Party and the Liberal Agrarian Party was a key factor in creating a political consensus about the universal welfare state (Kolstrup 1996: 18). Cultural radicalism, a key element in the ideology of the Radical Liberal Party, has influenced Danish political culture in the areas of free sexuality, women's rights, and the rights of children. Not a social movement, cultural radicalism was limited to a small group of influential intellectuals. Many were communists and socialists, their political struggle being motivated by anti-fascism (Lunde 1988: 31–2). The mix of communism and cultural radicalism influenced the working class and even inspired the strategies and visions of women in the National Association for Working Women's Education (Arbejderkvindernes Oplysningsforbund), who were organised as an opposition in all Danish union of unskilled workers between 1924 and 1935 (Caspersen 1978).

During the 1930s the coalition government was headed by the pop-ular social democratic Prime Minister T. H. Stauning, with the Radical Liberal P. Munch as Foreign Minister. A number of social and political reforms favourable to workers and farmers were initiated during the economic crisis, the most important of which was the social reform of 1933, adopted in alliance with the Right, which gave the state a more central position in social welfare (Kolstrup 1997: 298–321).

The reform introduced a new 'principle of right' in social legislation that reduced the number of 'undeserving' poor (who lost the right to vote) from 100 000 to about 5000. New rights in preventive health policies also improved the welfare of children and poor working families, for example the free help of a midwife for pregnant women, and increased public support for kindergartens.[6] In 1937 the Social Act equalised the legal position of legitimate and illegitimate children. Finally, from 1939, the private charity organisation Mothers' Help, founded in 1907 to help unmarried mothers with advice, money and shelter for themselves and their children, received public support with the objective of expanding the support to poor married mothers (Nørgård and Skalts 1982).

Women's campaigns for civil, political and social rights

Feminist scholarship has stressed the interconnection of women's demands for civil, political and social rights. Danish scholarship has shown the importance of women's activities in autonomous women's organisations, in the political parties as well as in the trade union movement, but there has been no systematic research about the role of women and women's organisations in the formation of the universal Danish welfare state. After the vote was won in 1915, women from different organisations formed alliances and networks around specific issues, although there were also profound differences and political conflicts between women over social and moral questions[7] (Christensen and Nielsen 1985; R. Christensen 1997).

The Danish case illustrates the cooperation and conflict between the labour movement and the feminist movement. The demand for women's suffrage was first raised by the Social Democratic Party in 1876, and in 1897 and again in 1907 the party proposed a law that included universal suffrage for women and men. The main agency for women's suffrage was, however, not the party but women's organisations, especially the Danish Women's Society's Suffrage Committee (Dansk Kvindeforenings Valgretsudvalg), which was based on cooperation between a number of women's associations and Social Democratic women like the Women's Dressmakers' Union (Damekonfektionssyerskernes Fagforening) (Liversage 1980: 118).

Two of the key advocates for women's rights during the last hundred years were the National Women's Rights Organisation, the Danish Women's Society (Dansk Kvindesamfund), and the Danish Women's National Council (Danske Kvinders Nationalråd), an umbrella organisation for a number of women's organisations. The members of the two organisations were mainly women from the middle classes, but the two cooperated with women in the political parties, especially from the Social Democratic Party and the Radical Liberal Party, and with women in the trade union movement (Ravn 1995; R. Christensen 1997).

The Danish Women's Society, founded in 1871 as part of the international women's rights organisation Association Internationale des Femmes, became the most important women's rights organisation in the interwar period. Bourgeois women formed the majority of its members, and equal rights between women and men became the official objective of the Danish organisation after 1900. The emphasis was on equal rights to wage work and to education, not on the struggle for the vote. The demand for full political rights was too controversial for the organisation. The vote was mentioned for the first time as late as 1906, two years before women gained the right to vote in local elections (1908), and nine years before women got the right to vote in national elections (1915). Many of the organisation's members became active in the Women's Progressive Association (Kvindelig Fremskridtsforening), which from 1888 had women's suffrage as part of their program. The struggle for the vote was taken up by women's organisations with relations to the trade union movement and the Social Democratic Party.[8] The united women's organisations were active in the struggle for the women's vote and published a journal, *What do we want?* (*Hvad vil vi? Organ for kvindesagen, fredssagen og arbejdersagen*). In 1907 the National Association for Women's Suffrage in Denmark was formed (Landforbundet For Kvinders Stemmeret), with women from different political parties, and by 1910 they had more members than the Danish Women's Society (Liversage 1980: 90–9; Kræmer 1990: 10–13). One of the main arguments for women's suffrage was society's need for women's special qualities connected with housework and motherhood (Rosenbeck 1987: 315; Ravn 1989: 12).

The Danish Women's Society adopted a new object clause in 1915 emphasising 'full equality with men in the family, society and the state and the need to improve women and children's situation through legislation'. According to Anna-Birte Ravn (1989: 14), the objective included a double focus on 'equality and difference'. This enabled the organisation to combine two different objectives: women's equality with men and women's difference from men. According to Ravn, many of the demands of the Danish Women's Society were fulfilled by 1925, for example equal pay for women and men in the public sector, and the equal right of women to positions in the public sector in 1921 (with the exception of the position of clergyman and positions in the military). Unmarried women had gained civil equality and the right to engage in economic activities in 1857, and in 1925 married women gained civil rights through a revision of the marriage laws proclaiming formal equality between the spouses.[9]

The Danish Women's Society was mainly a bourgeois organisation, but it is also an example of women's networking, because it included leading members of the Social Democratic and Radical Liberal Parties as well as women from the Right (R. Christensen 1997). During the interwar period the main struggle was about the equal right of women to wage work and to education. The consensus between women's organisations about the struggle for equality between women and men on the labour market contrasted with profound conflicts about social and moral issues like voluntary motherhood, contraceptives, and abortion (Borchorst 1985). The silence of the Danish Women's Society on important issues related to motherhood, sexuality and reproduction was due to the ambivalent ideologies and interests of its members. On the issue of children born out of wedlock the majority in the organisation defended what has been defined as 'the interests of married bourgeois women over unmarried working women' (Ravn 1989: 14).

Social democracy and women's agency

Historians have analysed the conflict and alliances between Social Democracy and women's organisations in relation to gender equality on the labour market. Two examples can illustrate the conflicts between women's interests and Social Democratic paternalism, as well as the alliances about equal rights in the labour market between women's rights organisations, women in the trade unions, and women in the Social Democratic Party: 1. the discourse on protective legislation[10] for women workers (see Ravn 1995, 1996), and 2. the discourse about the right of married women to work (Gertsen 1985). These two cases have been selected because they have played an important role in the feminist debate about women's interests and are both fairly well documented in feminist scholarship (Wickander et al. 1995).

Case 1. The debate about protective labour legislation in urban industries in connection with the revision of the Factory Act in 1899–1901 and again in 1911–13 illuminates the struggle of Danish women against the ban on night work. The case has been used as an example of what Ravn (1995: 210) has called Danish 'exceptionalism', which refers to the fact that there were only two exceptions to the general ban on women's night work adopted by 'all civilised nations'. Ravn (1996: 6) has traced the history of the two kinds of special protection for adult female workers introduced by Danish governments: maternity leave and prohibition of women working at night in factories. Maternity leave was included in the Factory Acts of 1901 and 1913, but prohibition of women's night work was omitted from the final text.

Ravn has asked why the government did not regulate women's hours or impose a night-work prohibition for women. Part of the answer was that the Social Democratic labour movement was divided. The Social Democratic Party, as well as the Danish Federation of Trade Unions, argued that the 'prohibition on women only' would be a big step forward and would improve the living conditions of working-class families. This was strongly opposed by leading female trade unionists. Women organised in the Women's Branch of the Printers' Union (Dansk Typografforbunds Kvindelige Afdeling) and the Union of (Unskilled) Women Workers in Denmark (Kvindeligt Arbejderforbund i Danmark) were opposed to the prohibition only because it was against the interests of the better-off women workers. Social Democratic women formed a unique alliance with the Danish Women's Society to protest against the night-work prohibition on women only. The three organised large public meetings in Copenhagen in 1900 and 1911 and signed protest resolutions to the government. The protest was supported by other female trade unions, among them the Women Tailors' Union (De Kvindelige Herreskrædderes Fagforening) and the Women's Dressmakers' Union (Damekonfektionssyerskernes Fagforening) (see Ravn 1995, 1996: 6–10).

The successful female alliance between Social Democratic and middle-class women contrasts with the situation in Sweden, where a night-work prohibition for women alone was included in the Swedish Factory Act of 1909, despite the opposition of socialist and bourgeois women. In Norway, parliament decided not to include any special legislation in the Norwegian factory acts; here it was mainly the bourgeois women's movement that opposed special legislation.

Was the regulation prohibiting night work for women in the interests of women? Recently, comparative feminist scholarship has challenged the maternalist discourse that support for the prohibition of night work was in the interests of women workers. The argument is that 'legislation shackled women to a male standard that substituted sameness for equality and turned difference into subordination' (Wickander 1995: 19). In Denmark, the main argument from the two leading opponents of the prohibition was that women would lose their jobs. According to Ravn (1996: 13), Denmark and Norway were 'the exception that proves the rule' that legislation generally reduces women to a male standard and turns difference into subordination.

Case 2. The second example is the successful cooperation between women's organisations during the 1930s against attempts to restrict the right of married women to work. This was a unique interclass alliance between the Danish Women's Society, Danish Women's National Council (Danske Kvinders Nationalråd), Danish Women's Business Council (Danske Kvinders Erhvervsråd), the local union of teachers in Copenhagen (Københavns Kommunelærerinder) and leading Social Democratic women in the party and the trade unions. The background was arguments put forward by leading men within the Social Democratic Party and in the Federation of Trade Unions for the need to restrict married women's rights to work in order to protect the jobs of male workers in times of mass unemployment. The campaign against married women working was directed mainly at women employed in the public sector, especially teachers, nurses and office workers. Measures against married women in jobs were taken by local authorities preferring unmarried to married women, and dismissals were directed towards individual female workers (Aarhus and Muusman 1981).

Feminist research has shown that the Danish Women's Society played the crucial role in this alliance. The arguments supporting married women in jobs were women's need of wage work, their right to personal development through wage work, and the conviction that women should keep their jobs as a matter of justice (Gertsen 1982: 141–2). The alliance succeeded in influencing both the discourse and the practice of the Social Democratic Party towards married women in wage work, and no restrictions were ever passed in legislation on the right of married women to work in Denmark.[11]

Protecting this right played a crucial role in the discourses of gender equality, and feminist scholars have been discussing how to interpret the national differences (Hobson 1993; Ravn 1996). According to Ravn (1996: 14), Danish women succeeded in making their voices heard in the two cases that 'constructed women as workers who were also in periods of their lives mothers'. One argument refers to the class structure, especially the strong organisation of the rural middle class of farmers and smallholders, which, in contrast to the urban middle class, perceived both men and women as producers (ibid.). Another argument stresses the role of women's agency, especially alliances between women across party and class lines, which in Denmark as well as Sweden played a crucial role in the successful protection of the right of married women to work (Hobson 1993; R. Christensen 1997).

Feminist scholars agree that the Danish welfare model cannot be explained by the class argument alone but by the interplay between class and gender. Feminist historians have noticed that the woman's role as producer is rooted in the agrarian past. They have suggested that the split between the private and the public sector, between women's roles as mothers and producers, has never been as acute in Denmark, a country dominated by small middle-class farmers, as in countries with a strong bourgeoisie (Rosenbeck 1989; Ravn 1996).

I have suggested that political institutional factors must be added to the class and gender arguments (Siim 1998a). In contrast to Sweden, Danish women lacked organisational resources within the Social Democratic Party (Hobson 1993; Dahlerup 1979). Therefore alliances and networks between the Danish Women's Society and women organised in the trade union movement, in the Social Democratic Party and Radical Liberal Party, came to play a major role in the fight for gender equality on the labour market (Nielsen 1996). Research indicates that the political discourse of social democracy about gender equality in wage work was ambivalent towards women workers in the interwar period. The dominant position claimed that women's primary role was to be a mother, and that men were the breadwinners. At the same time formal equality between women and men was institutionalised in legislation, with the Factory Laws recognising that women were often forced to earn their living as wage workers in order to support their family (Ravn 1997). The discourse and politics of the Social Democratic

Party were directed towards economic support and social concerns for the welfare of children and poor families, including lone mothers. Social policies rested on a notion of class solidarity as well as on an ideology of paternalism, with the implication that the interests of men as workers generally came before those of women workers.

To sum up, Danish research has stressed the important role of the working-class movement in the development of the welfare state and the determining role of the Social Democratic and Radical Liberal Party, in some cases in alliance with the Liberal Party. Kolstrup's study has illuminated the key role played by voluntary associations in the formation of the universal welfare state. The study opens new questions about women's active citizenship and about the role of women's voluntary organisations as well as about the influence of women in the Social Democratic and Radical Liberal Parties in the struggle for social rights and equal rights between women and men.

Feminist scholarship has only recently started to explore the impact of women's alliances and networking on the discourse and politics on gender and work, albeit only on the basis of a few selected cases. Unfortunately there is still no comprehensive analysis of the role of women's agency in the development of the Danish welfare state.[12] On the basis of the available research I conclude that the Danish model of citizenship has historically been ambivalent towards including women. On the one hand, social democracy has been dominated by a class discourse that has put men's interests over women's; on the other, there has been a space for women's agency to mobilise women and to influence politics.

In the Danish case women's active citizenship included their multiple activities in voluntary organisations, political parties and the trade union movement. One example is the successful alliance between women's organisations across party and class lines about the protection of women's rights as producers.

Universal Social Rights and the Dual-breadwinner Model

The breakthrough for the universal Danish welfare state after World War II was followed by a gradual transformation to a dual-breadwinner norm that was premised on the obligation for women and men to become wage workers. During the last thirty years there has been a shift in the language of social equality ('lighed') to include equality between women and men ('ligestilling'). The expansion of the public sector since the 1970s has been accompanied by a parallel inclusion of married women in the labour market. The development of the universal welfare state where social rights are predominantly based on citizenship has usually been regarded as beneficial for working mothers and their children. Contested, however, is the role of women's agency in the institutionalisation of the universal welfare state as well as the implications of the present restructuring of the welfare state for women's position on the labour market (Siim 1998a).

Since 1960 Denmark has gradually moved towards a high degree of universalism in health, education and welfare in the sense that both social services and benefits have been directed towards all citizens independently of income. There has been a high degree of political consensus about the welfare strategy advocated by the Social Democratic Party, which combined Keynesian economics with preventive social politics (Kolstrup 1996: 385). Since the 1970s, the expansion of the public sector has been connected with the changing role of families and social networks, and especially with the integration of married women into the labour market (R. Andersen 1989: 124). The inclusion of women as the majority of wage workers in the public sector was not a conscious strategy but rather an unintended effect of the welfare strategy of social democracy and the gradual transformation to a service economy with a large public sector financed by taxes.

The cornerstones of the universal Danish welfare state have been the old-age pension (1956), public health care reform (1960 and 1971) and public schools and higher education free of charge (Andersen 1992). Public regulation based on institutionalisation was a crucial element of social democratic reform policy, and citizen entitlement provided the nexus of distribution, not the market or the individual family (Esping-Andersen 1985: 159). Social programs have been financed by progressive income taxes and flat-rate, or even means-tested, benefits rather than by allowances proportional to previous income. The gradual expansion of social rights culminated with the social reform in 1974 that safeguarded all citizens against sudden drops in income and living standard, and institutionalised a guaranteed social income irrespective of the cause of hardship.[13]

In the past thirty years, the classical social policies of income transfers have been combined with a high degree of public responsibility for providing social services, including kindergartens, creches and other institutions for children at low charges, and services for the sick, the handicapped and the elderly. The expansion of social services was followed by a politics of decentralising social services to local and regional governments, which has become a defining characteristic of the Danish model (R. Andersen 1993). As a result, social services such as care of the elderly, including all kinds of home care services, nursing homes and other institutions are today the responsibility of 275 local governments. Social services such as nursery schools, child protection, sickness allowance, services to the disabled, rehabilitation, and the administration of public pensions have been placed under the same umbrella, and fourteen regional governments administer the health services, primary services and hospitals. On this basis, the former Danish Minister for Social Affairs, Bent Rold Andersen (1993: 111), concludes that in a way what was formally a 'Nordic' model, in contrast to the 'Bismarckian' insurance model, is becoming less Nordic and more Danish.

Feminist scholarship has stressed the importance of publicly financed and organised childcare for the move towards a dual-breadwinner norm (Borchorst and Siim 1987; Borchorst 1989a; Siim 1997a). Since the reform in 1965, childcare has in principle been a social service directed towards all children. And from the 1970s the political consensus on public policies designed to help families reconcile working and family life through the expansion of childcare centres and child/family benefits has been followed by a dramatic expansion in the number of child-care centres. Since the beginning of the 1970s, the basic unit in social legislation has been the individual, not the household or the family, and all individuals, women and men, have a duty to provide for themselves through wage work (Koch-Nielsen 1996). Today, Denmark has the highest coverage of childcare institutions for 0–3-year-olds in the EU (Jensen 1994).

During the last thirty years there has been a unique political consensus about social policies as well as gender equality policies. During the 1980s bipartisan policies continued to increase public support for childcare centres despite high unemployment and the takeover of a new bourgeois-centre government, in power from 1982 to 1993.[14] A new political consensus about universal family policies was forged, based on a combination of expanding existing day-care centres and increasing direct financial support for families with children, including common-law marriages and lone mothers (Koch-Nielsen 1996; Siim 1997a).

In Denmark the shift from the male-breadwinner norm to a two-worker family form was not the result of a 'master-plan' developed by social democracy. Recent research indicates that women's massive entry into the labour market and the explosion of the public sector was not an intended effect in the Social Democratic welfare strategy (Christiansen 1996: 8). The parallel growth in women's wage work and the expansion of childcare institutions have meant thorough-going changes in gender relations. One of the results is that Denmark today has the highest activity rates of all OECD countries; by 1992 about 90 per cent of all mothers with small children are in wage work (Carlsen and Larsen 1994; and see Figures 1, 2 and 3 in the Appendix).

From the late 1980s and 1990s the change from a male-breadwinner norm to a *dual-breadwinner* norm, where both mothers and fathers are obliged to work, and care, has been followed by a new debate about the new problems for parents of reconciling working life and family life.[15] Research shows that parents have scheduling problems in their daily lives when both parents are working full time and that these are experienced most acutely by mothers, especially lone mothers (Bak 1986). Dual-earner families are able to employ different strategies to deal with this problem, for instance part-time work for the mother and overtime for the father.

The leave schemes in relation to childcare and education, which have become very popular since they were first adopted in 1993, have been motivated by strategies to combat unemployment and to help families with young children (Siim 1999b). One reason for this is no doubt a public recognition of the growing needs of parents to spend more time with their children. The leave schemes are gender-neutral, but women make up the large majority of parents on parental leave. The construction of the leave schemes has recently been criticised by feminist scholars as a barrier to women's equality on the labour market and to men's use, and the Minister of Labour has recently proposed making them more flexible (Siim 1998a).

The dual-breadwinner norm has profound implications for the meaning and practice of the family and of motherhood (and indeed fatherhood), and the new problems reconciling working and family life is one of the key issues of public discourse in the 1990s. The changes have also affected political participation and the meaning of politics. Parents have gained new citizens' rights in relation to schools and childcare centres, and research indicates that motherhood is no longer a barrier for women's political participation. Instead motherhood, and indeed parenthood, has become a potential for citizenship (Siim 1994a). Both parents have become active as citizens in their daily life, and in relation to schools parent participation is high and expanding for all social groups (Nyseth and Torpe 1997).

Social democracy and the new discourse on gender equality

Lewis and Ostner (1994: 17–19) suggest that the Scandinavian welfare states are 'weak male-breadwinner models' that have brought benefits to women because the large public sector has increased their ability to provide for themselves through wage work. The male-breadwinner model has been important in explaining the variations in welfare states from the perspective of women. It has been criticised because it fails to provide an understanding of the internal dynamic and political history of the Scandinavian welfare states, for example that motherhood and mothering can be the basis for entitlements (Sainsbury 1994: 168). From a feminist perspective, the political development that occurred after World War II expresses a dramatic change in women's citizenship, but it is not clear what the driving force has been.

In Denmark, the Social Democratic Party became one of the key agents in the transformation of the socio-economic situation of women, often along with the Radical Liberal Party. The appointment of a Women's Commission in 1965 by the Social Democratic Prime Minister was supported by all the political parties and marked the beginning of the institutionalisation of women question. The commission was initiated by women from the Social Democratic Party, who created a cross-party pressure group in parliament (Borchorst 1997). Its objective was to investigate the changes taking place in the situation of women in society and to propose public policies for women. One of the conclusions of the reports published by the commission was that married women could be expected to join the labour force if places in day-care institutions and part-time work were available (Final Report concerning Women's Position in Society 1974).

Gender equality on the labour market became the new political discourse, and social policies a means to support women's wage work. In 1966 a Family Ministry was formed to improve the situation of families and single mothers, but it lasted only a year, the only tangible result being the adoption of a universal children's grant and a small benefit to all mothers in 1967 (Markussen 1977: 110).

As a result of alliances and networks among women organised in the national women's rights organisations and the Social Democratic Party, the discourse on gender in the political parties gradually changed from 'women as mothers and housewives' to 'women as equal partners in work, family and society' (Markussen 1977: 94). The notion of social equality also changed and came to include equal rights between women and men as wage earners and in society.

The debate about family policy and women's double roles started within the Social Democratic Party, but there has been considerable political consensus about the 'women question' in Denmark compared to Britain and France. Since 1960, and for different reasons, all political groups have been in favour of an increase in wage work opportunities for married women and an expansion of childcare centres in order to facilitate this (Borchorst 1989a).

The abortion issue was one of the few controversial issues within both the political parties and the women's rights organisation and thus represents the exception to the rule of political consensus around gender issues. The debate about abortion was initiated by the Youth Movement of the Danish Women's Society (Thilderne), and the bill to liberate abortion was introduced in parliament not by the Social

Democratic Party but by the Socialist People's Party (Socialistisk Folke-parti, formed in 1959 by former members of the Communist Party). From 1969, the Social Democratic Party was in favour of abortion on demand and the party introduced the Bill that was adopted by parliament in 1973. The Christian Folk Party (Kristelig Folkeparti) provided the only organised opposition to the new law, but the party never really gained popular significance.

During the past twenty years there has been a further institutionalisation of gender equality policies. One of the main suggestions of the Women's Commission was a proposal to form a permanent Equality Council. The proposal was discussed in parliament in 1974 and got the support of the Left, including the Social Democrats, the Radical Liberal Party and the Socialist People's Party. The Right, however, opposed it, and as a consequence the new Social Democratic Prime Minister formed the Equality Council administratively in 1975. The council was formed in law in 1978 with the support of the majority of the political parties from the Right and Left, and its powers/authority was increased in 1988. Today, the council has nine members, who represent both women's organisations and organised labour and employers; one member is an independent feminist scholar, and the government appoints the chairman (Borchorst 1997).

Since the 1980s, equality policies have been institutionalised and the equality discourse has become a consensus issue with the broad cross-party support of women of the political elite. The Danish Equality Council has gradually increased its power and resources since the mid-1980s, but it is less institutionalised and has less resources than the Swedish and Norwegian councils (Borchorst 1999).

According to Borchorst (1997), there are three problems with the Danish design compared with the other Nordic equality councils: it has only limited power; the employers' organisation has a veto power; and it has only limited resources to research. Another problem is the deradicalisation of gender equality and the demobilisation of the women's movement in Denmark during the 1990s.

I suggest that today one of the key problems with gender equality politics in Denmark is that the discourse of gender equality has become separated not only from the old 'emancipation' politics of the women's movement but also from the new forms of cultural politics – what Nancy Fraser (1997) has called 'identity politics'. Gender equality has become associated with the older generation of state feminists, and this has made it difficult to mobilise women, especially younger women, around it. Below I focus on the inclusion of women in politics and on the interplay between women's social and political citizenship.

The Transformation of Women's Democratic Citizenship

During the past thirty years one of the most dramatic changes in Denmark, indeed in Scandinavia, has been the democratisation of citizenship, with women becoming active in politics. In Danish political culture, active citizenship is about the ability of citizens to form political communities in civil society as well as their ability to influence political decisions. Women in Denmark, and Scandinavia, have become mobilised politically and women have increased their presence in all spheres of political life, and they have gained a new influence in the political elite.

> In the Nordic countries, even if there are still differences across sectors, women are by now fully integrated in all main walks of public decision-making, even if not to an equal extent. The improvement of their position over the last two decades has been so dramatic that it has changed the whole face of politics. It is perhaps not an exaggeration to say that the increased proportion of women in political life is the most important single change in Scandinavian social life in the post-war era. (Karvonen and Selle 1995: 21)

It is unique to Scandinavia that women's mobilisation in the women's movement in the 1970s was followed by an incorporation of women in the political elite. The recent development has been followed by a shift in paradigms in feminist research from a focus on women's political marginalisation to one on their political empowerment (Raaum 1997; Siim 1997b). Although the general picture of women's participation and representation is similar today, comparative Nordic feminist research indicates that the political processes of mobilisation and integration have been different within the five Nordic countries. Recent research contrasts the 'movement-oriented' Danish 'gender profile' with the more 'institutional' Swedish gender profile (Bergquist et al. 1999).

In Denmark, women's political representation increased dramatically from 17 per cent in 1970 to 34 per cent in 1990 (Christensen and Knopp 1998: Table 3), and since the last election (in March 1998) women make up 38 per cent in parliament. During the 1990s, between a quarter and a third of ministers have been women. In what follows I discuss the nature and implications of the specific Danish combination of what Hernes (1987: 15) has called 'mobilisation from below' and incorporation 'from above'.

The interplay between feminism and political institutions

Since the 1970s the new feminist movement has become the key element in the transformation of women's democratic citizenship.

Feminist scholarship has shown that the New Women's Liberation Movement in Denmark has played a crucial role in the mobilisation and empowerment of women as well as in cultural transformations of the discourse about gender equality (Dahlerup 1988; Christensen and Siim 1989; Togeby 1994a,b). In Denmark, the New Women's Liberation Movement (NWLM), known as the Redstocking Movement (Rødstrømpebevægelsen), was formed in the spring of 1970. According to a recent study by Dahlerup (1998), the movement represented a new thinking and practice, its main characteristic being a left-wing feminism based on an anti-hierarchical principle of organisation. The defining element was a new understanding of women's oppression, the objective no longer defined as 'equality' between women and men but as the 'emancipation' of women and their 'liberation' from male oppression.

The Redstocking Movement thus challenged the former women's rights organisations in terms of both ideology and organisational form and attitudes towards abortion, and wage work became the first ideological battleground. During the 1960s open conflicts broke out in the Danish Women's Society about issues of abortion as well as about the value of housework (Borchorst 1989b: 28–9). In contrast to the Danish Women's Society, the NWLM showed an ambivalent attitude towards the state, which was described as both capitalist and patriarchal.

According to Dahlerup (1993, 1998), the NWLM developed in three stages in Denmark: a period of direct activism in 1970–73; a period of a vigorous new feminist counterculture in 1975–80; and a period of specialisation and professionalisation from about 1980. During the first phase the new women's movement participated in three major reform movements: the campaign for free abortion; the fight for equal pay; and the campaign against Denmark's entry into the EU.

From an ideological point of view, the NWLM has been described as one of the most successful social movements in Denmark in that it influenced politics as well as contributed to changes in people's daily lives (Gundelach 1988: 195). The movement declined during the 1980s and almost disappeared during the 1990s, but its ideas lived on and spread to all parts of society. In Århus, the second biggest town in Denmark, a big party celebrated the formal dissolution of the movement in 1985. It gradually lost its appeal during the 1980s, but at this time feminist ideas were spreading to new groups of women in the political parties, in the trade union movement, political organisations and at the universities (Christensen and Siim 1989; Togeby 1994a,b).

The NWLM also tried to influence politics and policies, abortion and equal pay for example, but it did not try to gain any *direct* impact on public policies (Dahlerup 1998). According to Dahlerup (1998: 788–91) the main impact of the Redstocking Movement has been to get feminist issues onto the public agenda and change the discursive opportunity structure of political reform.

On the main issues of abortion, equal pay and Danish membership of the EU, feminists were not the main actors but worked alongside women from political parties, trade unions and the former women's rights organisation. In the campaign for abortion on demand and another for equal pay between women and men, there was a high degree of political consensus in Denmark during the 1970s. A liberal abortion law of 1970 had prepared the acceptance of free abortion on demand in 1973, and the issue never raised the same profound conflicts between citizens – or between women – as in other societies where religion has played a major role.

In the campaign for equal pay in the private sector, women in the trade union organisations as well as including women in the Social Democratic Party, were the main actors in cooperation with the NWLM. Women in the private sector gained equal pay from 1976, that is, fifty-four years after equal pay was instituted for women and men employed in the public sector. Danish feminists lost only one fight, Denmark's membership of the EC. The majority of feminists as well as the (New) Left tended to vote against Danish membership of the EC in the referendum of 1972 (Dahlerup 1998: 158).

According to Dahlerup (1998: 227–47), ambivalent attitudes to public policy can be explained by the anti-capitalist nature of the feminist movement, indicating that activities were not directed primarily at the state but rather at the mobilisation of women. Danish political culture has always been open to demands from grassroots activists and social movements (Gundelach 1988; Nielsen 1991), and the nature of Danish political institutions explains the integration of feminist issues in the political parties and as part of the political agenda.

The mobilisation of women in the NWLM was followed by an expansion of feminism, from well-educated young women to a wider group of women, and by an institutionalisation of feminist ideas within the political culture (Christensen and Siim 1989). Dahlerup (1998: 788) has suggested that one of the unintended effects of the NWLM has been a radicalisation of moderate feminism inside formal political institutions. Feminist ideas have to a certain extent become integrated within political parties, trade union organisations, voluntary organisations, and so on, and the NWLM indirectly helped to put gender equality on the political agenda. One of the implications is that 'women' have become a political category and gender has acquired a new meaning in politics.

During the 1980s the growth of feminist ideas was followed by a disintegration of the women's movement as well as by a deradicalisation of women's issues (Togeby 1994a, no. 6: 15). Today many women still call themselves feminists, although they do not necessarily share the same left-wing values and anti-hierarchical ideas of organisations. The quantitative investigation by the Danish political scientist Lise Togeby (ibid.: 31) indicates that there has been a dispersion of feminist attitudes between 1965 and 1990 from the feminist core group to other social groups, as well as a differentiation between feminist issues such as equality in the family and the labour market, and women's empowerment.

Gender equality became a political issue and was taken over by women in the political parties, included in the political discourses, and integrated into public policies. This was followed by the growth of what Hernes (1987: 153) first called 'state feminism', the interplay of 'feminism from above' (gender equality and social policies) and 'feminism from below' (women activists). Recent research has shown that the specific connection between the collective mobilisation of women and strategies to integrate women into political institutions has been different in Denmark, Norway and Sweden (Skjeie 1992; Rauum 1997; Bergquist et al. 1999). In Denmark, state feminism was the indirect not the direct effect of the NWLM (Dahlerup 1998: 189). The new women's movement was fairly critical of the 'reformist' Social Democratic welfare state. State feminism in the form of social policies and gender policies, including the adoption of a quota system in public committees and commissions, was initiated not by the feminist movement but by women in the political parties in cooperation with the old Danish equal rights organisation (Dansk Kvindesamfund). However, during the 1980s there were a number of examples of alliances, networks and cooperation around local women's projects and around equality policies between the old and new women's organisations, as well as between women inside and outside formal political institutions (Dahlerup 1998: 255–80).

Feminism changed during the 1990s to the more moderate feminism based on equality policies that is predominant today in public politics. From a focus on women's liberation, the main emphasis has shifted to the political and social reforms that influence the daily lives, working conditions and political representation of women (Kruchow 1996). In the 1980s and 1990s women have struggled unwaveringly towards women's 'politics' and gender equality within established political organisations and institutions; but women activists working for gender equality in the trade union movement, in the political parties and political institutions have seldom called themselves feminists. This development can be interpreted both as demobilisation of the feminist movement and as a spread of feminism to new arenas and to new issues.

*The Scandinavian feminist debate about women's
political presence*

Since 1970 the presence of women in political institutions has increased, particularly in political representation, which from 10 per cent in 1970 had increased to 38 per cent in 1998 (see Table 7 in the Appendix). This increase in women's political representation is similar to the political development in other Nordic countries (Karvonen and Selle 1995). While feminist scholars outside Scandinavia have been surprised by this (Phillips 1992: 83–91), Nordic researchers and feminist activists have taken it all for granted.

In Denmark women's political mobilisation in the feminist movement has been followed by a profound change in the political culture, in what Dahlerup (1998) calls the discursive opportunity structure. During the 1970s and 1980s the mobilisation of women also affected the political parties, especially the Social Democratic Party and the Socialist People's Party, which were considerably influenced by feminist ideas. Gender equality in politics became the official political goal. One of the implications was that the rationale for women in politics changed as all-male assemblies lost democratic legitimacy and women became a political category in elections (Dahlerup 1998).

In Denmark these two parties were committed to increasing the power of women in politics. They both adopted party quotas to internal elections in the party, reserving 40 per cent of all seats to women in all branches, and later they adopted candidate quotas in the promotion of candidates for elections to parliament (Borchorst 1999a), but both later abandoned them. Denmark is today the only Scandinavian country without a quota system to stimulate the number of women representatives to parliament, and in spite of this the number of women representatives to parliament continued to grow at the last election (1998). This indicates that in Denmark the formal rules have had only limited effects, although the symbolic effect of the quota system may have been important.

The abandoning of the quota system by the Left is surprising, since gender equality in politics has become an accepted norm. Quotas have always been controversial in Denmark. Opponents on the Right have called them undemocratic, and the system has never played the major role it has in politics in Norway (Dahlerup 1998). Today, quotas are no longer popular among young politicians, and it was actually young women who proposed abandoning them in the Socialist People's Party (Christensen and Knopp 1998).[16]

One of the major changes in Danish political culture has been the inclusion of women in the political elite. Feminist scholars have different explanations as to why women's political mobilisation in Denmark was transformed into an increase in political representation. One explanation has linked the increase in women's representation to the increase in women's wage work; another to the development of the universal welfare state, and yet a third to the political mobilisation of women in society. According to Dahlerup (1998: 615–16), the increase in women's political representation was an indirect rather than a direct effect of the activities of the feminist movement. Feminism contributed directly to creating new norms of legitimacy, to increasing women's mobilisation, and to shaping a new political discourse about women.

Scandinavian feminist research indicates that there is no determinism in the inclusion of women in politics (Skjeie 1992). Comparative Nordic research has recently confirmed that there is indeed a relative autonomy of politics and illustrates that women's inclusion in politics has taken different forms in the Nordic countries (Bergquist et al. 1999). In the Danish case I suggest that neither the increase in women's wage work nor the growth of the welfare state can alone explain the political transformation (Siim 1997b). Dahlerup's study illustrates the importance of politics, and indicates that the Danish political culture created a space that made it possible for women to influence political institutions and for political institutions to include women. From the Nordic comparative perspective, it has recently been argued that the Danish model of mobilisation is fairly unique, because it has been based primarily on women's mobilisation 'from below' and not, as in Norway and Sweden, on women's integration into political parties (Bergquist et al. 1999). This indicates that in order to explain the massive increase in women's political representation since 1970, we need a more systematic study of the connection between Danish political institutions and women's political activities.

Another major change has been the integration of women within corporatist organisations and political administration. Corporatism[17] has been a key aspect of the Danish/Scandinavian political culture, and until the mid-1980s feminist scholarship generally interpreted it as the main barrier to women's political representation (Hernes 1987). A number of feminist scholars still see the sex-segregated labour market and trade union movement as the main barriers to gender equality (Hirdman 1990, 1991), while others have argued that corporatism is changing (Bergquist 1994).

The paradox is that social democracy and corporatism in Scandinavia originally acted for the participation of workers in politics and administration against the participation of women, when today these powerful organisational and institutional structures to some extent act for women.

It was men in the political parties and in parliament who voted for gender equality legislation, but they would not have succeeded without the activities of women both inside and outside administrative and political institutions (Dahlerup 1988; Skjeie 1992).

In Denmark the first indication of a change in corporatism came with the adoption of the 1985 Act on Equality in Appointing Members to Public Committees. This legislation increased the number of women in the corporate decision-making process by ordaining the adoption of gender equality policies for the appointment of members to public committees. At the time there were only about 15 per cent of women in corporate institutions. According to the Danish Equal Status Council, in all new committees appointed from 1 July 1985, women comprise at least 30 per cent. Since the introduction of the equality law in public committees and commissions in 1986, it could be argued that corporatism can also be used as a means of increasing women's participation in the administrative elite (Borchorst 1998a; Bergquist 1994).

The adoption of the Act on Equality in Appointing Members to Public Committees can be interpreted as one of the successful effects of the increase in women's political representation. According to Dahlerup (1998: 632–6), there has been a network of women politicians from different parties with roots in the Danish Women's Society who have been influencing politics since the 1960s.

Hege Skjeie (1992) has discussed the paradox of the paternalist Scandinavian welfare states, where all male forums have adopted policies that have increased the welfare and power of women, for example through the adoption of a quota system favourable to their political integration. She has emphasised the different interaction between social rights and political participation in Scandinavia on the basis of the Norwegian case. According to Skjeie, the Danish and Swedish cases both illustrate how the increase in women's social rights, for example in relation to childcare, came before women's presence in the political elite. This contrasts with Norway, where women's inclusion in the political elite came before the expansion of childcare facilities. In this latter case, the adoption of social rights was the effect rather than the cause of public policies. Skjeie interprets the two cases as different ways of empowering women: through access to social benefits and through access to politics.

Scandinavian feminist scholars have different interpretations of the implications of the presence of women in politics. One group suggests that women have common interests and expects women to form alliances about social reforms in relation to childcare to make them increasingly economically independent of their husbands (Halsaa 1988; Leira 1992;

Skjeie 1992). Another group argues that women have common interests in being present and influencing the *form* not the *content* of politics (Hernes 1987; Jonasdottir 1988; Siim 1988, 1993). Scandinavian research does not yet give any clear indication what the effect will be of the presence of women in politics, but political developments in the 1990s do clearly indicate that women have different interpretations of their interests in relation to childcare. In Norway and Sweden, new conflicts have emerged around strategies towards childcare between Left and Right, one of which is to expand childcare institutions, another to increase direct financial support to parents (Leira 1998). In Denmark there is still a high degree of consensus around publicly funded childcare centres, but the Right would like to increase the right of parents to choose between different forms of care. There are also new conflict lines in relation to social rights. The new populist party on the Right (Dansk Folkeparti) promotes the right of Danish citizens to care against the threat of immigrant families with many children (Siim 1998a).

Feminist scholarship has also discussed the implications for power relations of women's political presence. The Swedish historian Yvonne Hirdman (1990, 1991b) has argued that the modern Scandinavian welfare states represent a new gender contract in which the gender system has been modernised, with gender equality being put on the political agenda. She suggests that women have not gained any power in the public sphere in relation to men. Rather what has happened is that a modernisation of the sex/gender system has reproduced sexual hierarchy and segregation in a new way in the public sphere. Skjeie (1992) has argued that women have gained new political resources and positions of power in the welfare state as workers and citizens, and that women's employment in the public sector is an alternative by which to control strategic resources. This may apply even more in the case of Denmark, where since 1970 women have gained a relatively strong position as professional social administrators in the large public sector (Sjørup 1996).

Scandinavian research indicates that access to political citizenship represents potential power and that political ideologies are usually stronger than gender, although there are also examples of women forming networks across party lines. Skjeie concludes on the basis of her own study of male and female members of the Norwegian parliament that both parties are convinced that gender matters in politics, in the sense that women politicians do agree on many political issues across party lines. She found, however, that the only issue where women had actually made an impact was around the issue of childcare. Here women formed alliances across political parties that combined support for two different political lines: an expansion of childcare centres (the Left) and an increase in support to women caring for dependants at home (the Right) (Skjeie 1992).

Dahlerup (1998: 634–5) has traced a network of women politicians in the Danish parliament,[18] and gives three examples of how they worked together successfully across party lines during the 1980s: the increase in maternity leave to six months in 1983; the adoption of affirmative action for women on public boards and committees in 1985; and the adoption of national action plans for equality in 1985. These examples indicate that women cooperating across party lines is the exception rather than the rule.

Research from the Danish Investigation of Citizenship indicates that there has been a connection between women's social and political citizenship in Denmark. In terms of social citizenship, the Danish model has been favourable to women: universal social policies based on the dual-breadwinner norm have improved women's ability to provide for themselves and to determine their own lives as mothers, workers and citizens (Siim 1994a,b). I suggest, however, that in order to explain the increase in women's political representation we need to add the *specific political culture and the nature of political institutions*. In terms of democratic citizenship, the increase in women's political participation and representation can be interpreted as an empowerment of women in the sense that it has given them 'a voice and a vote' within formal political institutions (Young 1990a).

To sum up, I find that there is a complex relationship between Danish women's social rights and political agency. There has been a connection between formal and informal politics. The changes in the political culture can thus be interpreted both as the *effect* of women's political mobilisation and as the *cause* of the integration of women in elite politics. The feminist movement has empowered women, but it played only an indirect role in the move towards the universal welfare state after 1965. I suggest, however, that during the 1970s and 1980s the New Women's Liberation Movement did contribute directly to changing the discourse about women's active citizenship and indirectly to changing the public discourse about gender equality. Women's political mobilisation was followed by their inclusion in the political elite and also in administrative institutions during the 1980s and 1990s. In that sense, social rights can be seen as having been the cause rather than the effect of women's political agency.

Changes in Women and Men's Political Participation and Identities

The political mobilisation of women in the new women's movement and in the political parties was followed by profound changes in women's participatory profiles, political identities and values on a mass level. The disappearing gender gap in political participation and values has recently been referred to in Nordic research (Karvonen and Selle 1995). Lise Togeby (1989) has called it a 'silent revolution' in women's relations to politics, and it was this that changed women from a 'passive, weak and alienated' group to a 'strong, active and angry' group. Danish research has identified growing support for feminist issues and a small gender gap in party identification in favour of women who support social democratic and leftist values to a greater extent than men do (Togeby 1992, 1994a,b; Christensen 1989, 1991; Andersen et al. 1993).

The 1990 Danish investigation of democratic citizenship (Andersen et al. 1993; Andersen and Torpe 1994) is an indication of the profound changes in political gender relations. A representative survey of about 2000 people was carried out by a research team at Aalborg University in cooperation with researchers from Aarhus University, Copenhagen and Oslo. 'Politics' was redefined to include the 'small' democracy that refers to problems in everyday life as well as in the local community. The interplay between 'small' and 'big' democracy[19] was one of the key questions; another was the connection between class, gender and generation. Democratic citizenship was defined as 'the relation of the individuals to the institutions and places where they meet to discuss and resolve matters of common concern' (Andersen et al. 1993: 18). Citizenship was seen as having a political-institutional dimension, delineating the rights and duties of individuals that enable them to influence the state, and a political-cultural dimension, describing the horizontal relations between citizens that enable them to form political communities and develop political identities. The results of the investigation give an indication of the effects of women's mass political mobilisation in Denmark. The investigation provided an overview of the development of women's political participation and values between 1980 and 1990, and included a comparison between Denmark and Sweden in relation to the area of the small democracy. The results also confirmed that there are still differences in the participatory profiles of women and men. In contrast to Sweden, there was no 'women-dominated' arena in Denmark with differences in participation in favour of women, for instance the small democracy (Petersson et al. 1989: Ch. 6).

In what follows I look in more detail at two cases: women and men as parent-citizens, and the gender gap in political attitudes towards the welfare state.

The case of the small democracy: the political participation of parent-citizens

Results from the Danish and Swedish investigations support the thesis that gender differences in political participation can be linked to the nature of the political arenas. Women are at least as active as men in 'small' democracy around issues related to problems in everyday life – schools and childcare institutions (except for the workplace) – while men are generally more active than women in 'big' democracy – in political parties (except in relation to political manifestations).

It is not yet possible to compare the development of citizen involvement in small democracy (schools, childcare institutions, hospitals, the local area and the workplace) over time because this area was excluded from previous investigations of political participation. The Danish study of citizen involvement in schools and childcare activities illustrates two points: a high level of participation, with between 40 and 50 per cent of all citizens concerned being active within the previous year; and gender equality in the level of participation (see Table 1). This is surprising, since a similar Swedish investigation found a gender difference on the side of women in small democracy (Petersson et al. 1989).

Table 1 gives the distribution of women and men who were active informally as parent-citizens in schools and childcare institutions in Denmark. The table was based on the following questions asked of all parents with children in schools and childcare institutions: 'Have you alone or with others done anything to exert influence on the conditions in the schools within the last twelve months?' 'Have you alone or along with others done anything to exert influence on the conditions in the childcare institutions within the last twelve months?'

The high level of citizen participation in Danish schools and childcare institutions is interesting from a comparative perspective. The table shows that parents who have tried to exert influence on the conditions in schools and day-care institutions are more numerous than in Sweden.

Table 1   Percentage of women and men active in schools and day-care institutions in Denmark, 1990, and Sweden, 1988 (%)

	Women	Men
Denmark		
Active in relation to schools	44	42
	(N=257)	(N=206)
Active in relation to childcare institutions	48	45
	(N=118)	(N=115)
Sweden		
Active in relation to schools	39	32
Active in relation to childcare institutions	28	26

Note: Women are overrepresented among parents, so the gender differences in the table are not statistically significant.

Source: Data from the Danish Investigation of Citizenship

And gender equality in parents' participation in the Danish case contrasts with the Swedish case, where small democracy is described as a 'women-dominated' area of participation (Petersson et al. 1989: 141, 149). The difference cannot be explained by macro-structural factors because in both countries there is a combination of married women's wage work and a high coverage of public childcare centres (Siim 1994b). In addition, since the 1974 introduction of the Parents' Insurance Law, Swedish family policies have been more advanced than Danish policies in promoting parents' rights and equality between women and men in relation to children (Åstrøm 1992: 188).

The differences between schools and childcare institutions in Denmark and Sweden can be explained by political institutional factors. Comparative Nordic research indicates that Danish institutions have a relatively open, participatory culture, and that both women and men experience great satisfaction with the effects of the informal participation of citizens (Andersen et al. 1993: Ch. 4). Furthermore, a statute introduced in 1990 has created formal channels of influence that have strengthened the roles of parents as users and citizens.[20]

Research indicates that men participate more than women on school boards, and the formal representation may therefore stimulate men more than women (Siim 1993; Torpe 1993). Nevertheless, the combined effect of the formal and informal channels of participation in Denmark has been to encourage both parents to participate and has enabled citizens to influence institutions to a higher degree than in Sweden (Andersen et al. 1993: Ch. 4). The chance to influence the provision of services as parent-citizens thus helps to explain why Danish citizens in general, and Danish men in particular, have become actively involved in schools and childcare institutions.

From a gender perspective, the fact that there are different levels of activity of men as parent-citizens in Denmark and Sweden is surprising, because Swedish public policies since the adoption of the Parents' Insurance Law in 1974 have had the explicit goal of stimulating equality among parents. In Sweden men have a right to take paid leave at the birth of their child; both parents have a right to take paid leave when the child is ill, along with economic compensation, and a right to reduce their working hours to six hours a day without such compensation (Åström 1992: 188).

Swedish research indicates that, contrary to political intentions, parent rights in Sweden have been claimed more frequently by women than by men. This is the basis of the feminist argument that the 'parent-friendly' policies have, inadvertently, helped to strengthen a sexual division of work in relation to children (Åström 1992: 193). This begs the question of why men do not use their rights to paid leave to take care of their children. Research points to the dual labour market, with different work cultures in the private and public sectors as one important barrier (Carlsen 1994). Another barrier is the wage differential between women and men, which means that the household generally loses money if men take leave (Åstrøm 1992). In the Danish case this supports the hypothesis that the participatory structure in relation to schools and childcare institutions tends to stimulate both women and men, while in Sweden parent-friendly social policies tend to stimulate women more than men.

The potential for women's participation as citizens in small democracy is contested in democratic and feminist theory. Optimists stress the possibilities of women's mobilisation to form new political communities and identities around the concern for children. This in turn may lead to an increased participation in national politics and an increase in their influence on public policies (Andersen et al. 1993). Pessimists focus on the possible fragmentation of the common good and fear that women's participation in small democracy may lead to a new gender segregation that tends to reproduce women's exclusion from big democracy (Hirdman 1990).

The results indicate that political participation in small democracy has potential from a citizenship as well as a gender perspective because it mobilises parents around issues of everyday life. The new rights of parent-citizens in relation to schools and childcare institutions can be interpreted as expanding the tradition for active citizenship that increases the autonomy of parents and has the potential to strengthen civic identities around concern for their children. Participation in small democracy can also be interpreted as a dangerous step towards a new gendered split between citizens' participation in small democracy as 'everyday-makers' and their participation in big democracy. One question is whether parent-citizens develop democratic identities. Another is whether the new rights actually give parents any real power to influence the schools. A recent case study of the democratic identities of parents elected to the Danish school boards during 1994–97 gives a rather pessimistic answer to both these questions (Kristensen 1998).

The gender gap in political attitudes towards the welfare state

Research indicates that there has been a trend towards a homogenisation of the political values and attitudes between women and men (Togeby 1994a,b). The Investigation of Citizenship, however, also points towards the growth of 'new' differences in the political profiles and identities of men and women (Andersen and Torpe 1994). The study of the connection between gender and class indicated that women have moved to the Left, especially employed women with three or more years of education after college. Young women were more post-materialist and voted more on the Left than young men, and young men were more materialist and voted more on the Right than young women (Christensen 1994).

There is a high degree of political consensus in Denmark on the need to expand childcare centres to correspond with citizen needs. This was confirmed by the survey, with more than 80 per cent supporting a claim for an expansion in order to meet the needs of parents; there was a gender difference of 11 percentage points on the side of women (Siim 1994b: 143).

The investigation confirmed the feminist hypothesis that women more than men favour the expansion of the welfare state, social reforms, social equality, and support for disadvantaged groups. The redistributive dimension was discussed on the basis of two questions, one concerning attitudes of citizens towards social reforms, the other attitudes to public support of disadvantaged groups. The results indicate (see Tables 2 and 3) that women tend to be more positive than men towards maintaining social reforms and more positive towards reducing income differences through redistribution. The gender difference on social and political issues was even more prominent in a recent study from 1998 where voters were asked what welfare issues they would give highest priority to. Thirty-nine per cent of women mentioned elderly care compared to 22 per cent of men, and 32 per cent of women mentioned childcare institutions compared to 19 per cent of men, whereas the gender difference was relatively small in relation to health care (Andersen 1999: 119).

Table 2 Attitudes towards social reform by gender, 1990 (%)

	Men	Women	N
Per cent most in agreement with A	56	44	616
Per cent most in agreement with B	46	54	1174
Neither/do not know	42	58	178

A says:　'The social "reforms" in this country have been taken too far. To a greater extent people should be able to manage for themselves, more than they do today, without social security and contributions from the state.'

B says:　'The social reforms instituted in our country ought to be maintained at least to the same extent they are at present.'

Source:　Data provided by the research project Democratic Citizenship in Denmark

Table 3   Attitudes towards social equality by gender, 1990 (total and %)

	Men	Women	N
Per cent most in agreement with B	57	43	523
Per cent most in agreement with A	45	55	1096
Neither, nor/do not know	38	60	249

A says: 'The differences in income and living standards are still too big in this country, so people with low incomes ought to have their standard of living improved more quickly than those with a higher income.'

B says: 'Income redistribution has gone far enough. Income differentials as they are at present should be maintained.'

Source: Data provided by the research project: Democratic Citizenship in Denmark

The investigation of citizenship also indicates that women in the well-educated employed groups are more positive about the preservation of social reforms than men. And privately employed women with three or more years of education after college are more favourable to social reform and redistribution than privately employed men at the same level. The gendered pattern of employment thus explains some of the gender difference in political attitudes towards the welfare state, because public employees are more favourable towards social reforms and redistribution than are private employees. However, in relation to social reforms and redistribution, the attitudes of women employed in the private sector resemble those of women in the public sector more than those of privately employed men (Siim 1994b: 142–7).

It is remarkable that the gender difference in the youngest generation on the question of social reforms is double the general average: 71 per cent of women and 55 per cent of men disagree with the statement that the social reforms have gone too far (see Christensen 1994: 187, Table 4). The pattern is the same for redistribution: here 66 per cent of the young women compared with 47 per cent of the young men say that differences in incomes are still excessive (see Christensen 1994: 188, Table 5). The gap between what has been interpreted as women's 'collectivism' and men's 'individualism' is strengthened in the attitudes towards the welfare state in the youngest generation. This indicates that the consensus in the political culture about the classic values of the welfare state, such as solidarity and redistribution, rests on women in the youngest generation, but the gender gap in the youngest generation is only to a limited extent translated to party choice (Christensen 1994).

Denmark has the highest union membership in Europe (above 90 per cent of all workers are union members). However, only a small minority of young women (17 per cent) and of men (24 per cent) under 30 – and only 10 per cent under 25 – considers that the reason for trade union membership is solidarity. More than 80 per cent of all union members support the idea that one of the most important demands for the trade union movement is to eliminate pay differentials between women and men. Solidaristic wage policy, which equalises wages between members with high and low education, has lower priority (ibid.: 204, Table 12).

The question is how to interpret these findings. Women's support for the welfare state is often interpreted as an expression of collectivism and as an indication of women's collective interests as workers, clients and consumers (Hernes 1987). It has also been interpreted as an indication of a new political conflict between women employed in the public sector and men in the private sector (Esping-Andersen 1990). The negative attitude of men to redistribution can be interpreted as either an expression of individualist liberalism or as a critical attitude towards the equality ideal of the welfare state (Christensen 1994).

Research indicates that feminist attitudes have spread and gender equality has today become integrated as part of the political culture and is no longer a progressive counterculture (Togeby 1994a,b). The change from radical to moderate feminism is illustrated in Dahlerup's recent investigation: 84 per cent of the old Redstockings still consider themselves feminists. Asked about what kind of feminism and gender politics they support – equal worth, equality or emancipation – only 25 per cent still support the old ideal of 'emancipation', and about 80 per cent that of 'equal worth' (1998).

The feminist debate about women's political mobilisation
and interests

In the Nordic countries the increase in women's participation in the labour market has been followed by an increase in their participation in politics. Women's integration within the labour market and their rising level of education has increased their political resources. In her dissertation, Togeby (1994a: 18) suggested that the increase in women's wage work could be seen as a necessary precondition for the collective mobilisation of women. Additional factors have been educational resources, the expansion of public service work, and a political opportunity structure favourable to new political actors, but social development was the primary cause. A successful integration of women into political life is dependent on women's agency.

The empirical basis for Togeby's dissertation is a survey investigation of the collective political mobilisation of women in Denmark during the 1970s and 1980s. The main concept is political mobilisation connected with the creation of a new women's consciousness and a new women's culture focusing on 'equality among women and men' and 'solidarity with the weak groups' (ibid.: 16). Togeby suggests that the gap between women's expectations and reality is a basis for the political mobilisation of young well-educated women and the growth of a new woman's culture. The result is described as a move from one form of society, where men and women are separated into a man's and a woman's world, to a society where 'men and women share wage work and family obligations' (ibid.: 27). This interpretation is an indication of the profound transformation in the relation between the public and private domains in Denmark. I believe that Togeby's conclusion overestimates the move towards equality, however, and that her approach tends to underestimate the political institutional factors as an explanation for women's mobilisation (Siim 1997b).

The comparative perspective raises important questions about women's labour market participation as the main explanation for women's political participation: the first about the notion of wage work as the factor explaining the mobilisation of young, educated women. The move towards women's integration in wage work is a general move that does not explain variations in women's political mobilisation. Indeed, women have a high mobilisation in countries where they do not have high levels of labour market participation, for instance in the Netherlands, a country that has the lowest activity rates of all European countries except Ireland (Drew et al. 1998).

A second explanation emphasises the expansion of the welfare state as a precondition for women's mobilisation. I consider that this has been important in the Danish case, but it is problematic as a (universal) explanation because the expansion of social services in the Danish case in Scandinavia has no parallel in countries like Britain, where women have also increased their political mobilisation. The lack of welfare state services has indeed been an important factor in the mobilisation of British (and American) women in the 1980s (Lovenduski and Randall 1993).

The comparative perspective challenges universal explanation for the increase in women's political participation: in contrast to Togeby, I suggest that women's wage work is neither a necessary nor a sufficient condition for explaining women's demands for equality in the family and in politics. This study of the French, British and Danish cases has emphasised the relative autonomy of politics and suggests that in the Danish case political, institutional and cultural factors have been the basis for the inclusion of women in political life (Siim 1997b).

The argument is that the impact of the New Women's Liberation Movement in Denmark was dependent on the response of political culture, institutions and organisations. The connection between Danish women's collective mobilisation, the participatory political culture and the open political institutions helps to explain women's specific mobilisation as well as their inclusion within politics. This contrasts with the barriers in French political culture and institutions that partly explain the political marginalisation of women in France and that have prevented the integration of women in political institutions.

I suggest that there is indeed a relative autonomy of politics that can explain the different national and historical patterns in women's political participation and presence in the political elite. The differences in women's inclusion in politics cannot be explained primarily by women's labour market participation or welfare state developments. I also suggest that there is the potential for women's agency to influence politics and political institutions. In the Danish case the interaction between women's agency and political institutions is a key factor explaining the unique character of the Danish feminist movement. Mobilisation does not by itself lead to gender equality in political participation or to an increased presence of women in political life. And the increase in women's political participation is not in itself an indication of gender equality in power and influence in political institutions and organisations. The structure of democratic institutions is an additional factor that can help to explain variations in women's political presence. The argument is that the different models of citizenship influence the perception of women's interests and the formation of women's agency, and they may stimulate or constrain the formation of women's agency as well as their ability to form alliances that look after their perceived interests.

Conclusion: Potential and Problems of Equal Citizenship

The story about women's citizenship in Denmark is no longer about women's exclusion and marginalisation from the public arena but rather about inclusion and participation. Male domination has been transformed, although there are still gender inequalities in political power. In contrast to Pateman's patriarchal hypothesis (see Chapter 1), gender inequalities in power are no longer based on the public/private split but rather on new divisions in the political arena and on the labour market, for instance between women employed in the public sector and men employed in the private sector.

From the perspective of the public/private divide, the Danish version of pluralism[21] is based on a mix of public and private organisations with an extensive cooperation between voluntary organisations, social movements, and political institutions. Political pluralism refers to the existence of a plurality of ideas and interests in political life. In Denmark social pluralism was historically expressed in the plurality of welfare agents in civil society and in the existence of many voluntary organisations in civil society based on a class structure with many independent smallholders. Cultural pluralism refers to the legitimacy of a plurality of opinions on cultural and moral questions. Danish social democratic pluralism refers to the tradition of cooperation between voluntary organisations and the state, and in Denmark is cultural pluralism connected with the ideals of human rights and sexual equality of cultural radicalism and the radical Left party. Political and cultural pluralism is expressed for instance in Danish school legislation, which allows for a high level of state support to private schools (called free schools, 'friskoler') according to religion, ethnicity, and ideological and cultural lifestyles (Lindbom 1995).

From the perspective of democracy, the Danish case illustrates the potential of and the limits to active social democratic citizenship for women. The discourse of active citizenship and the practice of open, participatory institutions have been an advantage for gender equality. Corporatism in the governance of society has reproduced unequal gender relations and has been a barrier for gender equality.

Welfare agents in civil society, municipal socialism, the political parties and the state were the driving forces in the formation of the welfare state in the 1930s. Women cooperated across classes and political parties in the interwar period for the advancement of women's right to work, and women's agency did successfully influence policies in selected cases, but women were not policy-makers. The expansion of the welfare state after 1965 was based on a dual-breadwinner norm as well as on universal social services that expanded what feminist scholars have called the caring dimension of the welfare state. The expansion of childcare services in particular has no doubt improved women's position as working mothers and empowered women in their daily lives. The old public/private divide has become degendered, but there is today a new gender segregation between men employed in the private sector and women employed in the public sector.

The Social Democratic Party played a major role in the development of the universal welfare state after 1965. Feminist scholarship has asked why the political discourse and politics of social democracy, in which class was the key concept and gender was subordinated to class, was transformed into a discourse where gender became a key concept in politics and social equality came to include gender equality. I suggest that Danish pluralism has both had the potential for and been a barrier to women's agency and the advancement of women's rights. Pluralism has opened up a space for women's organisations in civil society to influence politics at the national level 'from below' through alliances and networks across party lines.

Danish pluralism has been combined with pluralist corporatism, which until recently has been a constraint on the power of women's organisations to influence gender equality. Corporatism has changed as women have gained new political and administrative positions of power, but there are still inequalities of power between women and men connected with corporatist institutions (Borchorst 1998a). Research from Sweden (Bergquist 1994) indicates that today corporatism is not just a barrier for an increase in women's political power but may also become a means of increasing women's representation in political and administrative institutions.

I suggest that a combination of two factors can help to explain the radical changes in women's political roles in Denmark after 1970:

1. The political culture and political institutions have created a political opportunity structure, which was a precondition for the changes in women's democratic citizenship and the inclusion of women in the political elite.
2. Women's agency, including the political mobilisation of women in social movements, their participation in voluntary organisations, in trade unions and political parties as well as their political representation in parliament, has been the key factor changing the public discourse and political institutions.

This combination explains the changes in women's political roles and the shift in the political-cultural concept of equality from a focus on social equality to one that includes equality between women and men on the labour market and in politics.

In Denmark, modernisation has been accompanied by democratisation as well as by a high degree of individualisation and decentralisation. From the perspective of active citizens this represents both possibilities and limits: decentralisation of social services enables citizens to influence policies. On the other hand it may also lead to a fragmentation of the roles of citizens and an increase of inequality between citizen groups who live in different localities. Individualisation has created flexibility in everyday life and acceptance of differences among citizens as well as among women in political identities, lifestyles and generations. Many young women and men, however, have also become critical of public regulation of collective problems, for instance of forced paternity leave and affirmative action programs.

Today, new problems for women's equal citizenship have become visible. The restructuring of the welfare state and democracy place gender conflicts based on the sexual division of labour between women employed in the public sector and men in the private sector at the centre of political debate. Recent surveys indicate that there is also a large and persistent gender gap across political parties in the attitudes to the public sector: women tend to be more positive than men towards expanding public services. The gender gap can also be identified within the political parties, but in parliamentary politics gender differences tend to disappear and (party) discipline usually prevails.

New gender divisions between 'small' and 'big' democracy, between the national and the international level, may also lead to new gender hierarchies in political power. One of the main challenges for the Danish gender profile is the demobilisation of social movements, including the feminist movement. There is a growing activity of citizens as 'everyday-makers' in small democracy that is no longer transformed to participation in big democracy (Bang and Sørensen 1998). Women are active as ordinary citizens in relation to the politics of everyday life as well as in the political elite, but the bridge between women's political mobilisation 'from below' and integration 'from above' has been weakened.

In the 1990s the new problems of citizenship are connected with globalisation, immigration and the restructuring of the welfare state. The economic crises, unemployment and marginalisation of the 1980s have affected especially unskilled, older women, who have become long-term unemployed. This has created a tendency towards a new class polarisation between well-educated women on the one hand and unskilled, elderly women who tend to become marginalised economically and politically on the other. The present restructuring of the welfare state towards a new active line in labour market and social policy (Siim 1998a) has also raised new questions about the integration of immigrant women with different religious and ethnic backgrounds. One of the major challenges for the social democratic discourse is therefore to develop new forms of solidarity that are able to integrate differences in the language of citizenship – a reflexive solidarity that expresses 'support for the others in their difference' (Dean 1996: 30).

Today, European integration and transnational politics have made the contradiction of representation and power more visible in Scandinavia. There is a gap between women's active citizenship and their power positions in the centres of political and economic decision-making. There is a new tendency towards a gendered citizenship based on a division between small and big democracy – between local, national and transnational levels of politics. There is a growing tendency to separate democracy from power and governance, for example in the EU institutions where power lies with non-elected bodies like the Council of Ministers, from which women are absent. Finally, Scandinavian women are still marginal in relation to economic decision-making.

The conclusion is that there are new possibilities of and barriers to women's full and equal citizenship in Denmark. The possibilities are connected with women's activities as citizens, which today includes women as part of the legitimate political actors and gives women new capacity to form alliances and resolve conflicts around problems of common concern. This has put a new emphasis on the formation of women's political identities and on women's overlapping identities based on class, ethnicity and generation. The absence of gender equality as a mobilising issue for young women and the demobilisation of women's organisations are today political-cultural barriers to gender equality. The gendered labour market, male-dominated political institutions, and corporatist organisations represent institutional barriers to gender equality.

Conclusion:
Towards a Contextualised Feminist Theory of Citizenship

In the concluding chapter I confront feminist rethinking of citizenship with the discourses and politics of women's citizenship in different contexts and aim to develop a contextualised feminist theory of citizenship. I look first at the feminist rethinking of citizenship and discuss the different meanings of the key concepts of equality, care and participation in different contexts. The three feminist paradigms have all criticised the dominant male norm in civic republicanism, liberalism and socialism, but they have different perceptions of the potential for and limits to women's agency to influence politics. Despite the differences, one of the objectives of feminist scholarship is to develop a vision of citizenship that re-creates the link between democratic and social dimensions of citizenship, with women at the centre.

Second, I discuss the main questions concerning the interaction between discourses, institutions and agency raised by the three cases – France, Britain and Denmark. All three illustrate the importance of politics and the strength of the male norm embedded in institutions, discourses and policies as well as the attempts of women's agency to influence politics and change institutions. The French story is one of the political exclusion of women based on their sexual difference. It illustrates the contradictions of civic republicanism and the gap between male universalism and the perceived particularism of women. The British story is about gender inequality based on the roles of women as mothers and wives. It illustrates the contradictions of liberal pluralism and the gap between women's social activism at the local and national levels. The Danish case is a story of women's political inclusion based on their roles as women citizens. It illustrates the contradictions of social democracy as well as the gap between political representation and power.

Third, I discuss the shift in the political meaning of gender in France, Britain and Denmark and the changes in women's democratic citizenship during the last thirty years. The shift in the French discourse and institutions after 1981 marked a new discourse of class solidarity and gender equality. Mitterrand's presidency initiated a new state feminism that attempted but did not succeed in including women in politics. During the 1990s there has been a new mobilisation of women around demands for parity between women and men in politics.

Thatcherism, too, marked a fundamental shift in political discourse and institutions with implications for class solidarity and gender equality. Thatcherism has had contradictory effects on gender equality. Although women workers have increasingly participated in the labour market, at the same time social inequalities have grown. During the 1990s New Labour has introduced a notion about an active state which also includes a new program for social policies that intends to increase public child-care centres and make a conscious effort to integrate women in politics.

In Denmark, there have until recently been no radical shifts in political discourses and institutions. Social democracy played a key role in integrating gender equality as part of the political discourse and public policies after 1970, and women gradually increased their political presence in parliament. During the 1990s new problems for gender equality have become visible. One is the gap between political representation and the lack of mobilisation; another is the gap between political participation and new forms of governance.

Finally, I discuss the new social and political challenges to citizenship posed by European integration, immigration and unemployment, as well as the promises connected with the new social democratic governments in France, Britain and Denmark. Each of the three cases has illustrated that there are growing inequalities between women based on education and employment as well as on ethnicity and class. The new social democratic governments show tendencies towards convergence in relation to promises to include women in politics as well as to adopt policies to increase gender equality in the labour market and the family. At the same time there are still profound differences in the conception of the state, the family and civil society, which have implications for discourse and politics of gender and citizenship. Today, there is a new intermeshing of the social and political arenas in Europe. One of the new challenges is to redefine social citizenship to include women and marginalised ethnic groups and to create a new understanding of democracy based on the active participation of all groups in all arenas of society. One of the key questions is what will be the role of women's agency in the transformation of European welfare states as well as in relation to increased European integration.

Feminist Visions and Strategies

Feminist rethinking of citizenship expresses a paradigm shift, addressing new problems of citizenship. The feminist approaches discussed in this book have different vocabularies of gender and citizenship, vocabularies that have each illuminated particular aspects of women's citizenship. The key concepts in feminist rethinking are embedded in different theoretical traditions and have distinctive meanings in specific policy contexts. The main issues are centred around three axes: equality and difference, work and care, and participation and power.

Carole Pateman's framework has criticised the classical notions of citizenship based on women's exclusion and sexual difference. The powerful patriarchal figure conceptualises the role of the family in the social contract theory, indicating the limits of the liberal approach to sexual equality. Pateman's work shows how sexual difference founded on male domination and the subordination of women is an integral aspect of modern political thought. The feminist critique of the missing analysis of the family and care work and of the exclusion of women from democratic citizenship has been an important starting point for feminist critiques of the theory of democracy and citizenship.

Women's exclusion from the public arena and powerlessness in relation to political institutions is an important aspect of modern democracies, but the focus on the public/private divide is problematic as a universal theory. Pateman's focus on the reproduction of patriarchy further underestimates the significance of politics and the role of women's political agency. Women have been mobilised and empowered during the last thirty years through the New Women's Liberation Movement. The empowering of women as political agents is today most visible in the Danish/Scandinavian context, where women are now included in the political elite. The focus on patriarchy as the key concept is also problematic from a strategic perspective because it focuses on the reproduction of sexual power relations. The neglect of women's agency has thus made it difficult to understand how public patriarchy can be changed in modern democracies, as well as the importance of women's citizenship practice.

It is interesting that Pateman's approach has recently been rediscovered in the French context, where women's powerlessness in the public arena has been most visible. There the active, inclusive vocabulary of citizenship for men is contrasted with women's exclusion from the public domain. The French debate about parity has illustrated the strengths and weaknesses in Pateman's strategy for a feminist reconceptualisation of citizenship and the ambivalence of her vision of a 'sexually differentiated' citizenship that recognises sex as a basis for citizenship but ignores differences based on ethnicity and colour.

The ambivalence is illustrated in the French debate between the proponents and adversaries of the strategy of parity, which is interpreted in different ways. Proponents of parity argue that it represents a radical form of gender equality in politics, one based on the idea that women are not a minority but represent 'half the world'. Opponents argue that the vision of parity is ambiguous, because the solution reconstructs rather than deconstructs the essentialist opposition of men/women. The question is on what basis women are represented in parliament – as mothers or as women-citizens? If women are represented as 'mothers', it would seem to be on the basis of their biological sex and not as 'women-citizens'. Arguably parity is either a claim to break male power in politics, and should be transitory like the quota system, or it is based on biological sex and thus tends to reproduce gender differences in politics. From a democratic perspective, the problem is that parity is a static not a dynamic claim. The crucial question to French feminists is whether it is possible to have a permanent institutionalisation of gender difference without essentialist perspectives. Another question is how to connect the integration of women in politics with the integration of marginalised social groups based on ethnicity and colour.

The *maternalist-communitarian approach* has conceptualised women's caring work in the family as the basis for a new type of humanitarian politics that attempts to include caring as a central political value. Elshtain's model aims to change the language of politics to include informal care work. It does not aim to create gender equality in politics but rather to represent a conscious effort to (re)institutionalise sexual difference in politics. The British debate about social care that has conceptualised the relation between women's wage work and their caring work can illustrate the strength and weakness of this approach. The influential male-breadwinner model has been based on women's informal care work, and care work is an important aspect of women's social roles. The French and Danish cases illuminate the different ways the caring dimension has been incorporated into the vocabulary of citizenship. The private notion of care has been a crucial element of the British model of citizenship, but from the perspective of the European welfare states it seems to be the exception rather than the rule. The recent transformation of European welfare states has put the restructuring of social care provision on the political agenda, and women's agency has stimulated welfare states to rethink their care policies. However, it is still an open question how care work should be incorporated within the framework of citizenship and what care arrangements are in the best interests of women. Another question is to what extent all women can be expected to have the same interests in relation to their work as care-givers and to different kinds of care for children, the mentally ill, and disabled and elderly people.

The maternalist-communitarian model is based on a normative assumption about the value for democracy of women's caring responsibilities in the family. It has been argued that there is an affinity between the maternalist model based on the realities of everyday life and the ideas of modern communitarianism emphasising the 'embedded self' situated in existing social practices. In a communitarian society the 'common good' is conceived as a substantive conception of the good life that defines the community's 'way of life'. The idea rests on a belief that women have substantive interests 'as women' based on their obligation to care for dependants. It is interesting that in Norway, Sweden and Finland, women politicians during the 1980s have often voted for different childcare policies, and during the 1990s there has been a 'reprivatisation' of care through cash-for-care schemes in Norway and Sweden (Leira 1998; Bergquist et al. 1999). The arguments that women have common substantive interests in relation to care are thus challenged in the Danish/Scandinavian context, where women have been included in parliamentary politics as part of the political elite. In Denmark during the 1980s and 1990s there has been a remarkable consensus about support for childcare institutions, but today differences between women in relation to social policies have become visible as new conflict lines have emerged in relation to attitudes towards equal social rights for immigrant groups.

In contrast to Pateman's approach, the maternalist-communitarian model has not conceptualised unequal sexual power relations. I suggest that focusing on caring work as the key element in rethinking women's citizenship is problematic as a universal model. The maternalist approach is based on a dualistic model between men as wage workers and women as carers which is not an adequate description of women and men's lives. Research from Scandinavia indicates that both men and women today have responsibilities and identities as parents as well as workers and citizens. It is suggested that the emphasis on caring as the key notion is problematic as a universal strategy because it is based on the liberal division between public and private. I suggest that there is a growing need to deconstruct the family and to differentiate between different kinds of care work, for children, the elderly, and the handicapped and mentally disabled. The crucial question confronting British feminists is how care should be organised, and whether women should have the monopoly as care-givers.

The *feminist-pluralist approach* has conceptualised women's active citizenship, and one of the objects has been to deconstruct the gender difference in politics. The pluralist approach has stressed the need to create new political communities and identities based on alliances between women, and to form new solidarity between citizens through public dialogues between different social groups. The potential of and limits to the feminist-pluralist approach can be illuminated by the Danish experiences.

In Denmark the political developments indicate that women and men have a plurality of roles as citizens, and that the division between the public and private spheres has lost some of its gendered effects (Siim 1994a). The pluralist focus on women's *agency* is an important aspect of rethinking citizenship, but the three cases illustrate the need to combine agency with the notion of political power. The Danish case indicates that there is no guarantee that integrating women into the political elite will transform politics and put feminist issues on the political agenda. The pluralists tend to exaggerate the potential of women's agency to change public institutions and to underestimate the structural barriers to women's equal citizenship. Today, there is a growing need for transformative politics premised on a synthesis between social and political equality and on the creation of a new solidarity between women and marginalised social groups (Dean 1995; Lister 1997a).

The present debate about welfare state restructuring can illustrate the potential of and limits to women's political presence. In Denmark, women are in a position to influence the adoption and implementation of social policies as policy-makers and as administrators of the public social services, as well as providers and users of social services. There is still a persistent gender gap in the attitudes of ordinary citizens towards the welfare state, but the gap contrasts with attitudes in the political elite where politics is generally more important than gender. Women citizens across political parties are more positive than men are about expanding the public sector and increasing the number of public employees in welfare services to children, the sick and the elderly, but among women in the political elite, (party) politics tends to dominate divisions by gender. Social policies are formally gender-neutral, although they affect gender equality negatively. For example the recent leave policies are motivated by concerns for 'the family', 'parents' or 'children' rather than by gendered arguments.

The *postmodern approach* has conceptualised differences between women and women's overlapping identities. I find it important to continue the dialogue between post-structuralism, postmodernism and feminism. The strength of the postmodern approach is the objective of deconstructing essentialist categories like 'woman' and 'man', and directing attention to the many ways gender relations are constructed by public policies, institutions and discourses. The danger is that this approach tends to make the feminist agency and the feminist project disappear, with the result that the theoretical (and political) problem – how to end gender domination – also disappears from the analysis.

The potential of and limits to the post-structural approach can be illustrated by the Danish case. The dual-breadwinner model as well as the integration of women into politics represent a high degree of individualisation of public policies, which has been followed by a political discourse about the social organisation and quality of care and the rights and obligations of parents where gender tends to be absent. This can be interpreted as a deconstruction of the categories 'women' and 'men'. On the other hand, gender still appears to have a structuring effect on the labour market in combination with ethnicity and class, and there is a growing differentiation between women in terms of political power. In the homogeneous Danish welfare state, inequalities among women have become visible during the 1980s, connected with growing unemployment and increased immigration. There are also real power differences between women and men in the labour market and in politics that need to be addressed by feminist scholarship as well as by feminist politics.

Each of the feminist approaches thus represents different perspectives that illuminate key aspects of women's citizenship in modern societies. Pateman has conceptualised the notion of unequal power on a macro level, and she is right that gender inequalities in political power are still partly determined by the gendered division of work and male domination in society. I suggest, however, that feminist scholarship needs to develop a dynamic notion of power that includes a notion of citizens' ability to make a difference in their daily lives as well as in relation to political institutions. This implies a double understanding of power as oppression and empowerment.

The maternalist-communitarian model has conceptualised the notion of care, and its proponents are right about the need to integrate care work into the framework of citizenship. The family and the mother–child relationship, however, as well as the caring profession, can be a site of both caring and oppression. I agree with the need to conceptualise care in relation to restructuring the welfare state, but I have argued that there is not one feminist model of how care work should be integrated within this state. The cases show that women's agency has helped to put the issue of care for children and the elderly on the political agenda, but women often disagree about what is in women's and children's best interests – the Danish model of institutionalised care for children, the mixed model of institutionalised care and economic support to parents, or new combinations of public and private care.

I agree with the pluralists and post-structuralists that there is indeed a 'relative autonomy of politics' that includes discourses, institutions, laws, culture. The implications are that there is no universal theory about gender and citizenship. The potential for and limits to women's full citizenship on the political level need to be explored in further detail through systematic comparative studies as well as in-depth case studies. Results from cross-national studies show that there is a complex relationship between the state, the market, and civil society. The three cases indicate that the dynamic connection between the family, the state, and civil society create different gender logic and constructions of the political meaning of gender.

I suggest that *women's political presence on the public arena, including their political participation and representation,* is a necessary, though not sufficient, element in a multiple strategy to create gender equality. Strategies to secure women's access to equal citizenship need to address questions of equal civil, political and social rights for women and men as well as differences between citizens in terms of class and ethnicity. The asymmetry of power based on the interrelation of gender, class and ethnicity is one of the crucial challenges for feminist theory and politics that needs to be addressed at a structural, institutional and cultural level.

One important question is what concepts can be employed in studies across national and cultural boundaries. Another question concerns the different meaning of concepts like family, state and civil society in particular contexts. Citizenship has been one of the big unifying concepts, but the cases indicate that it has many meanings in different European discourses, in specific policy contexts and in different academic traditions. The same goes for the feminist vocabulary of equality, care and participation. The key concepts have normative implications and may be connected with both the private and public arena, with the family, civil society, and the state. The French notion of parity is influenced by civic republicanism and embedded in French political institutions. The British notion of care work is influenced by social liberalism and embedded in British political culture. The Danish notion of active citizenship is influenced by social democracy and embedded in Danish political institutions. In spite of the differences, I suggest that the potential of the feminist paradigms is the vision to re-establish the link between the political and social dimensions of citizenship. The democratic challenge is to place women's issues and concerns on the public agenda and to include women's agency in the public deliberation about the common good.

Including Gender Models in a Comparative Framework of Citizenship

From a feminist perspective, the strength of T. H. Marshall's framework has been his recognition of the connection between civil, political and social rights, and the problem has been that the contextual framework was based mainly on political development in Britain. Brian Turner's

ambition is to broaden Marshall's framework and make it truly comparative. The strength of Turner's model is the interaction of agency and
political institutions in different national contexts. His model indicates
the key role that political history, institutions and discourses play, and it
thus points towards both the dynamic formation of citizenship and the
importance of the interplay between actors and political institutions.
I find that the focus on political discourses, actors and institutions is
useful. One problem is Turner's focusing on the political development of
Europe that makes the framework Eurocentric. Another is the focus on
the formative period of democracy as well as the tendency to focus on the
continuities of political institutions and discourses and to undervalue
discontinuities and shifts in political discourses and institutions.

This study has illustrated that Turner's two dimensions need to be
reconstructed from a perspective of gender.

The *active/passive dimension* raises the question of the formation of
democracy 'from above' or 'from below', of their interconnection and
of how the two are defined in different contexts. From a feminist
perspective it is a question of who is excluded and who is included in
active citizenship, and what the democratic implications are of the
exclusion of women 'as women' on the basis of their biological difference from men. Women's exclusion from the public arena and political
rights in modern democracy after the French Revolution has been
described as a fundamental break compared to previous periods when
some groups of women were included and others were excluded. It can
be argued that political exclusion has given women as a group common
interests as outsiders in being included, which was the basis for feminist
demands for equality. From this perspective it follows that women, along
with marginalised social groups, have common interests in being present
in political forums to influence political decisions. Another question
concerns what groups are active and what groups are passive. The
dualism in Turner's framework between the dominant voice of the
monarchy 'from above' and the marginalised voices of democracy 'from
below' tends to underestimate new divisions in modern democracies
between social groups and between men and women based on gender.
After the formation of democracy, women were excluded from active
citizenship in all three cases, but there have been different models of
exclusion and different ways of including women as mothers, workers
and citizens in the French, British and Danish cases. The stories illustrate
the importance of politics and the key role played by alliances and
conflicts between collective actors in the development of women's social
and political rights.

The French case indicates that before World War II there was a
consensus among the dominant groups on the Right and the Left about

women's role in the family and about key elements like pronatalism in the French political culture. The British case shows that in the interwar period it was not enough for women's organisations to agree on social policies towards mothers, for example family allowances. One determining factor has been women's ability to form networks and alliances with dominant political forces such as the labour movement. The Danish case indicates that alliances and networks among women do matter. Before World War II, women's organisations in the selected cases were able to defend women's double roles as mothers and producers, although women were never able to form strong caucuses within the political parties. From a democratic perspective, one of the key questions is the kind of alliances that exist between feminism and the labour movement, and the extent to which and on what grounds there is consensus in political culture about social policies of care as well as about gender equality.

The *public/private dimension* raises the question about what the notions of 'public' and 'private' mean in different contexts and from different theoretical perspectives. The striking contrast between the liberal British perception of the 'public/private' divide and the republican notion of public/private has profound implications for women's civil, social and political rights. In the republican French context the public notion of solidarism is combined with a positive perception of public regulation of families, called familialism. The social democratic Danish perception of the public/private figure is different from both of these. There is, rather, a public/private mix that can be illustrated by the historical relation between social movements and voluntary organisations on the one side and the local and national state on the other. The family has not been perceived as a 'private' arena outside state intervention, as in Britain, nor has the state been perceived as being above the private family as in France. In Denmark there has been a public–private balance where the family has not been seen in opposition to the state but rather as a part of civil society that includes voluntary organisations. From a feminist perspective there is a need to transcend the dichotomy public/private and to reconceptualise the family and the relation between market, state and civil society.

In this study the notion of agency has been used as a bridge between the social and the political, and it is linked to political citizenship as well as to social citizenship and to the restructuring of the welfare state. It has raised the question of the relation between women as a social and political group. A key issue has been the role of women as collective actors and the conflicts and alliances between citizen groups and between women citizens. The results from the comparative study illustrate how women in all three countries were politically active in women's organisations and in political parties before they gained the formal right to vote. Historically, what has been a common feature is women's political exclusion motivated by their roles as mothers, but the study shows that the processes of women's inclusion have been very different in the three cases. The cases illustrate how women's issues have been shaped in the political process, and that organisations on the Right and the Left, including women's organisations, who had the authority to speak 'on behalf of women', had different gender profiles and interpretation of women's interests. When women enter parliamentary politics the differences between women's political identities and interests become visible, and the Danish case shows that politics has generally been more important than gender. It also indicates that women across political parties have formed alliances and networks in order to promote women's interests that in some cases have been able to influence public policies and increase gender equality.

The results further show the different role of women's organisations in transforming and reproducing discourses and policies through alliances and networks between women and between women and men. It is a common feature in political development that women have from the early 1970s been mobilised collectively in the new women's liberation movement in all three cases. This has changed the political meaning of gender as women have moved to the Left and have increasingly been included in democratic institutions during the 1980s and 1990s, and it has also rendered visible differences among women in terms of political identities, strategies and power. This has raised new questions about gender equality in political representation and about women's ability to influence policies through alliances and networks among different groups of women and between women inside and outside political institutions.

The Interplay of Women's Social and Political Rights

The present study illuminates the different interconnections of women's social and political rights embedded in three national configurations. They indicate how the perception of women is produced and reproduced by assumptions about gender inscribed in political discourses and institutions. They also indicate how women's agency in cooperation with political forces has contributed both to reproduce and to change dominant discourses about their roles as mothers, workers and citizens and to influence political institutions.

This study challenges the notion of a universal male-breadwinner model based on women's unpaid care work and their unequal social rights, and points towards different gender models of citizenship. The male-breadwinner model indicates that the key to women's citizenship is the relation between women's paid and unpaid work. This is a good conceptualisation of the British case, but it does not fit the French or the Danish case. In France the key to women's citizenship has been women's exclusion from political rights and married women's lack of civil rights in marriage. In Denmark the key to women's citizenship has been women's double role as producers and mothers.

The results indicate that political citizenship expresses an independent aspect of women's citizenship, and that France, Britain and Denmark represent three distinct models of citizenship, each with different assumptions about gender and about women's social and political rights. The French case illuminates the strengths and weaknesses of the republican version of citizenship and the notion of universalism. It tells a story about radical equality and the political inclusion of equal citizens premised on the exclusion of women from the public arena and their unequal inclusion as mothers. The cases further illustrate the dilemma between the ideology of familialism and the idea of gender equality.

The British case illuminates the strengths and weaknesses of social liberalism and the notion of liberal pluralism. It tells the story of women's second-class citizenship and their exclusion from equal social rights premised on their primary roles as mothers and wives. The case further illustrates persisting inequalities among women according to class and ethnicity, as well as the dilemmas between the private and public sector, between wage work and care work.

The Danish case is a story of the inclusion of citizens in the universal welfare state and the democratic participation of social groups. It illuminates the strengths and weaknesses of the notion of social democratic pluralism and of corporatism. Women have gained social rights as mothers and workers, and during the last thirty years the expansion of women's social rights has been followed by the inclusion of women as citizens. The case illustrates the potential for and limits to the inclusion of women citizens, which has created a new dilemma between mobilisation 'from below' and integration 'from above' and between participation and power.

Each of the three stories raises important methodological questions about the continuity as well as the shifts in notions of gender and citizenship in the last thirty years from different policy contexts. They indicate that political institutions and structures represent a strong continuity, or path-dependence, which has helped to reproduce gendered social and political rights. They also illustrate how political discourses represent an independent force that influences women's citizenship, and that shifting discourses contribute to constructing, reproducing and changing women's citizenship. Finally, they indicate that woman's agency in civil society and in relation to formal politics has in some cases been able to influence the discourse and politics of citizenship and improve women's civil, social and political rights. In crucial periods of transformation of welfare states and democracies, the alliances, networks or conflicts among women, and between women and major political forces, have been important elements in determining public policies towards women as workers, mothers and citizens.

The three cases illustrating the connection between civil, social and political rights have been different for women and men, which puts a question mark on the basic assumptions in both Marshall's and Turner's models. They further show that there have been three different patterns of civil, political and social rights for women in each of the three policy contexts, which question assumptions about a universal chronology between women's civil, political and social rights. The French case shows up a contrast between women's social rights as workers and mothers and gender inequality in political rights, and the problem of including women in politics. The British case illuminates the contrast between women's civil and political rights, and gender inequality in social rights, and the problem of social rights for working mothers. And the Danish case illuminates the link between women's roles as workers, mothers and citizens, and the problematic relation between political representation and power.

From a historical perspective, the French case illustrates the contradiction between universalism and particularism in French political life, especially the problem for voluntary organisations of influencing public policies. Women represent particularism and are therefore perceived as a threat to the discourse and politics of universalism. The vocabulary of universalism has thus been a constraint on women's independent organisation, and women's organisations have been subordinate to the dominant political organisations. The strong alliances between republican feminism and social Catholicism, as well as between women's organisations, and the dominant discourse about familialism and pronatalism during the interwar period, are one example. The implication is that in France there has historically been a strong link between pronatalism, familialism and feminist maternalism that partly explains women's lack of civil and political rights.

The British case illustrates the contradiction in British political life between centralism and decentralisation at the national and local level. While women have been active at the local level they have been unable to translate this to national policy. In Britain, the centralised state structure has been described as a separate barrier to women's access to citizenship which has put constraints on women's agency. There has been a long tradition of women's social activism in Britain, and one of the key questions for feminism has been how to transform this at the local level and increase women's influence on the central state. During the interwar period alliances among women about family allowances were not strong enough to influence policies because the alliance between women and the trade union movement did not succeed.

In the British case, one of the key questions has been how to open up formal to informal politics. On the positive side, feminist scholars have suggested that the principle of liberal pluralism has had potential for the self-organisation of citizens and has also encouraged women's involvement in voluntary organisations and strengthened their abilities to influence the local welfare state. During the 1980s local government became one of the major arenas of feminist activity, and the women's committees can be interpreted as an example of opening formal to informal politics. The New Labour government is committed to increasing the political influence of women, but the question remains of how to increase their political presence and power in the national arena.

In Denmark, the *pluralist* political culture is based on the cooperation between voluntary organisations, social movements and political institutions. The Danish case illustrates the dilemma of social democracy between participation 'from below' and incorporation 'from above'. I suggest that pluralism has been both a benefit and a barrier to the advancement of women's rights. Danish pluralism has opened up a space for women's organisations in civil society to influence politics at the national level 'from below', through alliances and networks across party lines, and it has been possible for social groups to influence public politics and the development of the welfare state 'from below'. The strength of social corporatism built on the cooperation of state institutions and the main organisations on the labour market has, on the other hand, given economic interest organisations a key role in economic policy, which has been a barrier to gender equality on the labour market and in society.

The Danish case also illustrates the limits of active citizenship. Women's organisations did not play a major role in the formation of the welfare state in the 1930s, and the new feminist liberation movement only indirectly influenced the development of the universal welfare state after 1965. Arguably the universal welfare state has improved the welfare of working mothers and children and has contributed to empowering women in their daily lives. Women's inclusion in politics has raised the question of the formation of women's political identities and the representation of their interests. One question is who has the voice and the authority to speak for women, and what is in women's best interests. Another question for feminists is what kind of issues can become the basis for a new mobilisation of women citizens, and whether women have the will and the ability to form alliances and networks across political parties to promote gender equality and influence the present transformation of the welfare state. Today, the homogeneous Danish welfare state is being challenged by a growing number of immigrants, followed by an ideological reorientation of citizens and new conflict lines inside and outside political parties in relation to social rights for immigrant groups.

Shifts in the Political Meaning of Gender

Political developments during the last thirty years illustrate dramatic shifts as well as continuities in the discourse and politics of citizenship in the three cases. In all three countries women's agency in the form of the women's liberation movement became a social and political force during the 1970s. It was followed by a new political meaning of gender as women moved to the Left, but the implications for gender equality were radically different. In France the victory of the first socialist president in 1981, followed by socialist governments during the 1980s, marked a dramatic swing to the Left. In Britain there was a dramatic swing to the Right with Margaret Thatcher's election victory in 1979. In Denmark political developments have been less dramatic and there has been a high degree of consensus about social policies and gender equality between conservative coalition governments from 1982 to1992 and social democratic coalition governments from 1993 to 1999.

The shift in French political institutions since 1981 has marked a new discourse of class solidarity and gender equality. During Mitterrand's presidency, a program for gender equality was adopted, with gender equality in the labour market as the key issue, and although the policies were not successful, French working mothers today have among the highest activity rates in Europe and the most extensive public provisions for childcare for the over 3-year-olds after Scandinavia. In spite of setbacks caused by economic crises and high unemployment, the republican promise of equality has had a major impact in education and the labour market. The integration of women in education and wage work contrasts with the constraint women still experience entering the political arena. State feminism has attempted to integrate women 'from above' in public administration, but women are still marginal in parliament. In this context the demand for parity between women and men in political institutions has been able to mobilise many women across the political spectrum as the road to political equality.

This book indicates that the notion of universalism in French political discourses and political institutions has been a barrier to the integration of women in politics. Universalism, however, has different meanings; it is open to change and, potentially, could lead to women's inclusion in politics if the political parties decide to adopt parity or quotas as a legal strategy. I suggest that the crucial differences in the notion of politics in Denmark and France in relation to political institutions and issues are both an expression of and the cause of differences in women's democratic citizenship. In terms of political issues, high politics connected with foreign politics and the 'common good' is separate from people's daily lives. In terms of political institutions, politics in France is closely linked with the classical political institutions at the national level, like the presidency, the government, parliament. This contrasts with the Danish case, where politics has increasingly become related to locally organised social services and associated with problems in people's daily lives, and where political participation includes the participation of parents in social service institutions, for example in relation to childcare and schools. The perception of politics as 'high politics' removed from the problems of people's daily lives can be seen as both the cause and the effect of women's exclusion from politics in France.

In Britain, the dominant values of non-intervention in private family matters in the political culture and in political discourse, as well as the recent neo-conservative interventionism, have been a barrier to the expansion of childcare centres and the adoption of social policies that would help working mothers to cope with work and care. The discourses of social liberalism and Thatcherism have been challenged by the report from the Commission of Social Justice from 1994 and by recent policy documents from the New Labour Party. The program for social and economic reforms in many ways expresses a political alternative to both the passive (welfare) state and the male-breadwinner model (Sassoon 1996). The report's reform program has been an inspiration for Labour's political debate about a renewal of the British welfare state and about the need for an active welfare state that combines individual responsibility with collective solidarity. The vision is to develop an intelligent welfare state that can prevent poverty through public policies that enable citizens to combine lifelong education with wage work and care for the weakest social groups (Social Justice 1994: 223).

The politics towards the family as well as strategies towards lone mothers represents a challenge for the discourse and policies of New Labour. One problem is whether working mothers should be supported by universal policies or by targeted social policies towards the family. Another is whether to change social policy and encourage lone mothers to take wage work.

In Denmark, the present gender gap in values concerning the welfare state is strengthened by the sexual division of labour between women employed mainly in the public sector and men employed in the private sector. And new gender divisions between small and big democracy, between the national and international arenas, can also lead to new gender hierarchies in political power. Corporatism is changing as women have gained new positions in public committees and commissions and in the welfare state as professional workers and citizens, but there are still inequalities of power connected with the power of economic interest organisations at the private labour market. Today, corporatism is not only a barrier to women's political power but may also be the means of increasing women's representation in political and administrative institutions.

In Denmark, the homogeneous welfare state is today challenged by new problems of ethnicity connected with immigration, and social and cultural differences between women according to ethnicity have been growing. The inclusion of women in politics has further made visible new differences between women in terms of political identity, profiles and power. Individualisation has created flexibility in everyday life and a growing acceptance of differences among citizens as well as among women in political identity, lifestyle and generation. Many young women and men have become critical of public regulation of everyday life problems, and there is a debate about forced paternity leave and mandatory affirmative action programs. During the 1990s the demobilisation of the women's organisations has contrasted with the increase in the activities of citizens in relation to problems in everyday life. This development has been followed by an academic debate about the new term 'everyday-makers', a reference to (women) citizens actively engaged in politics in relation to local everyday life problems. 'Everyday-makers' is a typically Danish phenomenon that can be interpreted as an example of the new reflectivity of citizens in relation to politics and everyday life, or as an illustration of the growing indifference of (women) citizens towards national politics and the EU.

New Challenges to Equal Citizenship in the European Welfare States

In the 1990s the new problems of citizenship are associated with globalisation, immigration and the restructuring of the welfare states. European integration is one of the new challenges changing the role of the European nation-states. EU policies about social rights have been ambiguous. The social dimension has strengthened the rights of workers, but at the same time its restrictive economic policies have contributed to cutting public spending and increasing unemployment, and central-isation in EU institutions has weakened their citizen roles and the national democratic processes. From a gender perspective, social and economic integration has also been ambiguous. Equality policies have increased gender equality on the labour market, but growing unemployment has adversely affected women more than men.

Feminist scholars debate what impact European integration has had on European social policies and what effect the strengthening of the economic and social dimensions of the European integration process will have on equality as well as on the relations between family and work (Borchorst 1998b; Walby 1998). Women generally have been more sceptical of the EU than men, but in Britain women have embraced it because social regulation of the labour market is good for women and because equality policies have given them new social rights, as manifested for example in the right to maternity leave. Danish women have been more sceptical because they fear that harmonisation of economic and social policies will lead to cuts in its large public service sector, and they are critical of women's absence from male-dominated political and administrative institutions.

On the European level, women's organisations and networks have been divided, but in the Nordic countries feminist organisations have generally been fairly negative towards the EU. In Denmark this is beginning to change, and today there is a new dialogue about the European Project among women's organisations and networks and a shift in the political identities of young women towards a more positive attitude towards the EU. One key question is to what extent women's groups and networks can be mobilised by the European project and will attempt to use the discourses of human rights and gender equality. Another is whether women's agency, that is, women's groups and networks, will have the potential to influence the EU discourse about social and civic citizenship and increase gender equality in EU institutions.

The three cases illustrate the growing inequalities between women in terms of education and employment, power and ethnicity, and this development challenges the dominant frameworks of citizenship, including feminist notions of women's common interests as a social group. The economic crises and growing employment of the 1980s have affected especially unskilled and elderly women, who have become poor, marginalised or long-term unemployed. This, in turn, has created a tendency towards a new class polarisation between well-educated, younger women and unskilled, elderly women, who tend to become marginalised economically and politically. Growing immigration has also exacerbated inequalities and differences between women based on ethnicity and colour. This development has created new problems of citizenship and new social and political challenges for the welfare states. One response to these challenges is the new politics of integration of unemployed and marginalised social groups through social policies of 'activation' emphasising the obligation on all citizens to work.

The present social democratic governments in France, Britain and Denmark illustrate fundamental differences in the political histories, discourses and institutions of the three nations, as well as new tendencies towards convergence. During the 1980s there was a demobilisation of social movements, including the labour movement, and in the 1990s there has been a growing need for ideological reorientation, including new notions of equality and solidarity. This is the basis for the recent debates about the inclusion and exclusion of citizens and about the relation between social, economic and political marginalisation of citizens in Europe.

Donald Sassoon has recently suggested that there is a convergence of the programs of the socialist parties in Northern and Southern Europe. He places the British and Nordic social democracies in the same family of the Left from the perspective of a modernisation of capitalism. He has not noticed that the British Labour Party till recently had radically different visions and policies in relation to childcare, the family and married women's employment from the Nordic social democratic parties. This study shows that from the perspective of family policies the Labour Party and Nordic social democratic parties did indeed belong to different families of the Left. During the 1990s there are signs of convergence of the social democratic parties in Europe. New Labour has adopted a program about democratic citizenship that includes women in active citizenship and a discourse about social citizenship that includes initiatives to integrate married women in the labour force through an expansion of childcare provisions.

The new government in France also represents a shift in the political programs and politics that brings it closer to the Nordic social democracies. The New Left coalition government of Socialists, Communists and Greens (from June 1997) has promised a more egalitarian and democratic public sphere, a sphere that includes the political participation of women and marginal groups in the governing of society. The new Socialist Prime Minister, Lionel Jospin, has recently committed himself to increasing women's political representation through the adoption of the principle of parity in legislation. This challenges the perception of universalism embedded in republican institutions and discourses and is a step towards accepting the ethos of democratic pluralism of political representation and ideas. I suggest that it would also imply rethinking politics and challenging the strict distinction between social and political aspects of citizenship in both discourse and politics and recognising the connection between the politics and social problems in people's daily lives.

The principles of the New Labour government towards a more active social state represent a break with the past in a number of policy areas. The ambition to support married women's employment, increase public childcare centres, and include women in politics, expresses a conscious break with the old masculine ethos of the labour movement. New Labour's social program intends to help working mothers. The proposals about an active line in social policy may also create problems for women, however, by strengthening the tendency for all mothers, including lone mothers, to be treated as workers who will only be able to get poorly paid jobs. New Labour has committed itself not to raise taxes, and during the first two and a half years has given priority to civil and political rights over social rights. One of the tests of New Labour will be whether the new line will indeed increase women's presence in parliament and strengthen the role of women's agency in the party and in society. Since the last election, in 1997, women now represent about 25 per cent of Labour MPs and about 20 per cent of Cabinet and other ministers. In spite of the growing number of women elected to parliament through the quota system, however, the prospects for an increase in women's democratic influence do not look too bright, because Tony Blair has announced that he does not want to use quotas in the coming elections.

In Denmark, the present Centre Left coalition government, in power since 1993, has begun to restructure the welfare state, and the social policies of integration directed explicitly towards immigrants have raised crucial questions about the unequal treatment of Danish citizens and immigrants with different ethnic and religious backgrounds. The homogeneity of the Danish/Scandinavian welfare states is increasingly under challenge from immigration and from political unification in Europe, and today there are new problems concerning how to integrate differences, and differences among women, in the struggle for equality. There are also new dilemmas in gender-neutral policies and gendered citizenship practices, for example in relation to childcare leave, which are gender-neutral but primarily used by women.

From the perspective of gender equality in politics, the program and policies of the new French and British Governments can be interpreted as a step towards convergence with the strategies of the Nordic welfare states supporting the inclusion of women in politics. From a perspective of gender equality in social policy, the program and policies of the New Labour government can be interpreted as a convergence towards the strategies of social democracy in the Nordic countries.

The notion of politics is also changing when problems in everyday life, like the rights of parents to public childcare, become the object of public policies. This is most visible in Denmark, where there is a discourse about the empowerment of citizens in relation to social policies at the local level as well as a tendency to a strengthening of the quality of local democracy. The point is, however, that public organisation and regulation of care work for children, the disabled and the elderly is today on the political agenda in all three countries, and indeed in all European welfare states regardless of whether the government is dominated by the Left or the Right. Democracy is changing, and while on the one hand there has been a demobilisation of social movements and the women's movement and an ideological reorientation of citizens, on the other, active citizenship has come to include women, and women's networks and feminist groups have the potential for playing a larger political role than ever before.

Women's increased political presence in parliament raises new questions about women's political identities, about alliances and conflicts among women and about who has the voice and the authority to represent women. There is everywhere a problematic gap between the visions and strategies of feminist groups and women's networks in civil society and the realpolitik of women represented in the political elite. From a feminist perspective, one of the main challenges for the discourse and practice of citizenship in all three countries is in reintegrating the link between civil, social and political rights and re-establishing the link between citizens' activities at the local, national and European levels. I suggest that one of the major challenges for feminist theory and politics is to develop new forms of solidarity that are able to integrate differences in the language of citizenship – a reflective solidarity that expresses 'support for the others in their difference'. The crucial question is whether we in the future will see a feminist mobilisation of women citizens around a new vision of equality and solidarity with the objective of transforming not only local and national politics but also European and transnational politics.

Appendix

Table 4 Childcare provisions in the European Union

Countries	Reference year	Age of compulsory schooling	Childcare* for children 0–3 %	Childcare* for children 3–6 %
Austria	1994	6	3	75
Belgium	1993	6	30	95
Denmark	1994	7	50	79
Finland	1994	7	21	43
France	1993	6	23	99
Germany (West)	1990	6	2	78
Germany (East)	1993	6	50	100
Greece	1993	6	3	64
Ireland	1993	6	2	58
Italy	1991	6	6	91
Luxembourg	1989	6	2	55–60
Netherlands	1993	5	8	71
Portugal	1993	6	12	48
Spain	1993	6	(2)	64
Sweden	1994	7	33	72
UK	1993	5	2	60

Source: *EUROSTAT* 1995, 1996 in Drew, Emerek and Mahon, 1998, p. 49

Note: *Places in childcare or children attending as percentage of children in that age group. For information on the method of measurement see Ruxton (1996).

Table 5   Women's representatives in France, 1945–97

The National Assembly   (Assemblée Nationale)

Elections	Places	Women	%
Fourth Republic			
October 1945	586	33	5.6
June 1946	586	30	5.1
November 1946	618	42	6.8
June 1951	627	22	3.5
January 1956	596	19	3.2
Fifth Republic			
November 1958	586	9	1.5
November 1962	482	8	1.6
March 1967	487	10	2.0
June 1968	487	9	1.8
March 1973	490	8	1.6
March 1978	491	18	3.7
June 1981	491	26	5.3
March 1986	577	34	5.9
June 1988	577	33	5.7
March 1993	577	35	6.0
June 1997	577	62	10.0

Source: Updated table from Jenson and Sineau, 1994–95, Annexe 8

Table 6 Labour women candidates and MPs in Britain, 1945–97

Election Year	Labour candidates		Labour MPs		All MPs	
	N	%	N	%	N	%
1945	41	7.5	21	5.3	24	3.8
1950	42	6.8	14	4.4	21	3.4
1951	41	6.3	11	3.7	17	2.7
1955	43	6.9	14	5.1	24	3.8
1959	36	5.8	13	5.0	25	4.0
1964	33	5.3	18	5.7	29	4.6
1966	30	4.8	19	5.2	26	4.1
1970	29	4.6	10	3.5	26	4.1
1974 (Feb.)	40	6.4	13	4.3	23	3.6
1974 (Oct.)	50	8.0	18	5.6	27	4.3
1979	52	8.3	11	4.1	19	3.0
1983	78	12.3	10	4.8	23	3.5
1987	92	14.5	21	9.2	41	6.3
1992	138	21.6	37	13.7	60	9.2
1997	158	24.7	101	24.2	120	18.2

Source: Original data provided by the British political scientist Simon Henig

Table 7 Development of women's representation in the Danish parliament, 1945–98, selected years

	1945	1950	1960	1968	1973	1975	1979	1987	1994	1998
Women	8	12	17	20	27	28	42	52	59	66
Men	141	137	158	155	148	147	133	123	116	109
Total	149	149	175	175	175	175	175	175	175	175
Women share (%)	5	8	10	11	15	16	24	30	34	38

Source: *Statistical Yearbook, Parliamentary Yearbook, The Yearly Report from the Equality Council 1997*

Comment: The data do not include the four North Atlantic members.

Source: Christensen & Knopf 1998, GEP working paper no. 7, table 3, p. 15

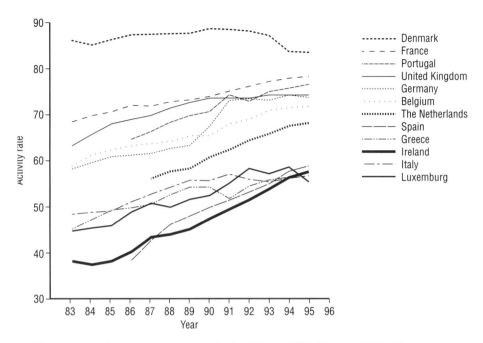

Figure 1   Activity rates for women in the EU aged 25–49 years, 1983–95
Source: EUROSTAT 1995, 1996 in Drew, Emerek and Mahon 1998, Fig. 8.3, p. 96

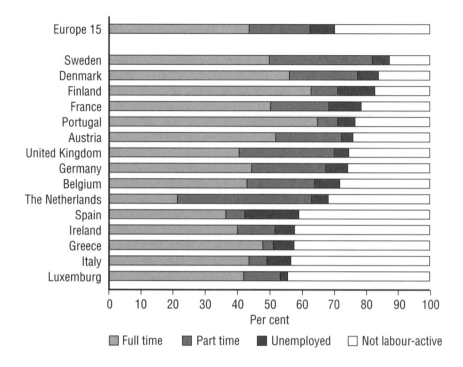

Figure 2   Women (aged 25–49 years) in the labour force in the European
Union, 1995. By full-time, part-time, unemployment and non-labour market
activity
Source: EUROSTAT 1995, 1996 in Drew, Emerek and Mahon 1998, Fig. 8.4, p. 97

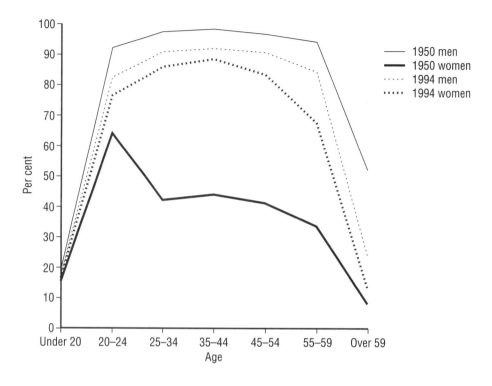

Figure 3   Employed women and men in the Danish labour market by age,
1950 and 1994
Source: 50-year review, Danish Statistical Bureau 1995

Notes

Introduction: Feminist Rethinking of Citizenship

1   Carole Pateman (1988) and Joan Scott (1988) represent two different theoretical traditions, disciplines and gender paradigms. Pateman's structural theory about modern patriarchy contrasts with Scott's post-structuralist paradigm. It is interesting that they both emphasise the new gender paradigm and the new political construction of gender in modern democracies – albeit with different arguments and from different perspectives.

2   In the national Investigation of Citizenship in Denmark the research group defined two different dimensions: the *vertical* dimension designating the relation between the individual and the state, and the *horizontal* dimension designating the relations of citizens to each other (see Andersen et al. 1993; Siim 1994a). This synthesis of the collective horizontal dimension of citizenship expressing the political organisation of citizens in civil society and the emphasis on individual rights transcends both the liberal rights tradition and the civic republican tradition. It is instead inspired by the socialist/social democratic tradition and is connected with the citizenship tradition of the Nordic democracies (Siim 1998a). In Nordic political history there is a long tradition of incorporation of social movements and voluntary organisations in politics which has led to a rather broad perception of the political and of democracy that transcends the public/private divide (Hernes 1987, 1988).

3   Feminist theorists like Hirdman (1990) define the sex/gender system primarily in terms of structural inequality of *power* as defined by the two principles of gender segregation of male and female activities/roles, and male hierarchy. Lewis and Ostner (1994) analyse the gender system in Britain and Germany mainly in terms of inequality of *welfare rights*, i.e. as a system dominated by the 'male-breadwinner' model. I will keep the two dimensions – the difference between male and female activities/roles as well as the male norm (hierarchy) – but in contrast to Hirdman, I maintain that the relation between the two is conceptually open.

4   There is a difference between the notion of agency in Giddens' framework and agency in Chantal Mouffe's (1992a) post-structuralist and Ruth Lister's (1997a) feminist thinking. In Giddens' framework agency is embedded in his theory of structuration and is part of the objective to transcend objectivism

and subjectivism in social theory (Giddens 1984: 14). Lister (1997a: 36–41) has reflected on a feminist perception of human agency with inspiration from human psychology, and her idea points towards the universal capacities of individual agency. She makes a useful distinction between *simple* agency – i.e. the capacity to act and choose – and *citizenship* agency, which is important to an individual's self-identity.

5 In Jean Cohen's recent definition of civil society, inspired by Jürgen Habermas, civil society refers to a third principle as distinct from the market and the state. It includes the church and the family as well as political and cultural organisations, i.e. all contexts where there is communication (Cohen in *Social Kritik* 1996: 31). This perception is close to the meaning given to the notion of civil society in Scandinavia, but different from the classical meaning given by Hegel and Marx, where civil society is associated with the market. In Scandinavia there has always been a connection between the state, the family, and civil society (Hernes 1988; Kolstrup 1997). In this book, civil society is used in a broad sense that includes the family, the church and voluntary organisations. The concept of civil society is an arena that is analytically different from the state and the market, but, in practice, voluntary organisations may be included as part of state institutions through corporatist structures (see Chapter 6).

6 Bodily rights, e.g. the right to abortion, which has a special relevance for women, has not been included in civil rights in equality before the law. Historically, women were excluded from political rights as women, and often women gained social rights not as individuals but as mothers or wives (Pateman 1988; Lewis 1993; Shaver 1997; Marques-Pereira 1998).

7 A political culture expresses the limits and content of politics in different national contexts. The classical understanding of political culture is the 'subjective dimension of politics', that is, the attitudes and values of citizens in different contexts, first developed in connection with comparative studies of 'civic virtues', with the objective of analysing the cultural conditions for stable democracies (Almond and Verba 1989a,b). In the Danish Investigation of Citizenship, we used the term 'political culture' broadly as the orientation of citizens in political life, including the patterns of their attitudes, values and participation, as well as the meaning of routines, procedures and practices of political institutions (Andersen and Torpe 1994: 7).

1 Towards a Gender-sensitive Framework of Citizenship

1 Lewis (1994) has an excellent discussion about the role of women's agency in the building of the British welfare state. She refutes both the argument that women have played a major role in building the British welfare state and the description of the British state as being 'weak'. The main argument is that although women's voluntary actions played an important role in Britain, women's agency has never influenced the core element of early British state legislation. See also Chapter 5.

3 Feminist Approaches to Citizenship

1 There are both similarities and differences between post-structuralism, inspired by Michel Foucault, and postmodernism, inspired by cultural and literary analysis, and there are many versions of feminist postmodernity. For a

discussion of the differences, see the feminist debate in Nicholson (1990) and in Benhabib et al. (1995). One of the differences is about the definition of agency and of politics. Scott (1988: 46) emphasises the collective meaning of agency, and defines the political meaning of gender as 'the particular and contextual ways in which politics constructs gender and gender constructs politics'. This is a useful definition, but it begs the question of what is the political.

2 Equality has been one of the key concepts in feminist thinking. Feminist scholarship has distinguished between formal and substantive equality (Gerhard 1997; Walby 1997). The German sociologist Ute Gerhard has developed a notion of dynamic equality which involves women as social actors in a decisive role as constantly renegotiating and reinterpreting law as equal participants (Gerhard 1997: 49). Anne Phillips' new book *Which Equalities Matter?* (1999) aims to reconnect the relation between political and economic equality in feminist and political theory. In political theory there has been a distinction between two aspects of equality called equality of democratic citizenship and equality of conditions or equality of life prospects (Arneson 1995: 489). The strong legal equal rights tradition includes affirmative actions to counter discrimination on the basis of such factors as race, creed, gender, sexual orientation, and ethnicity. Mouffe (1992a: 7–8) has recently referred to Michael Walzer's distinction between 'simple' and 'complex' equality. Simple equality is 'the concern to make people as equal as possible in all respects', and complex equality means that 'different social goods should be distributed in accordance with a variety of criteria reflecting the diversity of those goods and their social meanings'. This is a useful distinction based on the idea that the concept of equality should both be egalitarian and heterogeneous and compatible with a democratic and pluralistic conception of citizenship.

3 Fraser (1995: 5) has reached a similar conclusion in a recent paper analysing gender equity in the welfare state: 'With respect to social welfare, at least, the deconstruction of gender difference is a necessary condition for gender equity.'

4 The more general assumption is that there is indeed a relative autonomy, not only of politics but of the main arenas of society, the labour market, the state and civil society (see Connell 1987).

5 Bourdieu (1995, 1998) has analysed the significance of 'symbolic domination' in gender relations. He uses male domination as the paradigmatic case in relation to symbolic violence. His thesis is that there is a relative autonomy for the symbolic domain vis-à-vis the economy.

4 Gender and Citizenship: The French Case

1 According to Messu familialism is tainted with natalism, i.e. the belief in the virtues of the high birthrate, and it also joins in an ambiguous relation with solidarism, an ideology that emphasised the moral concern for justice based on reciprocal obligations between social actors. Messu (1998: 7) concludes that sociological thinkers about solidarity tended to forget that the family represents the earliest form of solidarity. Familialism can thus be seen as a specific form of familism. The notion of familism refers to state support for women's role as mothers but is not necessarily linked to natalism. In the following the term familialism is used only in the French case.

2   The history of women's rights to vote in France has been very strange. The right to vote had been blocked in the Senate during the 1930s, and women's suffrage was not legislated by parliament but was an initiative taken by de Gaulle and put forward in 1944 as a directive, not as a law (Jenson and Sineau 1995).

3   Auclert joined the organisation Avenir des Femmes in 1872 but created her own organisation, Droits de la Femme, in 1876, which changed its name to Suffrage des Femmes in 1872, and in 1881 she founded the journal *La Citoyenne*, which became a monthly in 1883 (see Ozouf 1995: 199–233).

4   In her comparison of the different legal systems in Europe, Sineau (1992) points out that the French legal tradition contrasts with both the Anglo-Saxon countries, like Britain, and the Scandinavian countries. French women's lack of civil rights in marriage under Code Napoléon contrasts with Scandinavia, where women gained civil rights in marriage as early as 1925.

5   The French social welfare system is complex. It is organised in different branches: healthcare and industrial accidents, old age, maternity and family affairs and unemployment insurance. The non-contributory means-tested sector was needed to provide for poor, vulnerable groups (children, disabled or elderly people) not covered by insurance, and the distinction between social insurance and social assistance (called solidarity today) is crucial (Bouget 1998: 158).

6   Simone de Beauvoir's ideas about radical equality have been influential and only a minority group around Luce Irigaray has supported the notion of 'sexual difference'. Radical egalitarian ideas are today defended by Christine Delphy and by feminists associated with the journal *Nouvelles questions féministes*. According to Jane Jenson (1993) there were three feminist tendencies in France: equality feminists active before 1968 (feminism égalitaire); revolutionary feminists organised in the MLF (feminism révolutionaire); and feminists in the labour movement (feminism syndicaliste).

7   Trat mentions three: a psychoanalytic tendency; a radical feminist tendency centred around *Nouvelles questions féministes*; and a socialist tendency that wanted to unite women's struggle with that of the working class.

5 Gender and Citizenship: The British Case

1   Liberalism is a slippery term that has many different meanings. It has often been associated with the belief in limited government and guarantees of civil liberties and has been defined as a 'theory of limited government aimed at securing personal liberty' (Lipset 1995: 756–76). According to Rosenblum (1995) there is a tension between liberalism and democracy, because liberal democratic citizenship is a legal concept, not a social or cultural one. Liberalism is contested and contextual, and liberalism has taken a different course in Britain, France, Italy, Germany and the USA. British social policy has been influenced by 'classical liberalism', 'new liberalism' as well as by 'neo-liberalism'. New liberalism puts a higher value on positive freedom and the collective role of the state in economic management advocated by the economist John Maynard Keynes. Neo-liberalism is influenced by conservative principles towards family values, which can be also be observed in the USA. (See also Orloff, O'Connor and Shaver 1999.)

2   According to Thane (1993), the Liberal Party by 1914 had a total membership of 115 097 women; the support organisation for the Conservatives had hundreds of thousands of women, and in 1913 women made up 43 per cent of the Fabian Society membership, which was quite small.

3   One key question concerns the extent to which women's organisations formed alliances and about what issues. Another is with whom they were able to form alliances among the political parties, social movements and trade unions, and about what issues. Clearly, class division between the feminist organisations and the lack of alliances between feminism and the labour movement were important factors explaining the defeat of family policy in Britain. Mary Daly (1997) has suggested that class stratification has been the main division in Britain, compared with gender, which has been the main division in Germany.

4   The three issues that dominated feminist campaigns during 1906–39 were the inclusion of women in national insurance, economic assistance to mothers through maternity benefits and some form of family allowances, and maternal and child health (Dale and Foster 1986: 1–38).

5   The male-breadwinner model was developed by Lewis (1992) on the basis of the British case, and the focus on the variations in the male breadwinner regimes fails to capture the specific logic of the different models. Sainsbury (1994) has argued that the model is too closely tied to the duality bread-winner/earner vs. dependent wife, and underestimates the roles of women as mothers and as citizens. (See also Lewis 1997b.)

6   Randall (1996: 502) suggests that British feminists had an ambivalent attitude to public childcare, and the issue of childcare failed to arouse feminist passions and mobilise feminist energies in contrast to issues like abortion, domestic violence and pornography. Second-wave feminism in Britain was not conductive to mobilisation on childcare, and therefore feminists in other countries have been more proactive towards the issue

7   London will soon again have its own government, with elements of pro-portional representation as part of the constitutional reforms of New Labour. These include a strengthening of autonomy for the local governments of Scotland, Wales and Northern Ireland, with elements of proportional representation (Hennig 1999).

8   The Commission of Social Justice was set up by the Labour Party in 1992 with the goal of analysing the need for economic and social reforms in the UK. The analysis was carried out by a group of independent experts, coordinated by the 'Institute for Public Policy Research', an independent Left of Centre think-tank (Social Justice 1994: Preface).

9   Sassoon (1998: 91) has recently suggested that there is a convergence of the programs of the Socialist parties in Northern and Southern Europe, and he places the British and Nordic social democracies in the same family of the Left from the perspective of a modernisation of capitalism. He thus ignores the fact that the British Labour Party had different visions and policies in relation to childcare, the family and married women's employment from those of the Nordic social democratic parties. I suggest that from the perspective of family policies, the Labour Party and Nordic social democratic parties did indeed belong to different families of the Left. The implication is that the thesis of convergence of the programs of the socialist parties in Europe becomes more complicated when issues of gender equality and family policy are included. The thesis of convergence will be discussed in further detail in the Conclusion.

6 Gender and Citizenship: The Danish Case

1 In the conclusion of a recent study of the Nordic democracies it is suggested that there are indeed five different models of mobilisation of women. The Danish model is described as unique, a model where the integration of women in politics was based primarily on the integration of social movements 'from below'. Danish women prefer grassroots organisations and are sceptical of political parties. In the Swedish and Norwegian model women have become integrated partly through the political parties and political institutions. From a comparative European perspective the commonalities between the gender models of the Nordic democracies and universal welfare states are still important, and the implications of the inter-Nordic differences for the development of women's social and political rights and for women's agency need further scrutiny. (See Borchost, Christensen and Raaum 1999.)

2 The Danish Investigation of Citizenship (1989-94) was inspired by T. H. Marshall's framework, although the emphasis was on democratic citizenship. The focus was on the political-cultural dimension of participation, which was seen as an expression of 'citizenship from below', that is, 'the norms, emotions and passions of citizens' in their daily lives (Mouffe 1992a). The key concepts were gender, class and generation, and one key question was the relation between the 'small' and the 'big' democracy. The investigation included a survey of the political participation and attitudes of citizens. Results from the investigation are published in two Danish books (Andersen et al. 1993; Andersen and Torpe 1994).

3 Corporatism designates the role of economic interest groups in political and administrative decision-making, which is formalised in the corporate channel, which implies an intersection between state-organised interests and various forms of expertise, for example government committees. Sweden, Norway and Austria are usually described as the most corporatist countries, while Denmark is more pluralist and less corporatist than the other Nordic countries. In the Nordic countries, the corporate channel has historically been designated as the most male-dominated political channel compared to the parliamentary channel, and in Denmark it is still male-dominated, although there have been important changes during the 1980s (Hernes 1987; Borchorst 1998b).

4 Between 1905 and 1940 the main split in the Danish political system was between the Right, based on an alliance between the United Farmers Party, the leftist Liberal Party and the Conservative People's Party, and the Left, built on an alliance between the Social Democratic Party and the Radical Liberal Party. In 1905 the United Farmers Party split into two: the Liberal Left, which represented the big farmers, and the Liberal Radicals, which represented the small farmers and teachers. After that the Danish political system was dominated by the four 'old' parties until the election of 1973: the Conservative Party, formed in 1915 with roots in the old Right (Højre), the Liberal (Left) Party (Venstre), the Social Democratic Party and the Radical Liberal Party (Det Radikale Venstre). During the 1960s and 1970s the Socialist People's Party played an important role in the New Left, representing the 'movements', especially the anti-nuclear movement, the opposition to the Common Market, the peace movement, the women's movement, and the environmental movement. Former members of the small Communist Party founded the Danish Socialist Party in 1958 as an independent and undogmatic party. The party has represented around 10 per cent of the

members of parliament since 1960, and today is a New Left party describing itself as 'red-green', combining the social and green dimensions and aiming to expand democracy in a socialist direction (Garodkin 1997).

5 Dahlerup has suggested that the main purpose of the committees was to educate and inform women about the policies of the party, not to develop a national Social Democratic policy for women. The committees had limited finance and few organisational resources, and the journal *Free Women* (*Frie Kvinder*), started in 1946, seemed directed primarily at housewives (Markussen 1977).

6 The Population Commission of 1937 put forward many new proposals for qualitative population policies to improve the situation of mothers and children, for instance family allowance to poor families. The immediate results were meagre in terms of legislation, but many of the proposals were taken up later in the 1950s and 1960s (Nielsen 1996). The leading Swedish Social Democrat, Alva Myrdal, who was married to Gunnar Myrdal, had put forward demands about universal childcare institutions as a means of improving the quality of the population and the number of children. These ideas were also held by teachers and reformers in Denmark, but they were not taken up until after World War II.

7 H. R. Christensen (1997) mentions the cooperation between the religious women's organisations, the housewives' organisations, and socialist organisations in connection with the trade union movement and the Social Democratic Party and women's rights organisations.

8 It has been noticed that women's trade unions, especially the Female Tailors' Union (Kvindelige Herreskræddere) formed a bridge between working-class women and bourgeois women's organisations in the struggle for the vote. The Female Tailors' Union formed the United Women's Organisations (De samlede kvindeforeninger) (1888–93) together with the Organisation for Women's Progress (Kvindelig Fremskridtsforening) (1885–).

9 The family laws of 1922–25 were the result of Nordic cooperation. It is interesting that they also equalised the obligations of spouses in relation to wage work and care work. Kirsten Gertsen (1985: 80) concluded that there was a contradiction between the formal equality in the marriage laws and married women's status as dependants in the tax laws.

10 In this context, there was debate about the meaning of protective legislation, i.e. about whether the prohibition of women working at night should be included in the legislation or not. This was part of an international discourse about protective legislation and a ban on women working at night, which was the basis of the Bern Convention from 1906 recommending the prohibition of night work for women (Wickander et al. 1995: Introduction). In Denmark, women's organisations formed successful alliances, and the prohibition of women's night work was not included in the discourse and policies of protective legislation (Ravn 1995).

11 In principle, the Social Democratic Party supported married women's right to wage work, but during the 1930s there were examples of not only private companies but also local governments dismissing married women with the active support of Social Democrats. The separate women's organisation of unskilled workers protested against this practice but they were not successful in the labour court. As a result, Social Democratic women from the trade union movement and the party protested to the leadership of the party, who sent out a circular to all Social Democratic members of local governments strongly opposing the practice as contravening the party's principles (Gertsen 1982: 143). For a detailed analysis of the Swedish case, see Hobson (1993).

12 For the older generation of women activists, women's networks were based on cross-party alliances between women organised in the Danish Women's Society. Women's networks thus rest on what has been defined as overlapping membership in political parties and in the women's rights organisations. The overlapping membership was characteristic of many women in the Radical Liberal Party, and from 1936 also for women from the Social Democratic Party, like Edel Saunte and Lis Groes (see R. Nielsen 1996; R. Christensen 1997; Dahlerup 1998).

13 Unfortunately this ambitious and expensive reform initiated by the Social Democratic Party was passed at the time the economic crises hit Denmark and there was growing support for the Progress Party (Fremskridtspartiet), a popular protest party that criticised high public spending and high taxes. The program became too expensive because of the growing numbers of un-employed and has been revised several times. However, the main idea of preventive social policies is still a key element in Danish political thinking.

14 The political conflicts surrounding childcare have been based on a split between the countryside and urban towns. Historically, the Agrarian Liberal Party (today the Liberal Party of Denmark) has supported a policy of free choice, where the public support to childcare would be given directly to the parents, i.e. 'the money should follow the children' and did not support the expansion of childcare centres until the reform in 1965. During the 1980s a new consensus was formed between the two different strategies: universal child allowance and expansion of public childcare centre. The coalition parties in government with the Liberal Left Party, i.e. the Conservative and Radical Party, supported an expansion of childcare centres, and women politicians across party lines formed networks around family and childcare policies (Borchorst 1989a).

15 Another problem is connected with mass unemployment, which during the 1980s resulted in problems of marginalisation for unskilled mothers. While households are generally less economically vulnerable with two wage earners, research shows that unskilled mothers are more vulnerable than unskilled fathers, especially lone mothers, who have higher unemployment rates than fathers (The Equality Dilemma, 1994; Siim 1997a).

16 This contrasts with Norway, where there are still quotas in the major political parties, and with Sweden, where the Social Democratic Party has recently adopted quotas in relation to the party organisations and also in relation to the selection of candidates (Christensen, ch. 4 in C. Bergquist et al. eds, *Likestilte demokratier? Køn og politik i Norden* (Equal democracies. Gender and Politics in the Nordic Countries) (1999). In Denmark there has been a decline in the membership of political parties during the last 20 years from 12 per cent in 1970 to 6 per cent in 1992, and women have remained a minority in the political parties. In Norway there are almost as many women as men, who are members of the political parties (Sundberg 1995; Christensen and Knopp 1998, Christensen 1999).

17 Since the 1970s the definition of corporatism has gradually been broadened in the Nordic countries from a narrow focus on the incorporation of the dominant interest groups of employers and trade unions in the decision-making process to a social corporatism that emphasises the incorporation of a plurality of interest groups, for instance parents, environmentalists, women and other groups (Raaum 1999).

18 According to Dahlerup, the network consists of women from the Social Democratic Party, the Socialist People's Party, the Radical Liberal Party and

the Conservative People's Party, and at times with women from the Liberal Party. Women from the two Leftist parties, the Left Socialists and the Communist Party, did have strong women's politics, but they generally followed the party line and did not want to form alliances with women from 'bourgeois parties'.

19 The results confirm that gender differences in political participation on a mass level have diminished during the 1980s, although they have not been totally abolished. Women, on average, participated with one activity less than men did during a one-year period (5.5 versus 6.5 on an overall participation scale). The persistent gender *difference* in favour of men in relation to political parties, political contacts, political communication and political discussion contrasts with the gender *equality* in relation to political manifestations and membership in organisations.

20 The Danish statute changed the school councils to governing bodies in which the parents have a majority of the seats. These new governing bodies have obtained greater power to decide things for themselves, so parents' representatives have become more important than previously (Torpe 1992). Anders Lindbom (1995) has given a good overview of the institutional history of the school system in Denmark.

21 Pluralism is about the plurality of ideas and interests in politics, but the term needs to be contextualised. Bussemaker and Voet (1998: 279) have recently referred to the notion of social pluralism. I find the distinction between social, political and cultural pluralism useful in the Danish context.

Bibliography

Aarhus, Marianne & Lars Muusmann. 1981. *Spørgsmålet om de gifte mellem-lagskvinders erhvervsrettigheder i hovedstadsområdet i 1930'erne* (The question of married women's right to wage work in the 1930s). Speciale, Historisk Institut, Århus Universitet.

Alestalo, Matti & Stein Kuhnle. 1987. The Scandinavian Route: economic, political and social developments in Denmark, Finland, Norway and Sweden. In Robert Eriksen et al. (eds). *The Scandinavian Model. Welfare State and Welfare Research.* New York: M.E. Sharpe.

Almond, G. A. & S. Verba. 1989a. *The Civic Culture. Political Attitudes and Democracy in Five Nations.* London: Sage (first printed in 1963).

Almond, G. A. & S. Verba (eds). 1989b. *The Civic Culture Revisited.* London: Sage Publications (first printed in 1980).

Andersen, B. Rold. 1989. Den offentlige vækst (The Public Growth). *Politica*, no. 2, pp. 120–32.

Andersen, B. Rold. 1991. *Velfærdsstaten i Danmark og Europa* (The Welfare State in Denmark and Europe). Copenhagen: Fremad.

Andersen, B. Rold. 1993. The Nordic Welfare State under Pressure: the Danish experience. *Policy and Politics*, vol. 21, no. 2, pp. 109–21.

Andersen, Johannes. 1999. Kvinder, mænd og mobilisering (Women, Men and Mobilisation). In J. Andersen et al., *Vælgere med omtanke*, pp. 61–5.

Andersen, Johannes, Ann-Dorte Christensen, Kamma Langberg, Birte Siim & Lars Torpe. 1993. *Medborgerskab – Demokrati og politisk deltagelse* (Citizenship, Democracy and Political Participation). Herning: Systime.

Andersen, J. & L. Torpe (eds). 1994. *Medborgeskab og politisk kultur* (Citizenship and Political Culture). Herning: Systime.

Andersen, J. & J. E. Larsen. 1998. Gender, Poverty and Empowerment. *Critical Social Policy*, vol. 18, no. 2, pp. 241–58.

Andersen, J., Ole Borre, J. G. Andersen & H. J. Jensen. 1999. *Vælgere med omtanke – en analyse af folketingsvalget 1998* (Responsible Voters – a study of the general election in 1998). Herning: Systime.

Arneson, R. J. 1995. Equality. In Goodin and Petit, *Companion to Contemporary Political Philosophy*, pp. 489–507.

Arrato, Andrew & Jean Cohen. 1992. *Civil Society and Political Theory.* Cambridge Mass. and London: Cambridge University Press.

Åström, Gertrud. 1992. Faste forbindelser. Om velfærdsstat og kvinders velfærd (Stable Relations. On the welfare state and women's welfare). In Y. Hirdman & G. Åström (eds). *Kontrakt i kris. Om kvinnors plats i velfärdsstaten*, Stockholm: Carlssons, pp. 183–204.

Badinter, E. & R. Badinter. 1988. *Condorcet. Un intellectuel en politique*. Paris: Fayard.

Bak, Maren. 1996. Enemorfamilien som senmoderne familieform (Lone-parent families as a postmodern form of the family), PhD diss., Aalborg University.

Baldwin, Peter. 1990. *The Politics of Social Solidarity. Class Bases of the European Welfare State 1875–1975*. Cambridge: Cambridge University Press.

Bang, H. & E. Sørensen. 1998. *The Everyday Maker: A New Challenge to Democratic Governance*. Working Paper, Department of Economics, Politics and Public Administration, Aalborg University, 1998: 2.

Bang, P. Henrik, Torben B. Dyrberg & Allan D. Hansen. 1997. Elite eller folkestyre – demokrati fra oven og/eller fra neden (Elite or Democracy – democracy from above and/or from below). *GRUS*, no. 51, pp. 5–32.

Barret, Michele & Anne Phillips (eds). 1992. *Destabilizing Theory. Contemporary Feminist Debates*. London: Polity Press.

Bauman, Zygmunt. 1997. *Postmodernity and its Discontents*. Oxford and Cambridge: Polity Press.

Beck, Ulrich. 1992. *The Risk Society*. London: Sage.

Beck, Ulrich. 1994. The Reinvention of Politics: towards a theory of reflexive modernization. In Beck et al., *Reflexive Modernization*, pp. 1–55.

Beck, Ulrich, Anthony Giddens & Scott Lash (eds). 1994. *Reflexive Modernization. Politics, Tradition and Aesthetics in the Modern Social Order*. London: Polity Press.

Benhabib, Seyla. 1992. *Situating the Self. Gender, Community and Postmodernism in Contemporary Ethics*. London: Polity Press.

Benhabib, Seyla. 1995. Feminism and Postmodernism: an uneasy alliance. In Benhabib et al., *Feminist Contentions*, pp. 17–34.

Benhabib, Seyla. 1999. *Citizens, Resident and Aliens in a Changing World. Political Membership in a Global Area*. Paper presented at conference 'Reimagining Belongings: Self and Community in the area of Nationalism and Postnationality', 6–8 May, Aalborg University.

Benhabib, S., J. Butler, D. Cornell & N. Fraser. 1995. *Feminist Contentions. A Philosophical Exchange*. London, New York: Routledge.

Benhabib, Seyla (ed.). 1996. *Democracy and Difference. Contesting the Boundaries of the Political*. Princeton: Princeton University Press.

Bergquist, Christina. 1994. *Mäns makt och kvinnors intressen* (Men's power and women's interests). Uppsala: Acta Universitatis Upsaliensis.

Bergquist, Christina. 1999. Familiepolitik i de nordiske velferdsstaterne, Del II (Family politics in the Nordic welfare states). In C. Bergquist et al. (eds), pp. 113–47.

Bergquist, C., A. Borchorst, A.-D. Christensen, N. Raaum, V. Ramnstedt-Silén & A. Styrkasdottir (eds). 1999. Equal Democracies? Gender and politics in the Nordic countries. Oslo: Scandinavian University Press.

Betænkning vedrørende ligestilling, no. 673. 1972. (Report concerning equality). Afgivet af udvalg under kommissionen vedrørende kvindernes stilling i samfundet.

Betænkning vedrørende kvindernes stilling i samfundet, No. 715. 1974. (Final report concerning women's position in society) Slutrapport afgivet af den af statsministeren nedsatte kommission vedrørende kvindernes stilling i samfundet. (Final report of the Prime Minister's Commission concerning women's position in society).

Bock, Gisela. 1992. Pauvreté feminisme, droits des mères et États-providence. In Duby & Perrot, *Histoire des femmes en occident*, vol. 5, pp. 381–409.

Bock, Gisela & Pat Thane (eds). 1991. *Maternity & Gender Policies. Women and the Rise of European Welfare States 1880s–1950s*. New York and London: Routledge.

Bock, Gisela & Susan James (eds). 1992. *Beyond Equality and Difference. Citizenship, Feminist Politics and Female Subjectivity*. London and New York: Routledge.

Borchorst, Anette. 1985. Moderskab og børnepasning i 1930'erne (Motherhood and childcare in the 1930s). In H. R. Christensen & H. R. Nielsen (eds). *Tidens Kvinder. Om Kvinder i mellemkrigstiden* (Women between the two World Wars). Aarhus; Håndbibliotekets veninder, pp. 36–57.

Borchorst, Anette. 1989a. Kvinderne, velfærdsstaten og omsorgarbejdet (Women, the welfare state and care work). *Politica*, no. 2, pp. 132–49.

Borchorst, Anette. 1989b. Kvindeinteresser og kvindekonflikter (Women's interests and women's conflicts). *Nyt Forum for Kvindeforskning*, October 1989, pp. 21–33.

Borchorst, Anette. 1994. Welfare State Regimes, Women's Interests and the EC. In Sainsbury, *Gendering Welfare States*, pp. 26–44.

Borchorst, Anette. 1997. *State of the Art Study of Research on Women and Political Decision-Making: Report on Denmark*. GEP Working Paper no. 2. Aalborg University.

Borchorst, Anette 1998a. Ligestillingsrådets historie (The story about the Equality Council). Memo.

Borchorst, Anette. 1998b. Arbejdsliv og familieliv i Vesteuropa (Work and family in the EC). *In Kvindeliv i EU. To bidrag fra Kvinfos kvindekonference i Faaborg den 14.-15. maj*, pp.19–37.

Borchorst, Anette. 1999. Ligestillingslovgivningen (Equality Legislation). In Bergquist et al., *Likestillte demokratier?*, pp. 176–91.

Borchorst, Anette & Birte Siim. 1984. *Kvinder og velfærdsstaten. Mellem moderskab og lønarbejde i 100 år* (Women and the welfare state). Aalborg University Press.

Borchorst, Anette & Birte Siim. 1987. Women and the Advanced Welfare State – a new kind of patriarchal power. In Sassoon, *Women and the State*, pp. 129–57.

Borchorst, Anette, Ann-Dorte Christensen & Nina C. Raaum. 1999. Ligestillede demokratier? Opsamling og perspektivering. (Equal democracies? Conclusion). In Bergquist et al., *Likestillte demokratier?*, pp.253–65.

Borre, Ole, & J. G. Andersen. 1997. *Voting and Political Attitudes in Denmark*. Aarhus University Press.

Bottomore, Tom. 1992. Citizenship and Social Class, Forty Years on. In Marshall & Bottomore, *Citizenship and Social Class*, pp. 55–93.

Bouget, Denis. 1998. The Juppé Plan and the Future of the French Social Welfare System. *Journal of European Social Policy*, vol. 8, pp. 155–72.

Bourdieu, Pierre. 1994. Nouvelles Reflections sur la Domination Masculine. In *Cahiers de Gedisst. Seminaire 1993–94 Division du Travail*. Rapports sociaux de sexe et de pouvoir, pp. 85–104.

Bourdieu, Pierre. 1998. *La Domination Masculine*. Paris: Seuil.

Bubech, Dietmut Elisabeth. 1995. *Care, Gender and Justice*. Oxford: Oxford University Press.

Bussemaker, J. & R. Voet (eds). 1998. Citizenship and Gender. Theoretical Approaches and Historical Legacies. *Critical Social Policy*, vol. 18, no. 3, pp. 277–307.

Bussemaker, J. (ed.). 1999. *Citizenship and the Transition of European Welfare States.* London: Routledge.

Butler, Judith. 1992. Contingent Foundations: feminism and the question of postmodernism. In Butler & Scott, *Feminist Theories of the Political*, pp. 3–21.

Butler, Judith. 1995. For a careful reading. In Benhabib et al., *Feminist Contentions*, pp. 127–43.

Butler, Judith & Joan Scott (eds). 1992. *Feminist Theories of the Political.* London: Routledge.

Callesen, G., S. Christensen & H. Grelle (eds). 1996. *Udfordring og Omstilling. Bidrag til Socialdemokratiets historie 1971–1996.* (Challenge and change: The history of social democracy) Fremad: Arbejderbevægelsens Bibliotek og Arkiv.

Carlsen, S., & J. E. Larsen (eds). 1995. *The Equality Dilemma. Reconciling Working Life and Family Life, Viewed in an Equality Perspective. The Danish Example.* Copenhagen: Munksgaars International Publishers.

Caspersen, Hanne. 1978. Arbejderkvindernes Oplysningsforening 1925–34. *Årbog for Arbejderbevægelsens historie 1978* (Yearbook for the history of the working class), SFAH, pp. 97–152.

Christensen, Ann-Dorte. 1989. *Ulydige kvinders magt. Kvindefredslejren ved Ravnstrup som politisk proces* (The power of disobedient women). Aalborg: Aalborg University Press.

Christensen, Ann-Dorte. 1991. Empowering and Identity. In T. Andersen et al. (eds). *Moving On. New Perspectives on the Women's Movement.* Århus: Århus University Press, pp. 155–75.

Christensen, Ann-Dorte. 1994. Køn, ungdom og værdiopbrud (Gender, youth and changing values). In J. Andersen & L. Torpe (eds). *Medborgerskab og politisk kultur.* (Citizenship and political culture). Herning: Systime, pp. 175–210.

Christensen, Ann-Dorte. 1997. De politisk-kulturelle betydninger af køn (The political-cultural meaning of gender). In Ann-Dorte Christensen, Anna-Birte Ravn & Iris Rittenhofer (eds). *Det kønnede samfund.* Aalborg Universitetsforlag, pp. 223–54.

Christensen, Ann-Dorte. 1999. Kvinder i de politiske partier (Women in the political parties). In Bergquist C. et al., *Likestillte demokratier?*, pp. 62–82.

Christensen, A.-D. & P. Knopp. 1998. *Kvinder og politisk repræsentation* (Women and political representation). GEP Working Paper no. 7, Aalborg University.

Christensen, Ann-Dorte & Birte Siim. 1989. Køn, magt og demokrati – mod et dynamisk magtbegreb (Gender, power and democracy – towards a dynamic concept of power). *Årbog for kvindeforskning* 1989, Århus Universitet, pp. 7–25.

Christensen, Ann-Dorte & Siim, Birte. 1995. Magt og medborgerskab – et feministisk perspektiv på frihed, lighed og broderskab (Power and citizenship – a feminist perspective on freedom, equality and brotherhood). Tidsskrifter *GRUS*, Aalborg University, vol. 16, no. 45, pp. 74–87.

Christensen, Hilda Rømer. 1997. *Med kvinderne til velfærdsstaten – kvindeorganisering i Danmark 1920–1940* (Women and the welfare state – women's organisation in Denmark 1920–1940). Paper presented at 23th Nordic Meeting of Historians, Tammerfors, 7–12 August.

Christensen, Hilda Rømer & Hanne Rimmen Nielsen (eds). 1985. *Tidens Kvinder. Om kvinder i mellemkrigstiden* (Women in the interwar period), Introduction. Århus, Håndbibliotekets veninder.

Christiansen, Niels Finn. 1996. Velfærdsststaten – et socialdemokratisk projekt? (The welfare state – a social democratic project?). *Social Kritik*, no. 44, June 1996, pp. 4–9.

Christiansen, Niels Finn, Karl Christian Lammers & Henrik S. Nissen. 1988. Vol. 7 of *Danmarks historie* (The History of Denmark), ed. Søren Mørch, Copenhagen: Gyldendal.

Cohen, Jean L. K. & Andrew Arrato. 1995. *Civil Society and Political Theory.* Cambridge, Mass.: MIT Press.

Connell, Robert. 1987. *Gender and Power. Society, the Person and Sexual Politics.* Oxford and Cambridge: Polity Press.

Cova, Abba. 1991. French Feminism and Maternity: theories and policies, 1890–1918. In Bock & Thane, *Maternity & Gender Policies*, pp. 93–119.

Critical Social Policy, vol. 18, no. 3, 1998. Special Issue: *Vocabularies of Citizenship and Gender in Northern Europe.*

Dahlerup, Drude. 1977. Et selvstændigt kvindeparti (An independent women's party). Den danske kvindebevægelse efter stemmeretten var vundet 1903–1918. En historie om stadigt bristede forventnminger. *Kvindestudier. Seks bidrag.* (Women's studies. Six contributions), Copenhagen: Fremad, pp. 149–96.

Dahlerup, Drude. 1979. Kvinders organisering i det danske socialdemokrati 1908–1969 (Women's organisation in the Danish Social Democratic Party 1909–1969). *Meddelelser om forskning i arbejderbevægelsens historie* no. 13, 1979, pp. 5–35.

Dahlerup, Drude. 1986. Is the new women's movement dead? Social movements decline and change: the case of the Danish feminist movement 1970 till today. In Drude Dahlerup (ed.). *The New Women's Movement. Feminism and Political Power in Europe and the U.S.* London: Sage Publications, pp. 217–44.

Dahlerup, Drude. 1988. From a Small to a Large Minority: women in Scandinavian politics. *Scandinavian Political Studies*, vol. 11, no. 4, pp. 275–98.

Dahlerup, Drude. 1993. From Movement Protest to State Feminism: the Women's Liberation Movement and unemployment policies in Denmark. *NORA, Nordic Journal of Women's Studies*, no. 1, 1993, pp. 4–20.

Dahlerup, Drude. 1994. Learning to Live with the State. State – market and civil society. Women's need for state intervention in East and West. *Women's Studies International Forum*, no. 2/3, pp. 117–27.

Dahlerup, Drude. 1998. *Rødstrømperne. Den danske rødstrømpebevægelses udvikling, nytænkning og gennemslag 1970–1985* (Redstockings. The Danish Women's Liberation Movement 1970–1985, with an English summary). Copenhagen: Gyldendal.

Dale, Jennifer & Peggy Foster. 1986. *Feminists and State Welfare.* London: Routledge & Kegan Paul.

Daly, Mary. 1997. Welfare States under Pressure. Cash benefits in European welfare states over the last ten years. *Journal of European Social Politics*, vol. 7, no. 2, 1997, pp. 129–46.

Daly, Mary & Jane Lewis. 1998. *Social Care and Welfare Restructuring.* TSER Report no. 4 of the EC Program 'Gender and Citizenship. Social Integration and Social Exclusion in European Welfare States, in Women's Empowerment and Political Presence'. Seminar Report, Aalborg University, 16–17 October 1998, pp. 87–109.

Daune-Richard, Anne-Marie. 1995. Travail et citoyenneté: Un enjeu esue hier et aujourd'hui. In Paul Bouffartigue & Henri Eckert (eds). *Le Travail à lépreve du salatiat.* Paris: Harmattan, pp. 93–108.

Daune-Richard, Anne-Marie. 1998. La Suède. Le modele egalitaire en danger?. In Jenson & Sineau, *Qui doit garder les jeune enfants?,* pp. 203–18.

Dean, Jodi. 1995. Reflective Solidarity. *Constellations,* vol. 2, no. 1, pp. 114–40.

Dean, Jodi. 1996. *Solidarity of Strangers. Feminism after Identity Politics.* Berkeley: University of California Press.

Del Re, Alisa. 1994. *Les femmes et l'État-providence. Les politiques sociales en France dans les années trente.* Paris: L'Harmattan.

Del Re, Alisa & Jacqueline Heinen (eds). 1996. *Quelle Citoyenneté pour les femmes? La crise des États-providence et de la représentation politique en Europe.* Paris: L'Harmattan.

Developments in National Family Policies in 1995. European Observatory on National Family Policies, Commission of the European Communities 1996.

Dietz, Mary. 1992. Context is all: Feminism and Theories of Citizenship. In Mouffe, *Dimensions of Radical Democracy,* pp. 63–85.

Drew, Eileen, Ruth Emerek & Evelyn Mahon (eds). 1998. *Women, Work and the Family in Europe.* London and New York: Routledge.

Duby, Georges & Michelle Perrot (eds). 1992. *Histoire des femmes en occident,* 5 vols, Paris: Plon.

Duby, Georges & Michelle Perrot (eds). 1993. *Femmes et histoire.* Colloque organisé par Georges Duby, Michelle Perrot et les directrices de l'historie des femmes en occident, la Sorbonne, 13–14 November 1992.

Eisenstadt, S. N. 1995. Civil Society. In Lipset, *Encyclopedia of Democracy,* vol. 1, pp. 240–42.

Elshtain, Jean Bethke. 1983. Antigone's Daughters. Reflections on Female Identity and the State. In Irene Diamond (ed.). *Families, Politics and Public Policy.* New York: Longman, pp. 300–11.

Elshtain, Jean Bethke. 1990. *Power Trips and Other Journeys: Essays in Feminism as Civic Discourse.* Madison: University of Wisconsin Press.

Elshtain, Jean Bethke. 1993. *Public Man, Private Women. Women in Social and Political Though.* Princeton: Princeton University Press, 2nd edn (first printed in 1981).

Eriksen, Erik Oddvar (ed.). 1995. *Deliberativ Politik. Demokrati i Teori og Praksis* (Deliberative Politics. Democracy in Theory and Practice). Otta: LOS-sentrets TANO-serie.

Esping-Andersen, G. 1985. *Politics Against Markets.* Cambridge: Cambridge University Press.

Esping-Andersen, G. 1990. *The Three Welfare Regimes.* Princeton: Princeton University Press.

Esping-Andersen, G. 1996. *Welfare States in Transition. National Adaptations in Global Economics.* Oxford: Oxford University Press.

Finneman, Niels Ole. 1985. *I broderskabets ånd. Den social-demokratiske arbejderbevægelses idéhistorie 1871–1977* (In the name of brotherhood. The ideas of the social democratic labour movement 1871–1977). Copenhagen: Gyldendal.

Flax, Jane. 1990. Postmodernism and Gender Relations in Feminist Theory. In Nicholson, *Feminism and Postmodernism,* pp. 39–62.

Flax, Jane. 1992. The End of Innocence. In Butler & Scott, *Feminist Theories of the Political,* pp. 445–63.

Frader, Laura. 1996. Social Citizens without Citizenship: working class women and social policy in interwar France. *Social Politics. International Studies in Gender, State and Society*, Summer/Fall 1996, pp. 111–35.

Fraisse, Geneviève. 1989. *Muse de la raison. La Democratie exclusive et la difference de sexe*, Aix en Provence: Edition Alièna.

Fraisse, Geneviève. 1995. L'exigence des féministes. *Le Monde des débats*, January 1995.

Fraser, Nancy. 1988. *Unruly Practices. Power and Discourse in Contemporary Social Theory*. Minneapolis: University of Minnesota Press.

Fraser, Nancy. 1995. Pragmatism, Feminism and the Linguistic Turn. In Benhabib et al., *Feminist Contentions*, pp. 157–71.

Fraser, Nancy 1997. *Justice Interruptions. Critical Reflections on the 'Postsocialist' Condition*. London: Routledge.

Fraser, Nancy & Linda Nicolson. 1990. Social Criticism without Philosophy. An encounter between feminism and postmodernism. In Nicholson, *Feminism and Postmodernism*, pp. 19–39.

Fraser, Nancy, & Linda Gordon. 1994. 'Dependency' Demystified. Inscriptions of power in a keyword of the welfare state. *Social Politics. International Studies in Gender, State and Society*, no. 1, 1994, pp. 4–31.

Garodkin, Ib. 1997. *Håndbog i dansk politik* (Handbook of Danish Politics). Copenhagen: Munksgård.

Gaspard, F., C. Servan-Schreiber & A. Le Gall. 1992. *Au pouvoir, Citoyennes! Liberté, Égalité, Parité*. Paris: Editions du Seuil.

Gaspard, Francaise. 1994. De la parité: genèse d'un concept, naissance d'un mouvement. *Nouvelle questions féministes:* La Parité 'pour', vol. 15, no. 4, pp. 29–44.

Gautier, Arlette & Jacqueline Heinen (eds). 1993. *Le sexe des politiques sociales*. Paris: Côté-femmes.

Geertsen, Kirsten. 1977. *Arbejderkvinder i Danmark 1914–1924* (Working-class women in Denmark). Grenå: GMT.

Geertsen, Kirsten. 1982. *Arbejderkvinder i Danmark. Vilkår og kamp 1924–1939.* Selskabet til forskning i arbejderbevægelsens historie (Society for Research in the Working-class Movement). Skriftserie no. 13.

Geertsen, Kirsten. 1985. Forsørgerbegrebet (the concept of the breadwinner). In Christensen & Nielsen, *Tidens Kvinder*, pp. 68–82.

Gerhard, Ute. 1997. Feminism and the Law. Towards a feminist and con-textualized concept of 'equality'. TSER Report no. 3 of the EC Program: 'Gender and Citizenship: Social Integration and Social Exclusion in European Welfare States' no. 3: *Equality Revisited*, Aalborg University, November 1997, pp. 39–51.

Giddens, Anthony. 1984. *The Construction of Society. Outline of the Theory of Structuration*. London: Polity Press.

Giddens, Anthony. 1991. *Modernity and Self-identity. Self and Society in the Late Modern Age*. London: Polity Press.

Giddens, Anthony. 1994. *Beyond Left and Right*. London: Polity Press.

Giddens, Anthony. 1998. *The Third Way. The Renewal of Social Democracy*. London: Polity Press.

Gilligan, Carol. 1982. *In a Different Voice. Psychoanalytic Theory and Women's Development*. Cambridge, Mass. and London: Harvard University Press.

Goodin, Robert E. & Philip Petit (eds). 1995. *A Companion to Contemporary Political Philosophy*. London: Basil Blackwell.

Gouges, Olympe de. 1988. *Oeuvre. Présentées par Benoite Groult*. Paris: Mercure de France.

Goul Andersen, J. 1996a. Marginalization, Citizenship and the Economy: the capacities of the universalist welfare state in Denmark. In E. Eriksen & J. Loftager (eds) *The Rationality of the Welfare State*. Oslo: Universitetsforlaget, pp. 155–202.

Goul Andersen, J. 1996b. Socialdemokratiets vælgertilslutning (The Attraction of Voters to the Social Democratic Party). In Callesen et al., *Udfordring og Omstilling*, pp. 174–219.

Goul Andersen, J. 1997. *Beyond Retrenchment: Welfare Policies in Denmark in the 1990s*. ECPR Round-table on 'The Survival of the Welfare State', Dept of Economics, Politics and Public Administration, Aalborg University.

Goul Andersen, Jørgen & Jens Hoff. 1999. *Democracy and Citizenship in Scandinavian Welfare States*. Forthcoming, Macmillan.

Gundelach, Peter. 1988. *Sociale Bevægelser og samfundsændringer* (Social movements and social change). Århus: Forlaget Politica.

Gustavsson, Gunnel, Maud Eduards & Malin Rönblom (eds) 1997. *Towards a new Democratic Order: Women's Organizing in Sweden in the 1990s*. Stockholm: Nordstedt Trykkeri.

Gutman, Amy. 1995. Democracy. In Goodin and Petit, *Companion to Contemporary Political Philosophy*, pp. 411–21.

Haavio-Mannila, E. et al. (eds). 1983. *Det uferdige demokrati. Kvinner i nordisk politik* (The unfinished democracy. Women in Nordic politics). Oslo: Nordisk Ministerråd.

Habermas, Jürgen. 1992. Further Reflections on the Public Sphere. In Craigh Calhoun (ed.). *Habermas and the Public Sphere*. Cambridge, Mass.: MIT Press, pp. 421–61.

Habermas, Jürgen. 1996. *Between Facts and Norms. Contributions to a Discourse Theory of Law and Democracy*. Cambridge, Mass.: MIT Press.

Halami, Gisèla. 1999. Parité, je n'écrit par ton nom ... *Le Monde Diplomatique*, September.

Halsaa, Beatrice. 1988. Har kvinnor gemensamme intressen? (Do women have common interests?). *Kvinnovetenskaplig tidskrift*, no. 4, pp. 323–36.

Hantrais, Linda. 1992. Les françaises et l'emploi. Portrait type ou prototype européen? In Duby & Perrot. *Femmes et histoire*, pp. 147–63.

Hantrais, Linda. 1993. Women, Work and Welfare in France. In Jane Lewis (ed.). *Women and Social Policies in Europe. Work, the Family and the State*. Aldershot, Hants: Edward Elgar, pp. 116–37.

Hantrais, Linda. 1995. *Social Policy in the European Union*. London: Macmillan.

Hantrais, Linda. 1996. France Squaring the Welfare Triangle. In Taylor-Gooby & George, *European Welfare Policy*, pp. 51–71.

Hantrais, Linda & Marie-Thérèse Letablier. 1996. *Families and Family Policies in Europe*. London: Longman.

Held, David. 1987. *Models of Democracy*. Cambridge: Polity Press.

Henig, Simon. 1999. The Labour Party and Women's Quotas. Paper forthcoming as GEP Working Paper, Aalborg University.

Hernes, Helga Maria. 1982. *Staten – Kvinner ingen adgang?* (The State – no access for women) Oslo and Bergen: Tromsø Universitetsforlaget.

Hernes, Helga Maria. 1987. *Welfare State and Women Power*. Oslo: Norwegian University Press.

Hernes, Helga Maria. 1988. Scandinavian Citizenship. *Acta Sociologica*, vol. 31, no. 3, pp. 199–215.

Hirdman, Yvonne. 1990. *Genussystemet* (The Gender System). In *Demokrati och Makt i Sverige. Maktudredningens huvudrapport*, SOU 1990: 44, ch. 3.

Hirdman, Yvonne. 1991. The Gender System. In T. Andreasen et al. (eds). *Moving On. New Perspectives on the Women's Movement.* Århus: Århus Univerity Press, pp. 187–207.

Hobson, Barbara. 1993. Feminist Strategies and Gendered Discourses in the Welfare States. Married women's right to work in the United States and Sweden. In Koven & Michel, *Mothers of the World*, pp. 398–429.

Hoff, J. 1993. Medborgerskab, brugerrolle og magt (Citizenship, citizens' involvement in social provision and power). In Andersen et al., *Medborgerskab*, pp. 75–107.

Hoskyns, Catherine. 1996. *Integrating Gender, Women, Law and Politics in the European Union.* London: Verso.

Jensen, J. J. 1994. Public Child Care in an Equality Perspective. In Carlsen & Larsen, *The Equality Dilemma*, pp. 103–17.

Jenson, Jane. 1993. Réprésentations des rapports sociaux de sexe dans trois domaine politiques en France. In Gautier & Heinen, *Le sexe des politiques sociales*, pp. 69–84.

Jenson, Jane. 1996. La citoyenneté à part entière. Peut-elle exister? In Del Re & Heinen, *Quelle Citoyenneté pour les femmes?*, pp. 25–46.

Jenson, Jane & Mariette Sineau. 1994–95. Le président qui aimait la famille. *Le nouveau Politis*, November/December 1994–January 1995, pp. 47–53.

Jenson, Jane & Mariette Sineau. 1995. *Mitterrand et les francaises. Un rendez-vous manqué.* Paris: Presse de Science PO.

Jenson, Jane & Mariette Sineau. 1997. D'une citoyenneté l'autre: la version neo-liberale de légalité républicaine. *Sextant, Revue du Groupe Interdisciplinaire D'Etudes sur les Femmes*, no. 7, pp. 121–39.

Jenson, Jane & Mariette Sineau. 1998. *Qui doit garder le jeune enfant? Modes d'accueil et travail des mères dans l'Europe en crise*, Librairie generale de droit et de jurisprudence. Paris: L G. D. J. Librairie Générale de Droit et de Jurisprudence

Jonasdottir, Anna G. 1988. On the Concept of Interest, Women's Interests and the Limitation of Interest Theory. In Jones & Jonasdottir, *The Political Interests of Women*, pp. 33–65.

Jonasdottir, Anna G. 1991. *Love Power and Political Interests. Towards a Theory of Patriarchy in Contemporary Western Societies.* Kumla: Ørebro Studies 7.

Jones, Kathleen B. 1990. Citizenship in a Women-friendly Polity. *Signs. Journal of Women in Culture and Society*, no. 4, pp. 761–93.

Jones, Kathleen B. 1994. Identity, Action, and Locale. Thinking citizenship, civic action, and feminism. *Social Politics. International Studies in Gender, State and Society*, no. 3, pp. 256–71.

Jones, Kathy & Anna Jonasdottir (eds). *The Political Interests of Women. Developing Theory and Research with a Feminist Face.* London: Sage Publications.

Jordan, Bill. 1989. *The Common Good. Citizenship, Morality and Self-Interest.* London: Basil Blackwell.

Karvonen, Lauri & Per Selle (eds). 1995. *Women in Nordic Politics. Closing the Gap.* Dartmouth: Aldershot.

Knibielher, Yvonne. 1992. Difference de sex et protection sociale (XIX–XX Siècles) *Culture et Société* sous la direction Leora Auslander et Michelle Zancarini-Fournel.

Knibielher, Yvonne. 1993. Mères, pouvoirs. In Riot-Sarcey, *Femmes, Pouvoirs*, pp. 32–43.

Knijn, T. & M. Kremer. 1997. Gender and the Caring Dimension of Welfare States: towards inclusive citizenship. *Social Politics. International Studies in Gender, State and Society*, vol. 4, no. 3, pp. 328–62.

Koch, H. 1991. *Hvad er demokrati?* (What is democracy?). Copenhagen: Gyldendal, 5th edn (first published 1945).

Koch, Henning & Kristian Hvidt. 1999. *Danmarks Riges Grundlove 1849, 1866, 1915, 1953* (The Danish Constitutions). Copenhagen: Christian Eilerts Forlag.

Koch-Nielsen, I. 1996. *Family Obligations in Denmark*. Copenhagen: Danish National Institute for Social Research, no. 3.

Kolstrup, S. 1996. *Velfærdsstatens rødder. Fra kommunesocialisme til folkepension*, (The Roots of the Welfare State. From municipal socialism to the old-age pension, with an English summary). Copenhagen: Selskabet til forskning i arbejderbevægelsens historie.

Kolstrup, S. 1997. Fra kommunesocialisme til velfærdsstat (From municipal socialism to the welfare state). *Social Kritik*, no. 49, pp. 5–21.

Koven, Seth & Sonya Michel (eds). 1993. *Mothers of the World. Maternalist Politics and the Origins of the Welfare State*. New York and London: Routledge.

Kræmer, Karin. 1990. *Dagligdagens kvinder. I kamp for valgret på vej mod ligestilling* (Everyday Women. The struggle for the vote for equality). Arbejderbevægelsens Bibliotek og Arkiv (The Library and Archive of the Working-class Movement). Copenhagen: Fremad.

Kristensen, Niels Nørgård. 1998. *Skolebestyrelser og demokratisk deltagelse – støvets fortælling* (School Boards and Democratic Participation). Copenhagen: Lawyers and Economists' Union Press.

Kruchow, Marianne. 1996. Kvinder i bevægelse. Socialdemokratiets kvindepolitik (Women in Movement. The gender policy of the Social Democratic Party). In Callesen et al., *Udfordring og Omstilling*, pp. 221–51.

Kvinden og Samfundet. 1996. Dansk Kvindesamfund i 125 år (Women and Society. Danish Women's Society in 125 Years).

Kymlicka, Will. 1990. *Contemporary Political Philosophy*. Oxford: Clarendon Press.

Kymlicka, Will & Wayne Norman. 1994. Return of the Citizen: A survey on recent work on citizen theory. *Ethics*, vol. 104, January 1994, pp. 352–81.

Laclau, Ernest. 1995. Discourse. In Goodin & Petit, *Companion to Contemporary Political Philosophy*, pp. 431–7.

Landes, Joan. 1988. *Women and the Public Sphere in the Age of the French Revolution*. Cornell: Cornell University Press.

Langberg, Kamma. 1994. Tiden, kønnet og politikken (Time, Gender and Politics). In Andersen & Torpe, *Medborgeskab og politisk kultur*, pp. 159–75.

Larsen, Øjvind. 1994. Interview with Jean Cohen. *Social Kritik*, no. 29, pp. 29–34.

Le nouveau Politis, November/December 1994–January 1995. Special issue: 'Famille je te hais, moi non plus'.

Le Monde, 31 October 1998. 'L'opinion souhaite l'égalité hommes–femmes plus que la parité'.

Le Monde diplomatique, March–April 1999. 'Femmes, le mauvais genre?'

Lefaucheur, Nadine. 1992. Maternité, famille, Ètat. In Duby & Perrot, *Histoire des femmes en occident*, pp. 411–30.

Leira, Arnlaug. 1992. *Models of Motherhood. Welfare State Policy and Scandinavian Experiences of Everyday Practices*. Cambridge: Cambridge University Press.

Leira, Arnlaug. 1994. Concepts of Caring, Loving, Thinking and Doing. *Social Service Review*, no. 2, pp. 187–201.

Leira, Arnlaug. 1996. *Parents, Children and the State: Family Obligations in Norway.* Oslo: Institute for Social Research, Report 96:23.

Leira, Arnlaug. 1998. Caring as a Social Right. Cash for care and daddy leave. *Social Politics. International Studies in Gender, State and Society,* no. 3, pp. 362–78.

Lewis, Jane. 1992. Gender and the Development of Welfare Regimes. *Journal of European Social Policy,* vol. 2, no. 3, pp. 159–73.

Lewis, Jane (ed.). 1993. *Women and Social Policies in Europe. Work, Family and the State.* London: Edward Elgar, Introduction.

Lewis, Jane. 1994. Gender, the Family and Women's Agency in the Building of 'Welfare States': The British case. *Social History,* vol. 19, no. 1, pp. 37–55.

Lewis, Jane. 1995. *Gender, Family and the Study of Welfare Regimes.* FREIA (Feminist Research Centre, Aalborg), Aalborg University paper series no. 25.

Lewis, Jane (ed.). 1997a. *Lone Mothers in European Welfare Regimes.* London: Jessica Kingsley Pub.

Lewis, Jane. 1997b. Gender and Welfare Regimes: Further Thoughts. *Social Politics. International Studies in Gender, State and Society,* vol. 4, no. 2, 1997, pp. 160–77.

Lewis, Jane & Ilona Ostner. 1994. *Gender and the Evolution of European Social Policies.* Centre for Social Policy Research, Bremen, working paper no. 4/94.

Lewis, Jane & Ilona Ostner. 1995. Gender and the Evolution of European Social Policy. In S. Leibfried & P. Pierson (eds). *European Social Policy. Between Fragmentation and Integration.* Washington: Brooking, pp. 159–194.

Lindbom, Anders. 1995. *Medborgerskapet i välfärdsstaten. Föräldrainflytande i skandinavisk grundskola* (Citizenship in the welfare state. The influence of parents in Scandinavian elementary schools). Acta Universitatis Upsaliensis, Statsvitenskabpliga föreningen i Uppsala, no. 123.

Lipset, Seymour Martin (ed.). 1995. *The Encyclopedia of Democracy,* 4 vols, London: Routledge.

Lister, Ruth. 1993. Tracing the Contours of Women's Citizenship. *Policy and Politics,* vol. 21, no. 1, pp. 3–16.

Lister, Ruth. 1995. Dilemmas in Engendering Citizenship? *Economy and Society,* vol. 24, no. 1, pp. 1–40.

Lister, Ruth. 1997a. *Citizenship. Feminist Perspectives.* Hong Kong: Macmillan.

Lister, Ruth. 1997b. Citizen or Stakeholder. Policies to combat social exclusion and promote social justice in the UK. FREIA, Aalborg University paper series no. 40.

Lister, Ruth. 1998a. Vocabularies of Citizenship and Gender: The UK. *Critical Social Policy,* vol. 18, no. 3, pp. 309–31.

Lister, Ruth. 1998b. To RIO via the Third Way: The equality and 'welfare' reform agenda in Blair and Brown's Britain. Paper presented at conference 'Equality and the Democratic State', Vancouver, November.

Liversage, Tony. 1975. *Da kvinderne måtte gå under jorden. Suffragetternes kamp for stemmeretten i England 1903–14* (When women had to go underground). Copenhagen: Gyldendal.

Liversage, Tony. 1980. *At erobre ordet* (To conquer a voice). Copenhagen: Tiderne Skifter.

Lovenduski, Joni & Vicki Randall, 1993. *Contemporary Feminist Politic. Women and Power in Britain.* Oxford: Oxford University Press.

Lunde, Helle. 1988. De kommunefarvede danskere – en nation af mindretal (The Danes – a nation of minorities). Tidsskrifter *GRUS* Aalborg University, no. 26, pp. 23–42.

Lykke, Nina, Anna-Birte Ravn & Birte Siim (eds). 1994. Introduction to the *Special Issue of Women's Studies International Forum* 'Images from Women in a Changing Europe', vols 2–3, March–June, pp. 111–16.

Mansbridge, Jane & Susan Moller Okin. 1995. Feminism. In Goodin & Petit, *Companion to Contemporary Political Philosophy*, pp. 269–90.

March, David & Garry Stoker (eds). 1995. *Theory and Methods of Political Science.* London: Macmillan.

Marcussen, Randi. 1980. Socialdemokratiets kvindeopfattelse og – politik fra 1960–1973 (Social democracy. Discourse and policies towards women). *Den jyske historiker* no. 18, pp. 13–168.

Marques-Pereira, Bérengère. 1998. The Representation of Women in Belgium. In TSER Report no. 4 of the EC Program 'Gender and Citizenship. Social Integration and Social Exclusion in European Welfare States, in Women's Empowerment and Political Presence', *Seminar Report*, Aalborg University, 16–17 October 1998, pp. 45–67.

Marshall, T. H. 1950. *Citizenship and Social Class.* Reprinted in Marshall & Bottomore, *Citizenship and Social Class.*

Marshall, T. H. & Tom Bottomore. 1992. *Citizenship and Social Class.* London: Pluto Press.

McClure, Kristie. 1992. On the subject of Rights: Pluralism, plurality and political identity. In Mouffe, pp. 108–28.

Meehan, Elisabeth. 1992. *Citizenship and the European Community.* London: Sage.

Messu, Michel. 1998. Solidarism and Familialism: the influence of ideological protection on the formation of French social protection. In *Comparing Social Welfare Systems in Nordic Europe and France*, Copenhagen Conference vol. 4, Paris: MIRE-DREES, pp. 113–26..

Mill, John Stuart. 1989. The Subjection of Women. Reprinted in Stefan Collini (ed.). *J. S. Mill. On Liberty and other Writings.* Cambridge: Cambridge University Press, pp. 119–217.

Millar, Jane & Andrea Warman (eds). 1996. *Defining Family Obligations in Europe.* Bath Social Policy Papers no. 23.

Mossuz-Lavau, Janine. 1993a. Les femmes et la sexualité. Nouveau droits, nouveau pouvoirs?. In Duby & Perrot, *Femmes et histoire*, pp. 89–90.

Mossuz-Lavau, Janine. 1993b. Le vote des francaises, 1945–1992. In Riot-Sarcey, *Femmes, Pouvoirs*, pp. 59–75.

Mossuz-Lavau, Janine. 1994a. Les electrices françaises de 1945 à 1993. XX siecle. *Revue d'histoire*, no. 42, Avril–June.

Mossuz-Lavau, Janine. 1994b. Les conceptions des hommes et des femmes ou le four de la RMIste. *Rapport établi pour la Commission des Communités Européennes.*

Mossuz-Lavau, Janine. 1994c. *Les français et la politique.* Paris: Odile Jacobs.

Mouffe, Chantal (ed.). 1992a. *Dimensions of Radical Democracy. Pluralism, Citizenship and Community.* London: Verso.

Mouffe, Chantal. 1992b. Feminism, Citizenship and Radical Democratic Politics. In Butler & Scott, *Feminist Theories of the Political*, pp. 369–84.

Mouffe, Chantal. 1993. *The Return of the Political.* London and New York: Verso.

Mouffe, Chantal. 1995. Citizenship. In Lipset, *Encyclopedia of Democracy*, vol. 1, pp. 217–22.

Nicholson, Linda (ed.). 1990. *Feminism and Postmodernism.* London: Routledge.

Nicholson, Linda. 1995. Introduction to Benhabib et al., *Feminist Contentions*.
Nielsen, Henrik Kaare. 1991. *Demokrati i bevægelse* (Democracy in Movement), Århus: Århus Universitetsforlag.
Nielsen, Hanne Rimmen. 1996. Livets lighed. Lis Groes og familiepolitikken (Equality. Lis Groes and family politics). In *Kvinden og Samfundet*. Dansk Kvindesamfund 125 år, pp. 25–34.
Nouvelles questions feministes, La Parité 'pour', vol. 15, no. 4, 1994.
Nouvelles questions feministes: La Parité 'contre', vol. 16, no. 2, 1995.
Nyseth, T. & L. Torpe 1997. Borgerstyre eller brugerstyre? – Institutionelle nydannelser i et demokratiperspektiv (Citizen-Users – institutional innovations from a perspective of democracy). In P. Gundelach, H. Jørgensen & K. K. Klausen (eds). *Det lokale. Decentral politik og forvaltning* (Local, decentralised politics and administration). Department of Politics, Economics and Public Administration, Aalborg University, pp. 235–65.
O'Connor, Julia S., Anne Orloff & Sheila Shaver. 1999. *States, Markets, Families: Gender Liberalism and Social Policy in Australia, Canada, Britain and the United States*. Cambridge: Cambridge University Press.
Offen, Karen. 1991. Body Politics; Women, work and the politics of motherhood in France, 1920–1950. In Bock & Thane, *Feminist Contentions*, pp. 138–59.
Offen, Karen. 1992. Defining Feminism. A comparative historical approach. In Bock & James, *Beyond Equality and Difference*, pp. 69–88.
Okin, Susan Moller. 1989. *Women in Western Political Thought*. Princeton: Princeton University Press.
Orloff, Anne. 1993. *Gender and the Social Rights of Citizenship: The Comparative Analysis of Gender Relations and the Welfare States*. IRP Reprint Series, Madison: University of Wisconsin.
Østergård, U. 1992. *Europas ansigter. Nationale stater i en ny og gammel verden* (The Faces of Europe. Nation States in a New and Old World). Copenhagen: Rosinante.
Ostner, Ilona. 1994. Independence and Dependence – options and constraints for women over a life course. *Women's International Studies Forum* 1994, no. 2/3, pp. 129–39.
Ozouf, Mona. 1995. *Les mots des femmes: Essai sur la singularité française*. Paris: Fayard.
Palier, Bruno. 1998. *French Social Protection System*. Paris: MIRE, Paris Rencontres et Recherches.
Parry, Geraint, George Moyser & Neil Day. 1991. *Political Participation and Democracy in Britain*. Cambridge: Cambridge University Press.
Pateman, Carole. 1985. Women and Democratic Citizenship. Jefferson Memorial Paper, University of California, Berkeley.
Pateman, Carole. 1988. *The Sexual Contract*. Stanford: Stanford University Press.
Pateman, Carole. 1989. *The Disorder of Women. Democracy, Feminism and Poltical Theory*. London: Polity Press.
Pateman, Carole. 1992. Equality, Difference and Subordination: the politics of motherhood and women's citizenship. In Bock & James, *Beyond Equality and Difference*, pp. 17–31.
Pateman, Carole. 1994. Three Questions about Womanhood Suffrage. In Carol Daley & Melanie Nolan (eds). *Suffrage and Beyond. International Feminist Perspectives*. New York: New York University Press, pp. 331–52.
Pateman, Carole. 1996. *Democratization and Citizenship in the 1990s: The Legacy of T. H. Marshall. Wilhelm Aubert Memorial Lecture 1996*. University of Oslo, Department of Sociology, Report 96:17.

Pedersen, Susan. 1993a. *Family, Dependence and The Origin of the Welfare State. Britain and France 1914–1945.* Cambridge: Cambridge University Press.

Pedersen, Susan. 1993b. Catholicism, Feminism, and the Politics of the Family during the late Third Republic. In Koven and Michel (eds), *Mothers of the World*, pp. 246–76.

Petersson, O., A. Westholm & G. Blomberg. 1989. *Medborgernas Makt* (The Power of Citizens). Stockholm: Carssons.

Phillips, Anne. 1992. *Engendering Democracy.* London: Polity Press.

Phillips, Anne. 1993. *Democracy and Difference.* London: Polity Press.

Phillips, Anne. 1995. *The Politics of Presence.* London: Polity Press.

Phillips, Anne. 1999. *Which Equalities Matter?* London: Polity Press.

Phillips, Anne (ed.). 1998. *Feminism and Politics.* Oxford: Oxford University Press.

Plough, Niels & Jon Kvist. 1994. *Recent Trends in Cash Benefits in Europe,* Social Security in Europe 4. Copenhagen: Danish National Institute of Social Research.

Pringle, Rosemary & Sophy Watson. 1992. 'Women's Interests' and the Post-structuralist State. In Michele Barrett & Anne Phillips (eds). *Destabilizing Theory. Contemporary Debates.* Oxford and Cambridge: Polity Press, pp. 53–73.

Pye, Lucien W. 1995. Political Culture. In Lipset, *Encyclopedia of Democracy,* vol. 3, pp. 756–61.

Raaum, Nina. 1995a. *Kjønn och politik.* (Gender and Politics) Det politiske medborgerskabet (Political citizenship) Oslo: TANO.

Raaum, Nina. 1995b. The Political Representation of Women: a bird's eye view. In Karvonen & Selle (eds). *Women in Nordic Politics,* pp. 25–75.

Raaum, Nina. 1999. Kvinner i offisiell politik: historiske utviklingslinier.(Women in formal politics: historical developments). In Bergquist et al., *Likestillte demokratier?,* pp. 27–45.

Randall, Vicky. 1982. *Women and Politics.* London: Macmillan Press.

Randall, Vicky. 1996. Feminism and child care. *International Social Politics,* vol. 25, no. 4, pp. 485–505.

Ravn, Anna-Birte. 1989. Mål og midler i den gamle og den nye kvindebevægelse (Objectives and means in the old and the new Women's Movement). *Nyt forum for kvindeforskning,* October, pp. 8–20.

Ravn, Anna-Birte. 1995. Lagging far Behind all Civilised Nations: the debate over protective labour legislation for women in Denmark. In Wickander et al., *Protecting Women,* pp. 210–35.

Ravn, Anna-Birte. 1996. *The Discourses of Gender and Work. The Danish Case.* Paper presented at First German–Nordic Conference on Gender History, Stockholm, 21–24 November.

Ravn, Anna-Birte. 1997. Køn i historisk forandring (Gender in historical change). In Ann-Dorte Christensen, Anna-Birte Ravn & Iris Rittenhofer (eds). *Det kønnede samfund.* Aalborg: Aalborg Universitetsforlag, pp. 51–75.

Rerup, Lorenz. 1989. Vol. 6 of *Danmarks historie* (The history of Denmark), ed. Søren Mørch, Copenhagen: Gyldendal.

Review of Services for Young Children in the European Union 1990–1995, European Commission Network on Childcare and Other Measures to Reconcile Employment and Family Responsibilities, January 1996.

Riley, Denis. 1983. *War in the Nursery. Theories of the Child and Mother.* London: Virago Press.

Riot-Sarcey, Michèle (ed.). 1993. *Femmes, Pouvoirs.* Paris: Edition Kimé.

Rosanvallon, P. 1981. *La Crise de l'Etat-providence.* Paris: Editions du Seuils.

Rosanvallon, P. 1992. *Le sacre du citoyen. Historie du suffrage universel en France.* Paris: Gallimard.

Rosanvallon, P. 1993. Histoire du vote des femmes. Reflection sur le specificité française. In Duby & Perrot, *Femmes et histoire*, pp. 81–6.

Rosanvallon, P. 1995. *La nouvelle question sociale. Repenser l'État-providence.* Paris: Editions du Seuils.

Rosenbeck, Bente. 1987. *Kvindekøn. Den moderne kvindeligheds historie 1880–1980* (*The Construction of Gender. The Modern History of Femininity*). Copenhagen: Gyldendal.

Rosenbeck, Bente. 1992. *Kroppens politik. Om køn, kultur og videnskab* (The politics of the body). Museum Tusculanums forlag, Københavns Universitet.

Rosenblum, Nancy. 1995. Liberalism. *In* Lipset, *Encyclopedia of Democracy*, vol. 3, pp. 756–61.

Ross, Alf. 1967. *Hvorfor demokrati?* (Why democracy?). Copenhagen: Nyt Nordisk Forlag (first printed 1946).

Ruggie, Mary. 1984. *The State and Working Women. A Comparative Study of Britain and Sweden.* Princeton: Princeton University Press.

Ryan, Allan. 1995. Liberalism. In Goodin & Petit, *Companion to Contemporary Political Philosophy*, pp. 291–311.

Sainsbury, Diane (ed.). 1994. *Gendering Welfare States.* London: Sage Publications.

Sarvasy, Wendy. 1985. A Reconsideration of the Development and Structure of John Stuart Mill's Socialism. *Western Political Quarterly*, vol. 38, no. 2, 1985, pp. 312–33.

Sarvasy, Wendy. 1994. From Man and Philanthropic Service to Feminist Social Citizenship. *Social Politics. International Studies in Gender, State and Society*, vol. 1, no. 3, pp. 306–25.

Sarvasy, Wendy. 1999. Transnational Citizenship through Daily Life. Paper presented at 1999 Annual Meeting of the Western Political Science Association, Seattle, 25–27 March.

Sarvasy, Wendy & Birte Siim (eds). 1994. Introduction to special issue on 'Gender, and the Transitions to Democracy'. *Social Politics. International Studies in Gender, State and Society*, vol. 1, no. 3, pp. 249–55.

Sassoon, Anne Showstack (ed.). 1987. *Women and the State. The Shifting Boundaries of Public and Private.* London: Hutchinson.

Sassoon, Anne Showstack. 1991. Equality and Difference. The Emergence of a New Concept of Citizenship. In D. McLellan & Sean Sayers (eds). *Socialism and Democracy.* London: Macmillan, pp. 87–105.

Sassoon, Anne Showstack. 1996. Beyond Pessimism of the Intellect: agendas for social justice and change. In M. Perriman (ed.). *The Blair Agenda.* London: Laurence & Wishart, pp. 147–69.

Sassoon, Anne Showstack. 1997. Complexities, Contradictions, Creativity: traditions in the voluntary sector. *Soundings*, no. 4, Autumn, pp. 183–95.

Sassoon, Donald. 1998. Fin-de Siècle Socialism: The united, modest Left. *New Left Review*, no. 227, Jan./Feb., pp. 88–124.

Schmied, Helmut. 1995. Velfærdsstatens solidaritetsformer (The solidarity forms of the welfare state). *Dansk Sociologi*, no. 3, pp. 30–52.

Schmied, Helmut. 1997. Den fornuftige solidaritet – om den franske solidarisme som bevægelse, filosofi og politisk ideologi (Rational Solidarity). *Dansk Sociologi*, no 1, pp. 17–35.

Scott, Joan W. 1988. *Gender and the Politics of History.* Columbia: Columbia University Press.

Scott, Joan W. 1997a. *Only Paradoxes to Offer. French feminists and the rights of man.* London: Harvard University Press.

Scott, Joan W. 1997b. 'La Querelle des Femmes' in the Late Twentieth Century. *New Left Review,* Nov./Dec., pp. 3–19.

Sen, Amartya. 1992. *Inequality Reexamined.* Oxford: Oxford University Press.

Shaver, Sheila. 1997. Comparing Gender Regimes in Liberal Welfare States. Paper presented at 3rd TSER conference, Stockholm, 2–5 October.

Siim, Birte. 1988. Towards a Feminist Rethinking of the Welfare State. In Jones & Jonasdottir, *The Political Interests of Women,* pp. 160–87.

Siim, Birte. 1990. Women and the Welfare State. Between public and private dependence. In Clare Ungerson (ed.). *Gender and Caring. Work and Welfare in Britain and Scandinavia.* London: Harvester/Wheatsheaf, pp. 80–109.

Siim, Birte. 1991. Welfare State, Gender Politics and Equality Policies. Women's citizenship in the Scandinavian welfare states. In E. Meehan & S. Sevenhuisen (eds). *Equality Politics and Gender.* London: Sage, pp. 154–75.

Siim, Birte. 1993. The Gendered Scandinavian Welfare States: the interplay between women's roles as mothers, workers and citizens in Denmark. In Lewis, *Women and Social Policies in Europe,* pp. 25–49.

Siim, Birte. 1994a. Engendering Democracy – the interplay between citizenship and political participation. *Social Politics. International Studies in Gender, State and Society,* vol. 1, no. 3, 1994, pp. 286–305.

Siim, Birte. 1994b. Køn, medborgerskab og politisk kultur (Gender, citizenship and political culture). In Andersen & Torpe, *Medborgeskab og politisk kultur,* pp. 125–59.

Siim, Birte. 1997a. Dilemmas of Citizenship in Denmark. Lone mothers between work and care. In Lewis, *Women and Social Policies in Europe,* pp. 140–70.

Siim, Birte. 1997b. Politisk medborgerskab og feministiske forståelser (Political citizenship and feminist theories). In A.-D. Christensen, A.-B. Ravn & I. Rittenhofer (eds). *Det kønnede samfund.* Aalborg: Aalborg Universitetsforlag, pp. 193–221.

Siim, Birte (ed.). 1997c. Report from the TSER project: 'Gender and Citizenship: social integration and social exclusion in European welfare states', no. 2: *The Causes of Women's Exclusion: Actors, Processes and Institutions,* Aalborg University, May 1997.

Siim, Birte (ed.). 1997d. Report from the TSER project 'Gender and Citizenship: social integration and social exclusion in European welfare states', no. 3: *Equality Revisited,* Aalborg University, November 1997.

Siim, Birte. 1998a. Vocabularies of Gender and Citizenship: The Danish case. *Critical Social Policy,* vol. 18, no. 3, pp. 375–96.

Siim, Birte (ed.). 1998b. 'Gender and Citizenship: social integration and social exclusion in European welfare states'. Report from the TSER project no. 4: *Women's Empowerment and Political Presence,* Aalborg University, November 1998.

Siim, Birte. 1999a. Gender, Power and Citizenship. In Ian Gough & Gunnar Olofsen (eds). *Capitalism and Social Cohesion. Essays on Integration and Exclusion.* London: Macmillan, pp. 107–24.

Siim, Birte. 1999b. Towards a Gender Sensitive Framework for Citizenship – Comparing Denmark, Britain and France. In Jet Bussemaker (ed.). *Citizenship and the Transition of European Welfare States,* pp. 85–100.

Siim, Birte (ed.). 1999c. 'Gender and Citizenship: social integration and social exclusion in European welfare states'. Report from the TSER project no. 5:

The Transition of Gender, Welfare States and Democracy in Europe, Aalborg University, May 1999.

Siim, Birte (ed.). 1999d. *Final Report: Gender and Citizenship,* Aalborg University, September 1999.

Siim, Birte. 1999e. Gender and Citizenship in France. In *Comparing Social Welfare Systems in Nordic Europe and France,* Copenhagen Conference vol. 4, Paris: MIRE-DREES, pp. 201–21.

Siim, Birte & Trudie Knijn (eds). 1996. Report from the TSER project 'Gender and Citizenship: social integration and social exclusion in European welfare states' no. 1: *Engendering Citizenship, Work and Care,* Aalborg University, August 1996.

Simonsen, D. G. 1996. Som et stykke vådt sæbe mellem fedtede fingre (As a piece of wet soap between slippery fingers). *Kvinder, Køn og Forskning* (Women, Gender and Research), no. 2, pp. 29–51.

Sineau, Mariette. 1988. *Des femmes politique.* Paris: Economica.

Sineau, Mariette. 1990. Gender and the French Electorate: A historical Review. In M. Katzenstein & H. Skjeie (eds). *Going Public. National Histories of Women's Enfranchisement and Women's Participation within State Institutions,* Institute for Social Research, no. 4, Oslo, pp. 79–103.

Sineau, Mariette. 1992. Pouvoir, modernité et monopole masculin de la politique: le cas francais. *Nouvelle questions feministes,* vol. 13, no. 1, pp. 39–61.

Sineau, Mariette. 1993. Droit et démocratie. In Duby & Perrot, *Historie des femmes en occident,* pp. 471–97.

Sineau, Mariette. 1994. Mise un Oeuvre de la Democratie Paritaire en France: Obstacles juridiques, voies et moyens pour les surmonter, pour Conseil d'Europe. Comité directeur pour légalité entre femmes et hommes, October.

Sineau, Mariette 1999. Les deux faces de la parité. *Le Monde Diplomatique,* December, p. 26.

Sjørup, Karen. 1996. Magt og kvindefrigørelse i den moderne velfærdsstat (Power and women's emancipation in the modern welfare state). *Arbejderhistorie,* no. 4 (Special Issue on the Welfare State), pp. 108–20.

Skalts, Vera & Magna Nørgård. 1982. *Mødrehjælpens epoke* (The epoch of Mothers' Help): Copenhagen: Forlaget Rhodos.

Skjeie, Hege. 1991. The Rhetorics of Difference. On women's inclusion in political elites. *Politics and Society,* vol. 19, no. 2, pp. 233–63.

Skjeie, Hege. 1992. *Den politiske betydningen av kjøn. En studie av norsk topp-politik* (The Political Meaning of Gender. A study in Norwegian elite politics). Oslo: Institute of Social Research, no. 11.

Skjeie, Hege & Birte Siim. Stating the Trouble. What do women want? Scandinavian Feminist debates about Citizenship. Forthcoming in *International Political Science Review.*

Sklar, Kitty. 1993. The Historical Foundation of the Creation of Women's Power in the American Welfare State 1830–1930. In Koven & Michel, *Mothers of the World,* pp. 43–93.

Skocpol, Theda. 1992. *Protecting Soldiers and Mothers. The Political Origin of Social Policy in the U.S.* Cambridge, Mass. and London: Harvard University Press.

Social Justice. Strategies for National Renewal, 1994. Report of the Commission on Social Justice, London: Vintage.

Stokes, Wendy. 1998. A Politics of Presence? Paper presented at 4th Seminar of the EC Program 'Gender and Citizenship. Social integration and social exclusion in European welfare states, in women's empowerment and political presence', *Seminar Report*, Aalborg University, 16–17 October 1998, pp. 117–36.

Sundberg, Jon. 1995. Women in Scandinavian Party Organisations. In Karvonen & Selle (eds). *Women in Nordic Politics*, pp. 83–111.

Taylor-Gooby, Peter. 1996. The United Kingdom. Radical departures and political consensus. In Taylor-Gooby & George, *European Welfare Policy*, pp. 95–116.

Taylor-Gooby, Peter, & Vic George (eds). 1996. *European Welfare Policy. Squaring the Circle*. London: Macmillan.

Thane, Pat. 1991. Visions of Gender in the Making of the British Welfare State. In Bock & Thane, *Maternity & Gender Policies*, pp. 93–118.

Thane, Pat. 1993. Women in the British Labour Party and the Construction of the Welfare State. In Koven & Michel, *Mothers of the World*, pp. 343–77.

Titmuss, Richard M. 1983. *Social Policy*. London: George Allen & Unwin (first published 1974).

Togeby, Lise. 1984. *Politik er også en kvindesag. En sammenlignende undersøgelse af unge kvinder og mænds politiske deltagelse* (Politics is also a women's issue. A comparative investigation of young men and women's political participation). Aarhus: Forlaget Politica, Aarhus Universitet.

Togeby, Lise. 1989. Politisering af kvinder og af kvindespørgsmålet (Politicising women and the women question). In J. Elklit & J. Tonsgård (eds). *To folketingsvalg. Vælgerholdninger og vælgeradfærd i 1987 og 1988* (Two general elections. The attitudes and participation of voters in 1987 and 1988). Aarhus: Forlaget Politica, Aarhus Universitet, pp. 227–54.

Togeby, Lise. 1992. The Nature of the Declining Party Membership in Denmark: causes and consequences. *Scandinavian Political Studies*, vol. 15, pp. 1–18.

Togeby, Lise. 1994a. *Fra tilskuere til deltagere. Den kollektive politiske mobilisering af kvinder i Danmark i 1970'erne og 1980'erne* (From spectators to participants). PhD Diss., 7 previously published articles. Aarhus: Politica.

Togeby, Lise. 1994b. *Fra tilskuere til deltagere. Den kollektive politiske mobilisering af kvinder i Danmark i 1970'erne og 1980'erne* (From spectators to participants). Summary Report, Aarhus: Politica.

Togeby, Lise. 1994c. The Disappearance of the Gender Gap: tolerance and liberalism in Denmark from 1971 to 1990. *Scandinavian Political Studies*, vol. 17 no. 1 , pp. 47–68.

Torpe, L. 1992. Citizen Involvement in Service Provision. Paper presented at ECPR Joint Session of Workshops, 1992.

Touraine, Alain. 1994. *Qu'est-ce que la démocratie?* Paris: Fayard.

Trat, Josette. 1992. 1970–1990: Les nouveaux rendez-vous marqués du feminisme et du mouvement ouvrier. In *Les Cahiers d'encrages*, deuxième trimester 1992, pp. 8–14.

Turner, Brian. 1992. Outline of a Theory of Citizenship. In Mouffe, *Dimensions of Radical Democracy*, pp. 33–62.

Turner, Brian. 1993. *Citizenship and Social Theory*. London: Sage Publications.

Ungerson, Clare & Mary Kemper (eds). 1997. *Women and Social Policy. A Reader*. London: Macmillan.

Varikas, Eleni. 1995. Une representation en tant que femme? Réflexions crtitiques sur la demande de la parité des sexes. *Nouvelle questions feministes: La Parité 'contre'*, vol. 16, no. 2, pp. 81–127.

Velstand og velfærd – en analysesammenfatning (Wealth and welfare – a summary). Kommisionen om fremtidens beskæftigelse og erhvervsmuligheder, Copenhagen, May 1995.

Viennot, Eliane. 1994. Parité: les féministes entre défis politiques et révolution culturelle. *Nouvelle questions feministes: La Parité 'pour'*, vol. 15, no. 4, pp. 65–88.

Vogel-Polsky, Eliane. 1997. Démocratie, femmes et citoyenneté européenne. *Sextant, Revue du Groupe Interdisciplinaire D'Etudes sur les Femmes*, no. 7, pp. 17–39.

Walby, Sylvia. 1994. Is citizenship gendered? *Sociology*, vol. 28, no. 2, pp. 379–95.

Walby, Sylvia. 1998. EU-reguleringens betydning for ligestillingspolitikken (The meaning of EC regulation for equality politics). *Kvindeliv i EU. To bidrag fra Kvinfos kvindekonference i Faaborg*, 14–15 May, pp. 3–18.

Walby, Sylvia. 1997. *Gender Transformations*. London and New York: Routledge.

Walzer, Michael. 1992. The Civil Society Argument. In Mouffe, *Dimensions of Radical Democracy*, pp. 89–107.

Wickander, Ulla, Alice Kessler-Harris & Jane Lewis (eds). 1995. *Protecting Women. Labour legislation in Europe, the U.S., and Australia 1880–1920*. Chicago: Chicago University Press.

Williams, Fiona. 1996. Postmodernism, Feminism and the Question of Difference. In N. Partou (ed.). *Social Theory, Social Work and Social Change*. London: Routledge, ch. 4.

Williams, Fiona. 1997. *Social Policy. A Critical Reader*. Cambridge: Polity Press.

Young, Iris M. 1989. Policy and Group Difference: a critique of the ideal of universal citizenship. *Ethics*, vol. 99, January, pp. 250–74.

Young, Iris M. 1990a. *Justice and the Political Difference*. Princeton: Princeton University Press.

Young, Iris M. 1990b. The Ideal of Community and the Politics of Difference. In Nicholson, *Feminism and Postmodernism*, pp. 300–24.

Young, Iris M. 1994. Gender as Seriality: thinking about women as a social collective. *Signs*, vol. 19, no. 3, pp. 713–38.

Yuval-Davis, Nira. 1997. Women, Citizenship and Difference – citizenship as a multitier construct. In *Causes of Women's Exclusion: Actors, Processes and Institutions*. Aalborg University Seminar 2 of EC program 'Gender and Citizenship', 4–6 April, Turin, pp. 49–70.

Index

Page numbers in **bold** type indicate detailed discussion of a topic.